D1351535

A Feminine Enlightenment

Edinburgh Critical Studies in Romanticism
Series Editors: Ian Duncan and Penny Fielding

A Feminine Enlightenment

British Women Writers and the Philosophy of Progress, 1759–1820

JoEllen DeLucia

EDINBURGH
University Press

To Nate

© JoEllen DeLucia, 2015

Edinburgh University Press Ltd
The Tun – Holyrood Road
12(2f) Jackson's Entry
Edinburgh EH8 8PJ
www.euppublishing.com

Typeset in 10.5/13 Sabon by
Servis Filmsetting Ltd, Stockport, Cheshire,
and printed and bound in Great Britain by
Printondemand-worldwide, Peterborough

A CIP record for this book is available from the
British Library

ISBN 978 0 7486 9594 2 (hardback)
ISBN 978 0 7486 9595 9 (webready PDF)
ISBN 978 1 4744 0426 6 (epub)

The right of JoEllen DeLucia to be identified as
Author of this work has been asserted in accordance
with the Copyright, Designs and Patents Act 1988,
and the Copyright and Related Rights Regulations
2003 (SI No. 2498).

Contents

Acknowledgments

Like the progress of Enlightenment this book traces, the progress of my own work has been, at times, uneven and uncertain. This project would not have been possible without the support of numerous teachers, colleagues, and friends. In its early stages, this project found encouragement and benefited from the insight of my brilliant dissertation committee. In her graduate courses, my director Janet Sorensen introduced me to an eighteenth century that I could love, and she patiently guided me through the writing process, always responding to my work with generosity and care. Deidre Lynch encouraged me to pursue my interest in women's writing and challenged me in her Richardson seminar to think about gender, emotion, and the eighteenth century in new ways. Mary Favret always asked the right question at the right time and invited me to rethink many of my assumptions about history and literature. Richard Nash and Ellen Mackay also provided helpful feedback at key moments. I would not have finished my graduate work in a timely manner without a dissertation fellowship from Indiana University's Center for Eighteenth-Century Studies. This important interdisciplinary group not only gave me time to write but also created an inspiring environment and provided resources for a community of scholars dedicated to the study of the long eighteenth century. I would like to thank my peers who travelled through the Ph.D. process alongside me and participated in the center's activities, particularly Melissa Adams-Campbell, Celia Barnes, Tim Campbell, Siobhan Carroll, Tobias Menely, the late Adrianne Wadewitz, Courtney Wennerstrom, and Paul Westover.

During my time as an assistant professor at John Jay College, City University of New York, my ideas about women's writing and Enlightenment evolved. I received support from smart and innovative colleagues in the English Department at John Jay College, who pushed me to think in interdisciplinary directions. I also benefited from the larger CUNY community. Course release from CUNY's Faculty Fellowship

Publishing Program allowed me to workshop my writing with a group of scholars that included Al Coppola, Ramesh Mallipeddi, Kristina Richardson, Brijraj Singh, Karl Steel, and Andrea Walkden. The CUNY Center for the Humanities provided additional course release for my year-long participation in their 2010–2011 Mellon seminar on emotion. During the course of the year, conversations with colleagues about affect theory and emotion proved invaluable. I would like to thank the seminar leaders Peter Liberman and Nancy Yousef and David Bahr, Noel Carroll, John Collins, Mikhal Dekel, Amy Hughes, Anupama Kapse, Nicola Masciandaro, Shea McManus, Eugenia Paulicelli, Stephen Pludwin, Ran Zwigenberg, and Elizabeth Wissinger. I would also like to thank the librarians at the New York Public Library, particularly Jay Barksdale, who makes the Wertheim Study a lovely and quiet retreat for scholars. The dedicated librarians at Central Michigan University, particularly Jane Morey, Anita Gordon, and Aparna Zambare, patiently fulfilled my many requests for books, articles, and microfilm.

My work in archives was also supported by a number of external grants. The Huntington Library generously granted me in the summer of 2008 a two-month fellowship that allowed me to read much of Elizabeth Montagu's correspondence. The Chawton Library supported my work in their unique collections in the fall of 2009, and I benefited greatly from time spent talking about British women's writing with Louise Curran, Christina Davidson, Gillian Dow, and Jacqui Grainger. Access to the novels of the Corvey Collection was made possible by my participation in Stephen Behrendt's 2010 NEH summer seminar, "The Aesthetics of British Romanticism, Then and Today." Stephen Behrendt's generosity and knowledge about Romantic-era women's writing provided the foundation for Chapter 5 of this book. I am also indebted to the encouragement of my fellow participants, including Kelly Battles, Kathy Beres Rogers, Soledad Caballero, Mercy Cannon, Molly Desjardins, Amanda Drake, Allison Dunshane, Lindsey Eckert, Kristin Girten, Kathy Harris, Jason Goldsmith, Seth Reno, Daniel Robinson, Catherine Ross, Jen Santos, and Joanne Tong. I would also like to thank the numerous librarians who assisted me in conducting research and the libraries and private individuals who granted me permission to publish from their collections, including the Huntington Library, the National Library of Scotland, the National Archives of Scotland, the British Library, and Mr. Drummond Moray.

Portions of Chapter 2 were previously published as "'Tales of Other Times': The Bluestockings in the Time of Ossian" in *Tulsa Studies in Women's Literature* 27.1 (2008), and sections of Chapter 4 appeared as "From the Female Gothic to a Feminist Theory of History: Ann Radcliffe and the Scottish Enlightenment" in *The Eighteenth Century: Theory and Interpretation* 50.1 (2009). I would like to thank both journals for their permission to republish. The final stages of this project benefited from the generosity and perceptive comments of both Penny Fielding and Ian Duncan on the final typescript. I also thank Edinburgh University Press, particularly the anonymous readers for their insights on my proposal and sample chapter, and Jackie Jones and Dhara Patel, who have helped bring this project to completion.

Although I know I have failed to acknowledge all of the debts acquired during the composition of this book, there are a handful of people who I owe personal as well as professional debts. Juliet Shields provided friendship and made herself available to a new Ph.D., patiently commenting on drafts and providing much-needed advice. While being both a roommate and colleague, Olivera Jokic responded generously to portions of the manuscript. Although this project was nearly complete when I arrived, colleagues at Central Michigan University, including Henry Fulton, Dean Pamela Gates, Susan Schiller, Melissa Sara Smith, and Nicole Sparling have also helped in various ways. My parents Carol and Joseph DeLucia both modeled a love of learning and literature and encouraged me to be independent and brave. Finally, I would like to thank my partner Nate Smith, who read every word and is at this very moment watching our beautiful son Simon on a Saturday, so I can meet my deadline.

Introduction:
A Feminine Enlightenment?

The Bluestocking writer Elizabeth Montagu and the Scottish philosopher, historian, and jurist Lord Kames met in Edinburgh in 1766. After their initial meeting, Montagu and Kames began a correspondence that would last until Kames's death in 1781. Ranging in tone from flirtatious to deeply philosophical, their letters document a significant instance of a woman writer's contribution to the development of Enlightenment thought. In her first letter to Kames, Montagu writes,

> I do not know when, nor indeed where; whether we met on the Orb of this Earth, had a short coquetry in the Planet Venus, or a sober Platonic love in Saturn, but I am sure we did not first meet at Edinburgh in the year 1766 . . . the first evening we supped together at our friend Dr. Gregory's; we took up our story, where it had perhaps indeed [begun] some thousand years before the creation of this Globe, if we gave it a prefatory complement, it was only the customary form to the edition of a work before published.[1]

In likening their first meeting to the resumption of an ongoing story or an already published book, Montagu presages their intellectual collaboration, which took the form of letters that included shared revisions to the fourth edition of Kames's *Elements of Criticism* (1769) and the co-writing of portions of his yet to be published *Sketches of the History of Man* (1774), which both Montagu and Kames considered his greatest work. Their subsequent letters debated the nature of progress and women's contributions to aesthetic and social development, making their correspondence an ideal "prefatory complement" to my own book and its exploration of women writers' contributions to and critiques of Enlightenment narratives of progress.

In a later letter celebrating the publication of Adam Ferguson's *Essay on Civil Society* in 1767, Montagu describes progress as a gendered and uneven movement. Although she admired Ferguson's effort to recover the Stoicism of the Ancients for a more emotive modern age, she had reservations about the ability of humanity to ever perfect itself and progress in a clear and linear direction:

> When he has been formed by institutions, instructed by Science, embellished by arts, as one may say, systematized and made suitable to the peculiarities of his Country and his condition of life when he is fit for councils or enterprises to be soldier, statesman, or philosopher, then we hope we may pronounce him perfect. But alas! Where then is the innocence of his childhood? Where the ardor, the ingenuous spirit of his youthfull days? Experience has intimidated him, he is effeminate, he is taught to employ cunning to gain his ends and to obtain wealth. He has a thousand artificial wants and weaknesses. He reasons like an angel, and acts like a Brute, becomes sensual as he grows intellectual; refines in doctrine and degenerates in action. Thus it is with the individual, and thus with societies. Can we esteem our savage ancestors, the first tyrants of the woods, or love our present brethren in Change Alley? Do we reverence the unpolicied Hord of Tartars or the too political Conclave of Cardinals? Man is great in various situations, perfect in none, at Athens wise and ingenious, at Lacedemon intrepid and firm. I cannot express to your Lordship the pleasure and delight with which I read Mr. Ferguson's elegant work, but as my admiration can do him little honour, I will give you, who are his friend, the pleasure of knowing it is admired and approved by all persons of judgment in literature, or who have that nobler taste, the love of virtue. But what a deal have I written about things I don't understand and I have not said a syllable of matters within my competency.[2]

Capturing the major tensions within the Scottish Enlightenment's efforts to map humankind's development, this letter poses a number of questions that will be key to this study. What is progress and how do we measure it? Who is more civilized: the cunning and modern commercial agents of "Change Alley" or the honorable and innocent "first tyrants of the woods"? If the institutions and systems that structure modernity and allow the arts and literature to flourish also create a "sensual" and feminine society, do we name this progress or regress? Notably, despite Montagu's concluding disavowal of her clearly admirable powers of synthesis and critique, Kames passed on her observations to Ferguson.

Letters on philosophy and literature, including extensive discussions of works by Adam Smith, David Hume, James Macpherson, and Hugh Blair followed, but Montagu reserved her most unqualified praise for Kames's *Sketches on the History of Man*, which was published in 1774. She had obviously read part of the work in draft and had corresponded with him extensively in regard to select sections, particularly his comments on Macpherson's Ossian poems and his discussion of poetic form as a gauge of historical progress. Although she deflects credit for her own contributions to the manuscript's development, she praises Kames's work for including women in the evolution of civil society that it maps: "With the History of Man, I dare say your Lordship has (con amore) written the History of Woman."[3] Upon its publication, she reiterates this sentiment: "I am much pleased with what you have said of the fair sex, you have spoken the sentiments of a Friend, and not the language of flattery or scorn."[4] Beyond her participation in the composition of the *Sketches*, Montagu also worked to disseminate Kames's work in England and beyond. In 1776, she informed Kames that she intended to bring his books with her on her trip to Paris: "I shall recommend myself to some of the first literati at Paris by carrying your works with me. Your last work will be perfectly relished by them, for their best philosophers are much employed on speculations of the same kind, tho they are not endowed with so happy talents for these nice disquisitions."[5] Montagu not only helped refine Kames's ideas about progress, gender, and art but also introduced his work to her powerful friends in England and France.

From this series of letters, an outline of an alternative portrait of women and Enlightenment begins to emerge. Montagu and Kames's correspondence makes visible the largely invisible contributions to Enlightenment thought of several British women writers from the mid-eighteenth century through the very early nineteenth century and invites a reconsideration of women's responses to Enlightenment, particularly the Scottish Enlightenment's gendered analyses of historical, economic, and aesthetic progress. Many studies of women and Enlightenment begin in the early part of the eighteenth century with Restoration writers like Mary Astell and Aphra Behn and their reactions to John Locke's social contract and the politics of consent,[6] or at the end of the century with Mary Wollstonecraft's "revolution of female manners" and her appeal in *A Vindication of the Rights of Woman* for the cultivation of women's powers of reason and a more expansive understanding of Thomas Paine's rights of man.[7] Although women writers' complex relationships and responses to Enlightenment notions of contract, consent, and rights are crucial to understanding the patriarchal biases of dominant political and social structures, these starting points often position women as critics of the work of their male contemporaries and outside or on the margins of Enlightenment. By beginning in the middle decades of the eighteenth century with Bluestockings such as Montagu, this book argues that the explosion of literary, philosophical, and historical narratives that investigate what Kames in his *Sketches* and John Millar in his *Origin of the Distinction of Ranks* (1777) called the "progress of women" provides a new perspective on women writers' relationship to Enlightenment thought. Kames, Millar, and other Scottish Enlightenment literati proposed that cultural and economic development was, at least in part, a result of a society's increased regard for the value of women, who were believed to be better equipped to express and cultivate the sentiments that were understood as markers of a morally and economically advanced society. Women writers such as Montagu both interrogated and helped develop Enlightenment ideas regarding the place of emotion and gender in the civilizing process. This book examines letters, poetry, and novels by women as part of these Enlightenment narratives of social and cultural progress; it also positions feminine genres such as Bluestocking poetry and the gothic novel, usually seen as outliers in a masculine Age of Reason, as central to theorizing women's and emotion's place in discussions of social and commercial progress in Enlightenment Britain.

Women writers were deeply engaged with the questions about gender and progress raised by Scottish philosophers and poets, foremost among them Adam Smith, David Hume, and James Macpherson. In his *Theory of Moral Sentiments* (1759), Smith declared humanity to be "the virtue of a woman,"[8] and Hume, in essays such as "Of the Rise and Progress of the Arts and Sciences" (1742), mapped women's contributions to the development of sentiment onto the progress of knowledge, writing "what better school for manners, than the company of virtuous women; where mutual endeavor to please must insensibly polish the mind."[9] Both writers suggested that the cultivation of feminine virtues required leisure time, which was only available in modern commercial society. Although, according to these writers, men could and did possess feminine virtues, women became the key transmitters of the refined and delicate feelings found in advanced commercial society. As a result, women's social status became a gauge of a culture's moral and economic development; according to this schema, a civilized and economically advanced society would have a greater appreciation for feminine virtues, such as humanity and sympathy. Alongside these historical and philosophical treatises, James Macpherson's Ossian poems offered a competing story. In the "savage" Highlands of the third century, Macpherson claimed to have recovered a body of poetry that documented an economically underdeveloped society in possession of refined and curiously "civilized" sentiments. While Ossian and his fellow warriors cried and mourned in modern terms, the women within the poems mourned, sang, and sometimes fought beside their husbands, lovers, fathers, and sons. The poems modeled a curious equality, creating an exception within the maps of development created by Smith, Hume, and their contemporaries. Later deemed to be forgeries, these poems not only spawned debates over literary originality and authenticity but also provoked philosophical conversations about the place of women and gender in historical narrative;[10] however, the lively scholarly debates surrounding the poems' authenticity have overshadowed the ways in which women writers adapted and discussed the poems in their own attempts to narrate and theorize Enlightenment understandings of progress.

These poetic and philosophical accounts of women's progress were well known by women writers of the late eighteenth century and, in some cases, Scottish literati discussed and refined their theories of social development in intellectual exchanges with their female contemporaries. Montagu and her Bluestocking circle corresponded and socialized with the major philosophers and poets of the Scottish Enlightenment, including Kames, Hugh Blair, Macpherson, and James Beattie. Together the Bluestockings and Scottish literati led the defense of the Ossian poems in the 1760s. Later in the century, Anna Seward read John Millar and Adam Smith, corresponded with Walter Scott, and contributed a poem to his *Minstrelsy of the Scottish Border*. The novelist Maria Edgeworth not only studied Adam Smith and allowed his accounts of uneven development and absenteeism to shape her Irish novels but also corresponded with Smith's pupil and later Chair of Moral Philosophy at Edinburgh Dugald Stewart. By uncovering the ways in which women writers incorporated Scottish poetry and philosophy into their letters, poetry, and fiction, this book suggests that British women writers made a significant contribution to Enlightenment discussions of gender and historical development, contributions that have been easy to overlook because of disciplinary and national boundaries.

Despite the extensive network connecting British women writers to Scottish literati, studies of the Scottish Enlightenment and literature rarely engage with women writers, particularly women writers outside of Scotland.[11] In important studies, James Chandler, Ian Duncan, and Ian Baucom have analyzed Scottish stadial history as a precursor to Marxist and postcolonial theories of economic and social progress and have also used stadial theory to develop new lenses for understanding the Romantic-era novel's economic and temporal dimensions.[12] Primarily studying novels by Scottish men, Juliet Shields has recently demonstrated the ways in which writers used Scottish theories of sentiment and sympathy to gender political relationships within the British Isles and shape British identities. Despite these studies' interest in the relationship between sentiment, historical progress, and literary culture, few scholars have explored the connections between this emergent understanding of historical progress and late eighteenth-century innovations in British women's writing, or studied women writers' efforts to theorize social and historical development.

Similarly, studies of eighteenth-century women's writing do not often address the influence of Scottish theories of development on women's literature. Women writers' contributions to a range of eighteenth-century and Enlightenment historical discourses have been well documented by Devoney Looser, Jane Rendall, and others.[13] Yet the Scottish Enlightenment and its influential stadial theory of history have only recently begun to figure in feminist literary critics' understanding of eighteenth-century literary culture. Harriet Guest and E. J. Clery have argued that, by equating economic achievement with the elevated status of women, the Scottish Enlightenment troubled the boundary between the public and private, but they stop short of associating Scottish philosophy and historiography with women writers' own representations of the female sex's position within narratives of imperial and commercial progress.[14] More recently, Karen O'Brien has argued for the centrality of women to Enlightenment narratives of the civilizing process and troubled the dominance of Locke's social contract in feminist readings of the Enlightenment. My study builds on her important work; however, instead of focusing on female historians such as Catherine Macaulay or Elizabeth Hamilton, or women's representation in historical and philosophical works, this study makes women's literature central to the Enlightenment debate over social progress and uncovers the engagement of feminine genres, particularly Bluestocking poetry, Radcliffe's gothic, and the early historical novel with Scottish Enlightenment philosophy.[15] I argue that the conversations in the Bluestocking salons of the 1760s and 1770s acted as a laboratory for the theories of sociability and sentiment developed by Scottish literati such as Adam Smith and James Millar; likewise, Catherine Talbot's and Anna Seward's Bluestocking poetry, which was inspired by James Macpherson's Ossian poems, tested alternative relationships between historical progress and the cultivation of emotion. Women writers' investment in Scottish theories of progress also exerted a shaping influence on Ann Radcliffe's gothic novels and Maria Edgeworth's historical fiction. Their novelistic innovations were made possible, I argue, by their own readings of the comparative studies of progress they found in Scottish poetry and historiography.

This study places these innovations in women's writing alongside the rapid mid-century development of the British Empire both inside and outside the British Isles, highlighting the engagement of these literary forms with the Scottish Enlightenment's effort to understand development and progress on a global instead of a national scale. Internally, Lord Bute's rise to power in the 1760s as George III's prime minister, despite the maelstrom of anti-Scottish sentiment it unleashed, signaled the successful assimilation of Scotland into Great Britain after the uneasy union of 1707 and the rebellion of 1745. The global dimensions of the Seven Years War, which expanded British power not only in Europe but also in the Americas and India, drastically altered the size and makeup of the

British Empire. The cross-cultural comparative methodology employed in the historical, philosophical, and literary texts of the mid-eighteenth century was an effort to find new forms and structures for processing a global empire that included the "underdeveloped" economies and social systems of the Scottish Highlands, the Native American cultures of the New World, and the highly developed cultures of the East.[16] Instead of focusing on abstract political formations such as the state, mid-century female and male writers analyzed the social practices and organizations of a host of cultures, employing a comparative methodology that forced them to take into consideration people and customs around the globe and theorize development on a global as well as national scale. Daniel Carey and Lynn Festa have suggested that "the tendency to constitute the agency of empire in terms of nation states has occluded categories of sex/gender, rank, language, ethnicity, religion, and region."[17] By privileging the realm of the social, the literary and historical texts in this study think outside the parameters of the nation-state and trace an eighteenth-century theory of global development in which gender and women become central instead of peripheral issues.

My approach to mid-century women's writing also builds on recent efforts to challenge depictions of Enlightenment as a monolithic whole. Scottish literati have figured largely in the efforts of J. G. A. Pocock and others to develop a more nuanced view of Enlightenment. In the first volume of *Barbarism and Religion*, Pocock writes,

> If there is a single target of my criticism it is the concept of "The Enlightenment," as a unified phenomenon with a single history and definition, but the criticism is directed more against the article than against the noun. I have no quarrel with the concept of Enlightenment; I merely contend that it occurred in too many forms to be comprised within a single definition and history, and that we do better to think of a family of Enlightenments, displaying both family resemblances and family quarrels (some of them bitter and bloody).[18]

The Scottish branch of this complex Enlightenment family distinguished itself by creating a stadial theory of human development that traced the emergence of society instead of the state. Indebted to French philosophes, particularly Voltaire and Montesquieu, the Scots turned history away from an exclusive focus on wars and great men. In works such as *The Spirit of the Laws* (1748) and *Essay on the Manners and Spirit of Nations* (1756), their French counterparts also traced the development of civil society; however, these treatises emphasized climate, politics, and religion instead of economics as primary measures of social development.[19] Using economic shifts to designate eras, the stadial method pioneered in the Scottish Enlightenment posited four stages of human development: beginning with hunting and gathering cultures, moving though pastoral and agrarian periods, and culminating in the commercial world of the contemporary British Empire.

The dominant narrative of these Scottish histories celebrated the public participation of women as philanthropists and patrons of the arts, and Britain's advanced commercial society as the final stage of human development. Alternatively, the "rude" economies of both Native Americans and the Highlanders of Scotland and their indifference to women relegated them to an earlier stage of history. The recognition that different stages of history could be contemporaneous also gave rise to the influential concept of uneven development, which, in turn, provided ideological justification for the expansion of the British Empire. The major historiographers of the Scottish Enlightenment, including David Hume and Adam Smith, as Pocock writes, "looked on undifferentiated primal energy as barbaric and dangerous, and on the progress of society as the progressive diversification of human nature into the multifarious specialized pursuits of a commercial civilization, where they would become refined, reflective, moderate and even – though it was dangerous to say so – feminised."[20] In Pocock's account of the Scottish Enlightenment, social progress is a gendered continuum that moves from masculine "undifferentiated primal energy," a state of barely controlled individual passions, to a "refined" and "feminized" modernity in which emotions are tempered by a feminine desire to reflect on the needs and feelings of others. The "feminized" nature of commercial civilization not only produced men of feeling,[21] but also provided women writers with a new opportunity to reflect on their particular contribution to the civilizing process.

Scottish literati also had little interest in a state of nature and instead understood humanity as always already social. By taking sociality and the artifice that often springs from it as defining aspects of the human condition, the writers I explore represent, for the most part, what Sankar Muthu has called an "anti-imperial" strain of the Enlightenment.[22] According to Muthu, the "anti-imperial" perspective employed a comparative approach to understanding "cultural difference" and saw non-European people – particularly Native Americans and Africans – not as "acultural" or "asocial" examples of natural man, but as representatives of alternative social orders formed through interactions with their different environments.[23] In an effort to recuperate Enlightenment thought as a means for understanding our increasingly global world, the philosopher Amartya Sen has also focused on this comparative strain of Enlightenment thought, what he calls the "other" Enlightenment of "realization based comparisons" used by Enlightenment thinkers such as Adam Smith as well as Mary Wollstonecraft. Sen recovers this "other" Enlightenment as an alternative to the "transcendental institutionalism" of contractarians such as Thomas Hobbes, John Locke, and Jean-Jacques Rousseau.[24] Like recent readings of the Enlightenment by Pocock, Muthu, and Sen, this study complicates our understanding of Enlightenment thought as a monolithic set of universalizing ideals by looking beyond the social contract theory of Hobbes, Locke, and Rousseau and toward Scottish literati and their female contemporaries. By finding examples of feminine and anti-imperial strains of Enlightenment in a range of sources, from Minerva Press novels to philosophical treatises, my study also makes a case for the necessity of understanding Enlightenment as a disparate and often contradictory phenomena that understood humanity and theorized its development in a number of registers and genres.

The more complex understanding of Enlightenment that emerges from a study of these literary, historical, and philosophical texts also challenges the standard view of Enlightenment in feminist theory. For example, the attention paid to feelings and their effects within the Scottish Enlightenment has made it possible to see emotion as an important framework through which eighteenth-century history and progress was imagined. William Reddy in *The Navigation of Feeling* has argued that standard histories of the eighteenth century impose a Cartesian dualism on the period that creates a strict distinction between the mind and body, reason and emotion. These binaries are incompatible with the influential work of Shaftesbury, Adam Smith, and David Hume. Reddy uses this framework to investigate how the cultivation of emotion instead of reason was "the best protection against unruly passions."[25] In a similar vein, Mark Salber Philips has investigated the ways in which sentimental culture shifted historical discourse in the eighteenth century away from an exclusive focus on the state and politics and toward a greater understanding of the social realm; he traces this shift to eighteenth-century historians' engagement with the developing genre of the novel. He argues that the techniques the early novel used for representing the interior emotional states of characters migrated into historical discourse and helped historians understand history not as a record of battles and rulers but as a means of chronicling the development of humanity as a whole. Both Reddy and Philips see reason as secondary to emotion and understand Enlightenment as tracing or uncovering the ways in which emotions have been refined, cultivated, and understood across temporal and cultural divides.

Also interested in troubling hard and fast distinctions between reason and emotion or the mind and the body, feminist and queer literary and cultural theorists have contributed to what has been called the emotional or affective turn. Critics such as Ann Cvetkovich and Sara Ahmed have resisted seeing emotion as a purely psychological state and instead have concentrated on the ways in which emotion functions as a diagnostic for largely social and political problems.[26] Ahmed writes, "emotional states should not be regarded as psychological states, but as social and cultural practices."[27] I borrow from feminist theory's engagement with emotion and embodiment, but at the same time, I hope to complicate the status of Enlightenment thought within feminist theory. Viewed monolithically, Enlightenment has been understood as advocating an abstract masculine reason at the expense of embodied and feminine modes of thought. By complicating this view of Enlightenment, my study provides important background for contemporary conversations in feminist and queer theory surrounding emotion. The literary and historiographical forms created by the eighteenth-century writers and philosophers I study were an effort to narrativize the social evolution of "emotional states" and their complex relationship to economic and cultural variables. By investigating Enlightenment engagements with emotion as a productive social force, I hope to trouble entrenched feminist narratives, particularly liberal feminist ones, that often use the Enlightenment as a masculine and rational straw man, wholly responsible for destructive modern attitudes toward the body and emotion and the nemesis of post-Enlightenment women writers. The feminine Enlightenment I describe privileged emotion above reason and saw progress as a move toward a more feminine world marked by heightened emotional states, which were produced by modernity and the commercial, imperial, and artistic developments that gave it shape.

Undeniably, the persistent association of women and femininity with emotion has been problematic. Since Mary Wollstonecraft, feminists have been drawn to the negative consequences of late eighteenth-century discourses surrounding women and emotion. "Civilized women" crippled by "overstretched sensibilit[ies]" fill Wollstonecraft's *Vindication of the Rights of Women*.[28] Wollstonecraft turns to reason continually to reform women's affective defects and prepare them to contribute positively to the modern nation. Also haunted by emotion's deleterious impact, the Victorian narrative of separate spheres figures the delicate and emotional woman in the "angel in the house," who is too sensitive to circulate in a callous public world. Significantly, this figure has been attributed at least in part to late eighteenth-century books such as *A Father's Legacy to his Daughters*, which was written by Elizabeth Montagu's friend the Scottish Dr. John Gregory. Despite these powerful literary and philosophical characterizations of feeling women, I believe that it is possible to read women's association with emotion in alternative ways that do not necessarily presage these familiar nineteenth-century and twentieth-century narratives.

Late eighteenth- and early nineteenth-century women writers treated femininity in ways that challenge Wollstonecraft's one-dimensional characterization of feminine sensibility. Femininity's relationship to feeling made it a powerful historical force that functioned to gauge progress. In this context, delicate sentiments were not a weakness of women but a set of social practices that were cultivated within a culture over time to foster greater humanity in men and women. These writers explored the utility of feminine emotions in various time periods and cultures in order to mark progress and interrogate women's position in a larger world. The cultivation of humanity, the elevation of the feminine, and the progress of humankind were gauged by women's status, which was thought to correspond with a society's level of economic development. Often "underdeveloped" cultures' "rude" or "savage" treatment of women was used as a justification within imperial ideology. My study investigates how women both embraced their position within this narrative and looked for ways to trouble this continuum and to separate a feminine humanity from the disturbing imperial narrative it often underpinned.

Inspired by the comparative methodology used by the women writers and Scottish philosophers I study, *A Feminine Enlightenment* challenges conventional generic and historical boundaries that have separated feminine literary genres from the supposedly masculine realm of philosophy, poetry from novels, and the Romantic period from literature of the eighteenth century. In doing so, I invite readers to consider unlikely pairings. I begin with Adam Smith's philosophical meditation on feeling in his *Theory of Moral Sentiments* and reach into the early nineteenth century, connecting Smith's theory of feeling to the sentimental poems and novels of Anna Seward and Regina Maria Roche, two writers who have rarely been considered outside the context of women's literary history. Likewise, I track discussions of "women's progress" and historical and commercial development from the rarefied atmosphere of mid-eighteenth-century Bluestocking salons and the masculine domain of the Scottish university system to the popular Minerva Press novels of the early nineteenth century. The effect of these pairings is twofold: to show how developments in eighteenth-century women's literature engaged with Enlightenment discussions of emotion, sentiment, and commercial and imperial expansion; and to provide a new literary historical context for contemporary conversations that continue to use "women's progress" as well as the cultivation of sentiment to assign cultures and societies around the globe a place in universalizing schemas of development.

My first chapter pairs the Ossian poems and Adam Smith's *Theory of Moral Sentiments* (1759). I contend that Macpherson and Smith created a temporal map of emotion that gauged social development from "primitive" to "developed" cultures and offered women writers and Scottish philosophers a new field upon which they could experiment with the relationship between gender and historical progress. For example, in the *Theory of Moral Sentiments*, Smith paradoxically expresses reservations about a too feminine modernity and bemoans the diminution of the masculine in Europe, while theorizing the beneficial force of a feminine "humanity" as characteristic of more highly developed nations. Also engaging with this emerging theory of social progress, Macpherson complicates the relationship between gender and historical progress by allowing feminine sentiments to flourish in the "rude" Highlands of the third century. Despite their obvious differences, Macpherson and Smith used women's social status and the feminine values they were thought to impart to their male counterparts as tools for charting, evaluating, and questioning emerging theories of historical change.

My second chapter examines the Bluestockings' role in the development of the Scottish Enlightenment's cross-cultural theories of human development and in the popularization of their literary equivalent, Macpherson's Ossian poems. In addition to recovering the epistolary record of Montagu's influence on major figures of the Scottish Enlightenment as well as the popular Ossianic feasts she incorporated into her London salons, I also discuss the Ossianic imitations of the poet Catherine Talbot, Montagu's friend and contemporary. Montagu's Ossian-themed feasts – attended by her Bluestocking circle, which included James Macpherson and other Scottish literati – enacted the equivalent social relationships and produced the refined social sentiments conjectured by Macpherson's poems and theorized in the Scottish Enlightenment. Montagu's celebration and defense of Ossian also led to her correspondence and friendship with several Scots literati, including Dr. John Gregory, Lord Kames, Hugh Blair, and William Robertson. Her correspondence documents the Bluestockings' responses to the work of their Scottish contemporaries as well as their contribution to the new maps of historical development generated by the Scots at mid-century. The final portion of this chapter argues that Catherine Talbot tested this emergent historical consciousness in her Ossianic imitations, which reflect on the Seven Years War and women's role in the civilizing process. Talbot's imitations of Ossian's affect and perspective make visible the feminine and colonial histories that the English center – in its efforts to represent a homogeneous body politic – often elided.

My third chapter continues to explore the Bluestockings' theory of historical progress through a close reading of Anna Seward's *Llangollen Vale* (1796) as well as the extensive body of her published and unpublished correspondence. I argue that Seward's immersion in Enlightenment theories of aesthetic progress as well as her devotion to Ossianic sentiment shaped her *Llangollen Vale*. In describing this picturesque Welsh valley and celebrating its famous occupants, from the Welsh national hero Owen of Glendower to Seward's contemporaries and close friends the Ladies of Llangollen, Sarah Ponsonby and Eleanor Butler, Seward's poem critiques established narratives of historical progress and tests the possibility that the refined feelings and sentiments produced by female friendship might flourish outside modern commercial society and the heterosexual family. One of Seward's most popular long poems, *Llangollen Vale* patches together a non-linear history for this rural Welsh location that mixes antiquarian and bardic histories with the eighteenth-century tale of Butler and Ponsonby, members of the Irish gentry who ran away from Ireland, their families, and the prospect of financially advantageous marriages to live together in relative isolation in the Welsh countryside. Building on the work of theorists of queer history and affect such as Carolyn Dinshaw and Judith Halberstam, I claim that Seward creates a "new time" for the ladies of Llangollen that aligns their experience of queer exile from their families and nation with antiquarian and bardic accounts of Welsh resistance to English hegemony. In doing so, Seward explores alternatives to progressive accounts of economic and imperial development as well as normative temporalities of reproduction, family, and inheritance.

My fourth and fifth chapters demonstrate how these theories of historical progress migrated from poetry into the novel. The fourth chapter argues that attention to Ann Radcliffe's use of Scots poetry in the epigraphs of *The Mysteries of Udolpho* (1794) transforms the female gothic into an historical instead of a psychological analytic. In the tension between *Udolpho*'s representations of female sensibility and its paratext – what Gerard Genette calls the "border" or "threshold" of the text – this chapter finds an uneven and non-linear feminist historiography capable of producing unconventional accounts of women's experiences of British imperial and commercial growth. Specifically, Radcliffe uses James Thomson's *Castle of Indolence* (1748) and James Beattie's *The Minstrel* (1771) as signposts for Emily's journey, grafting Emily's "progress" onto eighteenth-century debates about history, the relationship between manners and economic structures, and the place of women in history. Drawing on discussions of gothic and modern women found in Richard Hurd's *Letters on Chivalry and Romance* in addition to the work of Adam Ferguson and Lord Kames, the first part of the chapter situates Emily St. Aubert, *The Mysteries of Udolpho*'s heroine, in the context of eighteenth-century histories of gender and emotion. The second part turns to Radcliffe's debt to the Scots poetry found on the borders of her novels and the impact of the Scottish Enlightenment's treatment of time on the new feminist literary tradition she is in the process of creating. Ultimately, by setting her heroine's progress against the historical debates that are staged in the novel's paratext, Radcliffe's gothic not only challenges the possibility of a universal or singular British history but also proposes a new historical and literary method for representing the multiple histories found within the construct of Great Britain.

In my final chapter, I argue that the questions about women and civilization first raised in the relatively elite milieu of Montagu's Bluestocking salons migrated into the popular fiction of the circulating libraries of the Romantic era, shaping conversations about women and historical progress into the early nineteenth century. The term stadial fiction, which I coin in this chapter through an analysis of Regina Maria Roche's hugely popular Minerva Press novel *The Children of the Abbey* (1796) as well as her lesser-known *The Contrast* (1828), draws attention to women writers' fictional adaptations of the multi-stage historical method developed during the Scottish Enlightenment. Stadial fiction highlights how Roche positions the feminine and aesthetic categories of delicacy, elegance, and beauty in relation to changing historical and economic conditions. To demonstrate Roche's potential contribution to a discussion of the aesthetics of progress, I illustrate how she was engaged with the same questions that occupied other Romantic-era novelists who have fared better in literary history. Like Maria Edgeworth's novels, particularly *The Absentee* and *Patronage*, Roche's heroines often embody feminine aesthetic categories such as elegance and delicacy. In fact, both Roche and Edgeworth have their heroines travel through a variety of social and economic environments within the British Isles and test the value of these feminine aesthetic categories in each place in order to assess each region's placement in their maps of the civilizing process. This comparative approach to charting progress, which was developed in the history, poetry, and philosophy of the Scottish Enlightenment, also appeared in aesthetic theories from the same period, including Hugh Blair's *Lectures on Rhetoric and Belles Lettres*, Kames's *Elements of Criticism*, and Dugald Stewart's *Philosophical Essays*. By reading these theories of the progress of aesthetics against Romantic-era fiction, this chapter also develops a new context for understanding the Romantic-era novel's stock heroines, who have often been dismissed as flat and market-driven creations designed only to please a popular audience.

I hope this account of women's writing and the Scottish Enlightenment's conception of progress might generate new questions about entrenched narratives that have been used to explain women's relationship to social progress and economic development. In his influential *Origin of the Family, Private Property and the State*, Friedrich Engels famously wrote:

> Peoples whose women have to work much harder than we would consider proper often have far more real respect for women than our Europeans have for theirs. The social status of the lady of civilization, surrounded by sham homage and estranged from all real work, is socially infinitely lower than that of the hard-working woman of barbarism, who was regarded among her people as a real lady and was such by the nature of her position.[29]

By recovering the Enlightenment origins of the comparative method Engels employs to theorize women's placement in world historical development, this study argues for a more nuanced depiction of the "lady of civilization" and the "hard-working woman of barbarism." Reconsidering the history of Engels's classic narrative of progress and gender in a range of eighteenth- and nineteenth-century literary and philosophical sources sheds new light on categories which have troubled feminism, such as femininity, delicacy, and refinement – categories often associated with the progress of the arts, the elevation of literature, as well as the general advance of civilization. The chapters that follow provide a literary historical context for the relationships Engels attempted to map, and raise a set of related questions that will be pursued in the course of this study. How do the women in the Ossian poems who both weep and wield a bow challenge our understanding of progress? When the Ladies of Llangollen refuse marriage and instead spend a lifetime cultivating sentimental attachments to ruins and books, do we read this as progress or regress? Is the stoic self-command of heroines in gothic and historical fiction a means of correcting over-indulgent moderns, an anachronism, or both? Finally, by comparing women's status across cultures and regions, can we map women's progress, or do these comparisons ultimately point to the futility of creating a universal women's history?

Notes

1. Elizabeth Montagu to Lord Kames, 11 February 1767, Abercairny Collection.
2. Montagu to Kames, 24 March 1767, Abercairny Collection.
3. Montagu to Kames, 27 October 1773, Abercairny Collection.
4. Montagu to Kames, 12 September 1774, Abercairny Collection.

5. Montagu to Kames, 7 May 1776, Abercairny Collection.
6. Although Toni Bowers in her recent and important study troubles our understanding of how liberal consent works through her reading of the seduction fiction of Tory writers like Behn, Manley, and Haywood, her study still adopts consent as a starting point. See Bowers, *Force or Fraud*; see also Helen Thompson's *Ingenuous Subjection: Compliance and Power in the Eighteenth-Century Domestic Novel* (Philadelphia: University of Pennsylvania Press, 2005) for an important discussion of the eighteenth-century domestic novel's negotiation of the politics of consent.
7. Important discussions of Wollstonecraft's work include Gary Kelly's *Revolutionary Feminism* and Barbara Taylor's *Mary Wollstonecraft and the Feminist Imagination*.
8. Adam Smith, *Theory of Moral Sentiments*, p. 222.
9. David Hume, "Of the Rise of the Arts and the Progress of Science," *Essays Moral, Political, and Literary*, p. 134.
10. See, for example, Kathryn Temple, *Scandal Nation*. The next chapter discusses the debates over literary originality and the Ossian poems at greater length.
11. Pam Perkins in *Women Writers and the Edinburgh Enlightenment* investigates Scottish women writers' engagement with the ideas of male literati. She argues that women's elevation in Scottish Enlightenment theory constructed a less rigid public and private divide than existed in England, and that public displays of intellectual achievement and private expressions of domestic virtues were not seen as mutually exclusive in turn-of-the-century Edinburgh. See also Katharine Glover's *Elite Women and Polite Society in Eighteenth-Century Scotland* for a discussion of Scottish women's participation in the culture of Enlightenment Edinburgh and their responses to major Scottish Enlightenment texts.
12. See Ian Baucom, *Specters of the Atlantic*; James Chandler, *England in 1819*; and Ian Duncan, *Scott's Shadow*.
13. Devoney Looser's *British Women Writers and the Writing of History* argues that shifts in the discipline of history allowed women to participate in the writing of history and created women as the ideal readers of general histories. According to Looser, reading history also allowed women to become acquainted with public life without acquiring the taint of exposure. She also suggests that examining women writers' relationship to eighteenth-century historiographical practices deepens our understanding of women intellectuals' investments and takes feminist criticism beyond a potentially anachronistic recovery of protofeminists.
14. The historian Jane Rendall has made the Scottish Enlightenment central in a series of books and essays on women and gender. See, for example, "Virtue and Commerce: Women and the Making of Adam Smith's Political Economy" and "Clio, Mars and Minerva: The Scottish Enlightenment and the Writing of Women's History."
15. See Karen O'Brien, *Women and Enlightenment in Eighteenth-Century Britain*.
16. See Penny Fielding, *Scotland and the Fictions of Geography*, for a discussion of the ways in which representations of "Scotland seemed to offer in miniature the key to a complete global understanding that would

make time and space simultaneously available as a subject of inquiry" (p. 2).

17. Daniel Carey and Lynn Festa, *The Postcolonial Enlightenment*, p. 24.
18. See J. G. A. Pocock, *Barbarism and Religion: The Enlightenments of Edward Gibbon, 1737–1764*, vol. 1, p. 9. Although they complicate and challenge Pocock's multiple Enlightenments, influential recent discussions of Enlightenment include Jonathan Israel, *Radical Enlightenment: Philosophy and the Making of Modernity 1650–1750* (New York: Oxford University Press, 2002) and Clifford Siskin and William Warner's collection *This is Enlightenment* (Chicago: University of Chicago Press, 2010).
19. Although a full discussion of the debt of Scottish history to the work of Montesquieu and Voltaire is outside the scope of this book, useful comparisons of the similarities and differences between these two approaches can be found in Silvia Sebastiani's *The Scottish Enlightenment: Race, Gender, and the Limits of Progress*. Her second chapter, "Hume versus Montesquieu: Race against Climate" (pp. 23–43), includes a particularly useful discussion of Hume and his fellow Scots literati's objections to Montesquieu's use of climate as a gauge of cultural difference; see also Karen O'Brien's *Narratives of Enlightenment: Cosmopolitan History from Voltaire to Gibbon* (Cambridge: Cambridge University Press, 1997) and Richard Sher's "From Troglodytes to Americans: Montesquieu and the Scottish Enlightenment on Liberty, Virtue, and Commerce," in David Wootton (ed.), *Republicanism, Liberty, and Commerical Society, 1649–1776* (Stanford: Stanford University Press, 1994), pp. 368–402.
20. Pocock, *Barbarism and Religion: Narratives of Civil Government*, vol. 2, p. 331.
21. For important discussions of the man of feeling, see Claudia Johnson, *Equivocal Beings* and Julie Ellison, *Cato's Tears and the Making of Anglo-American Emotion* (Chicago: University of Chicago Press, 1999).
22. Although Muthu focuses on Herder, Diderot, and Kant, he mentions Adam Smith and Adam Ferguson in the course of his study. See *Enlightenment against Empire*, pp. 3 and 70. See also Silvia Sebastiani, whose *The Scottish Enlightenment* parses the differences between Scottish literati's approaches to history. Notably, she argues that Kames's theory of polygenesis served as a foundation for modern racism and contributed to the imperial discourse of the eighteenth and nineteenth centuries.
23. Ibid., p. 39.
24. Amartya Sen, *The Idea of Justice*: "In contrast with transcendental institutionalism, a number of other Enlightenment theorists took a variety of comparative approaches that were concerned with social realizations . . . they were all involved in comparisons of societies that already existed or could feasibly emerge, rather than confining their analyses to transcendental searches for a perfectly just society. Those focusing on realization-focused comparisons were often interested primarily in the removal of manifest injustice from the world that they saw" (p. 7).
25. William Reddy, *The Navigation of Feeling*, p. 164.
26. Ann Cvetkovich, *An Archive of Feelings*, and Sara Ahmed, *The Cultural Politics of Emotion*.

27. Ahmed, *Cultural Politics of Emotion*, p. 9.
28. Mary Wollstonecraft, *A Vindication of the Rights of Woman*, pp. 65–6.
29. Friedrich Engels, *The Origin of the Family, Private Property and the State* (New York: International Publishers, 1942), p. 77.

Chapter 1

The Progress of Feeling:
The Ossian Poems and Adam
Smith's *Theory of Moral Sentiments*

Although James Macpherson and Adam Smith earned their places in the British cultural pantheon almost simultaneously, they appear to inhabit two different worlds: the Ossian poems (1760–3) imagine a Scottish past of Highland mists and long-gone Gaelic heroes, while *Theory of Moral Sentiments* (1759) belongs to the present and future of eighteenth-century Britain, the expanding commercial empire theorized in Smith's more famous treatise *The Wealth of Nations* (1776). Superficially, Macpherson's translation and reconstruction of fragmented Celtic legends still circulating in the Highlands and Smith's study of modern sensibility appear unlikely companions. The Ossian poems recount the epic battles of a group of third-century Highland warriors and attempt to capture in print the existence of a particularly Scottish literary and cultural heritage. In contrast, Smith's study of modern sensibility creates a global map of feeling, charting the ways in which we feel for people we have never met and in some cases never even seen. Yet Smith and Macpherson's texts characterize the same historical moment and were hugely popular throughout the eighteenth and early nineteenth centuries, going through several editions. Smith revised and reworked his theory of feeling in six editions from 1759–90; similarly, Macpherson's poems went through several editions and were translated into numerous languages, including Polish and Greek.[1] Both texts grappled with the internal and external expansion of the British Empire, particularly the changes wrought by the 1707 Act of Union, which united England and Scotland under one parliament, the failed Jacobite Rebellion in 1745, and the expansion of the British Empire after the Seven Years War.[2]

Most importantly, for the purposes of this book, both texts have been cited by historians and literary critics as key to understanding the eighteenth century as an Age of Sensibility, a period that valued the cultivation of feeling as much as reasoned discourse.[3] In the eighteenth century, discussions of the "progress of feeling" or "manners" were also debates about a civilizing process that mapped human development from the "rude" age depicted by Macpherson to the developed commercial society represented by Smith. Smith laid the groundwork for this debate in his *Theory of Moral Sentiments*. Throughout the text, Smith attempts to balance the stoic quality of self-command that he sees as dominant in the masculine societies found in the ancient world, as well as in the recently discovered cultures of the New World, with the more feminine and softer virtues of the modern European man of feeling. As a result, he has difficulty wholly embracing the emotional practices of either ancient or modern cultures: "The hardiness demanded of savages diminishes their humanity; and, perhaps, the delicate sensibility required in civilized nations sometimes destroys the masculine firmness of behavior."[4] The ambivalence Smith expresses about the civilizing process, which results in a feminized yet "humane" modernity that relegates masculine "firmness" to underdeveloped nations and their "rude" economies, is reflected in debates over the gender of progress and the status of women in commercial society throughout the later eighteenth century.

Macpherson moved in the same intellectual circles as Smith, and Smith, when a professor at the University of Glasgow, mentioned Ossian's poetry in his lectures on jurisprudence and rhetoric and *belles lettres* in the early 1760s.[5] Registering as an exception within Smith's overarching narrative of progress, Macpherson's verse depicts feminine sentiments as flourishing in the "rude" Highlands of the third century. In the preface to the first edition of *Fingal*, Macpherson used the Ossian poems to articulate questions about Smith's civilizing process, which aligns the development of "moral sentiments" with historical and economic progress. In the preface to the first edition of *Fingal*, he claims that "the prejudices of the present age against the ancient inhabitants of Britain" lead many readers to believe that the occupants of ancient Scotland were "incapable of the generous sentiments to be met with in the poems of Ossian."[6] According to Macpherson, this skepticism about the Ossian poems arose from the prejudices of commercial society. Only members of an advanced commercial society who were accustomed to a "well provided" table and "soft" bed would "place their ultimate happiness in those conveniences of life" and believe that only commerce could improve or refine feeling.[7] He undoes the dependence of fine feeling on the advance of commerce by arguing that "the general poverty of a nation has not the same influence, that the indigence of individuals in an opulent country, has upon the manners of the community" and claims that commerce, instead of increasing our capacity for fellow feeling, created "the idea of meanness" which did not exist until "commerce had thrown too much property into the hands of a few."[8] Macpherson's poems explore the possibility that

Smith's theory of the progress of moral sentiments might depend too heavily on an economic motor that distorts instead of develops the fine and feminine feelings so valued by Scots literati. Macpherson's poetry reinforces the argument of his preface by mixing stories of bloody, even "barbaric" hand-to-hand combat with scenes of men and women crying over poetry that would not be out of place in contemporary sentimental novels. In Macpherson's premodern world, feminine sentiments exist without an economic impetus – undoing the ideological work of British imperial expansion, which justifies its own progress with claims to improve the morals, manners, and feelings of those it encounters. The Ossian poems test the hypothesis that sensibility and sympathy are not dependent on economic development. In fact, Macpherson suggests that feminine sentiments can flourish in civil society without the existence of advanced commercial structures. This chapter explores Smith and Macpherson's understanding of feeling or sentiment as a means of gendering historical difference and progress for two related reasons: to demonstrate the centrality of gender to the Scottish Enlightenment, and to establish the grounds for women writers' engagement with the narratives of progress found in the literature and philosophy of Scottish literati.

Critics have traditionally read the tears and fine feelings that characterize Ossian's lays as intrusions of modern sentiments that reveal Macpherson's poems to be forgeries instead of translations of authentic third-century documents.[9] Depending on what side of the debate a critic takes, James Macpherson can either emerge as a brazen liar or a defender of Scottish national identity, just as his most famous critic Samuel Johnson can appear as either a canny defender of literary originality or an English xenophobe fueled by anti-Scottish sentiment.[10] Recent critical attention has complicated Ossianic verse's status in literary history, focusing on the poems' negotiation of the divide between oral culture and the world of print and on their contribution to developing understandings of race and empire;[11] yet, debates over the Ossian poems' authenticity still overshadow their important influence on the historiographic methods pioneered by Macpherson's Scottish contemporaries and their reception among women writers who were, by and large, unconcerned with originality and authorship. The Ossian craze, which began in the 1760s and lasted well into the nineteenth century, was contemporaneous with the social histories that were written by Smith's students and interlocutors, including Lord Kames, Hugh Blair, James Millar, and Adam Ferguson. All of these writers discussed the poems, and often incorporated portions of Ossianic verse into their own philosophical works, which have been read as foundational texts for the modern disciplines of sociology, anthropology, and political economy.[12] Although the poems' authenticity was hotly debated in the years following their publication and, in some quarters, continues to be debated today,[13] these mid-century literati often accepted their third-century provenance, and the poems became an important laboratory for thinking through the relationship of feeling to economic structures and developing notions of historical progress. The indelible mark the Ossian poems left on the philosophical and historiographic methods pioneered by Scots literati and developed in the nineteenth and twentieth centuries transcends the issues of authenticity that are so central for scholars interested in the nature of literary originality and property or changing understandings of authorship. Focusing on the influence on historiography of the affective histories, which were pioneered in the Scottish Enlightenment in verse and prose, creates a new lens for understanding the contributions of late eighteenth- and early nineteenth-century women writers, who frequently referenced Ossian and Smith in their letters, poetry, and fiction, not as a means of considering questions of their own originality or authorship but as a tool for framing questions about gender and historical development.

In this chapter, I read the Ossian poems alongside Smith's theory of feeling as a context for the work of the women writers who are the subject of this book. In particular, I focus on the ways in which Smith used shifts in social attitudes toward gender and women's status to develop a universal scale of development, a measure that I suggest falls apart in his own theory of the impartial spectator whose temporal and gender ambivalence undermines Smith's theory of history. I am also interested in this chapter in seeing how Macpherson's poetry worked alongside Smith's philosophy, inviting readers to reassess the gendered dynamics of historical progress and reconsider the role of feeling in universalizing narratives of historical development. By suggesting that in ancient Caledonia the rude technologies associated with other premodern cultures coexisted alongside the cultivated feelings that were thought to be markers of modern commercial society,[14] Macpherson questioned the nature of progress and the relationship between developed economic structures and the fine feelings they were thought to produce. Ossianic women possessed masculine and feminine attributes and contributed to society in ways that most thinkers assumed impossible in "primitive societies." Unlike other premodern societies familiar to eighteenth-century readers from travel writing and historical surveys, such as the Native Americans of the New World or the Spartans of Ancient Greece, the Caledonian warriors encountered in Ossian's poetry not only cultivated the expression of emotion, they also valued women's perceived ability to inspire their male counterparts with sympathy and humanity and allowed women to participate actively in the public and private realms. The anachronistic sentiments and manners of Ancient Caledonians threatened to undermine the logic of imperialism, which depended on understanding expansion as not just a commercial but a moral development. These anomalous feelings also challenged reductive understandings of the "progress" of women that often equated imperial progress with an increased regard for women and feminine traits. The refined and delicate sentiments and the rude and violent passions discussed by Smith and Macpherson create the foundation for the following chapters of this book, which traces the ways women writers, including first and second generation Bluestockings as well as gothic and historical novelists of a slightly later period, engaged with these Enlightenment debates about the progress of feeling and the development of commercial society articulated by Smith, Macpherson, and their contemporaries.

Adam Smith's Historiographies of Feeling

The emphasis Adam Smith places on the progress of feeling in the *Theory of Moral Sentiments* might best be understood in the context of his theory of history, bits and pieces of which are found throughout his writings as well as his unpublished treatise on jurisprudence, the manuscript of which Smith had destroyed after his death. The student notes that have survived from Smith's lectures on law and civil society, which were given at the University of Glasgow from 1762–3, articulate in broad strokes the way in which Smith restructured existing understandings of social development and departed from the social contract tradition which had dominated British philosophy since Thomas Hobbes's *Leviathan*. Instead of assuming that sociability only begins when man consents to a social contract, Smith argues that to be social is to be human, and that manners and behavior change as the economic structures of the society being studied develop.[15] He breaks human history into four stages: "the first, the Age of Hunters, second, the Age of Shepherds, third, the Age of Agriculture, fourth the Age of Commerce."[16] His materialist history mapped economic "progress," what Karl Marx would later call shifts in "modes of production," onto the development of civil society. Although Smith was not an active participant in the debate over Ossian as were his peers Blair, Ferguson, and even David Hume, the Ossian poems appear in the lectures as an example of the first age. In contrasting Ancient Romans with their less advanced contemporaries, he says, "the Scots and Picts . . . as we see from the poems of Ossian were much in the same state as the Americans, tho they don't appear to have had the custom of roasting men alive."[17] Smith's stadial history – or what his biographer and student Dugald Stewart, using a more capacious term, named "conjectural history" – traced human development through four stages of social and economic growth, from the rude manners and often violent feelings that characterized hunting and gathering societies to the refined and polite sentiments that shaped the complex exchanges of modern commercial society.[18] According to Stewart, conjectural history captures the trajectory of human development from "uncultivated nature, to a state of things so wonderfully artificial and complicated."[19]

Recent interest in Adam Smith's contributions to the disciplines of history and anthropology have changed the way we understand him as both an economist and a moral philosopher. Attention to Smith's historical method has led critics such as James Chandler and Ian Duncan to identify Smith as deeply aware of the "uneven" power relationships and geographical hierarchies created by global commerce. They argue that Smith's theory of history found in his *Lectures on Jurisprudence* as well as his *Theory of Moral Sentiments* reflects his ambivalence about progress and the commercial expansion of the British Empire.[20] By separating human development into four stages, Smith's theory of history allowed for comparisons between, for example, the "rude" societies of Native Americans and Highlanders and the refined culture of modern Britain. These comparisons resulted in the production of a conceptual framework for Marxist discussions of uneven development as well as what Chandler has called "comparative contemporaneities."[21] For Chandler, "comparative contemporaneities" are the distinguishing feature of Romantic historicism, evident in its tendency to measure the present moment against distant places as well as previous ages. As Chandler argues, time and the mapping of human development in the eighteenth century became as much a function of geography as chronology.

Although capital overshadows sentiment in his *Wealth of Nations*, Smith's theory of history also shapes his theory of political economy, which equates economic transformations with historical ones. In describing commerce's relationship to development, Smith uses Scotland and England as an example of two different temporal stages existing side by side. When discussing the different demands for labor in Scotland and England, Smith writes, "The wages of labour, it has already been observed, are lower in Scotland than in England. The country too is not only much poorer, but the steps by which it advances to a better condition, for it is evidently advancing, seem to be much slower and more tardy."[22] When speaking of the "super-abundant" material for making cloth available in Scotland, specifically wool, Smith cites the Highlands as failing to cultivate the industry necessary to maximize its natural resources, describing the Highlands of Scotland "now" as England "was then" in a distant past.[23] Although he describes both nations in 1776, Scotland exists in a past left behind by England. The disjunction between the two countries emerges as a temporal one explained by stadial history, and the construct of Great Britain appears capable of accommodating the polyvalent time this disjunction creates. In the *Theory of Moral Sentiments*, Smith ties these economic differences to the development of social sentiments and feelings:

> The different situations of different ages and countries are apt, in the same manner, to give different characters to the generality of those who live in them, and their sentiments concerning the particular degree of each quality that is either blameable or praiseworthy, vary according to that degree which is usual in their own country and in their own times.[24]

Although many of the cultural comparisons introduced by Smith and developed in the conjectural histories of other Scottish literati such as Lord Kames, John Millar, and Adam Ferguson reinforced stadial history's universalizing narrative of human history, other examples used by these writers raised questions about the idea of progress and troubled modern Britain's position as a developmental endpoint.

The inconsistencies inherent in Smith's brand of comparative history can be seen in the brief history of women that Smith includes in his *Lectures on Jurisprudence*. In a passage that compares women in Turkey, Greece, France, and North America, Smith offers two competing understandings of women's progress. At one point, he argues that women are taken more seriously in earlier ages: "Tho' there was little regard paid to women in the first state of society as objects of pleasure, yet there never was more regard paid them as rational creatures."[25] In an age where there is no time for "pleasure" and the cultivation of feeling, women are not valued for their feminine attractions but for their ability to function in a masculine and "rational" sphere; for example, he describes women in North America as being "consulted concerning the carrying on of war, and in every important undertaking."[26] Yet Smith introduces a slightly different account earlier in the same passage, when he argues that women in modern society enjoy greater liberty and fear none of the dangers associated with being mere possessions of their spouses: "In Sparta it was common for them to borrow and lend their wives. When manners become more refined, jealousy began and rose at length to such a height that wives were shut up, as they are among the Turks at this day. As mankind became more refined, the same fondness which made them shut up women made them allow them liberties."[27] Women's progress emerges as erratic and inconsistent. Although in some "rude" cultures women are treated as rational, they run the risk of being "borrowed," traded, and later imprisoned. In the modern world, they are not viewed as rational equals, but they enjoy greater liberty because of their ability to add pleasure to man's social environment. His account of women's progress, as Karen O'Brien argues, "remains complex and contradictory,"[28] filled with paradoxes that were taken up repeatedly in both the philosophy and fiction of the later eighteenth century.

Although Smith mentions women only sparingly in his *Theory of Moral Sentiments* – and references to the impartial spectator, the central figure of his treatise, mark it as clearly male – Smith's focus on the hard and soft characteristics of feeling, particularly the violent, delicate, or stoic ways in which feeling might be expressed, result in a gendering of not only particular emotions but also stages of history, as Jane Rendall has argued.[29] Smith's ambivalence about commercial progress in *The Theory of Moral Sentiments* becomes most pronounced when he departs from his analysis of modern man, particularly in the section "Of the Influence of Custom and Fashion Upon the Sentiments of Moral Approbation and Disapprobation." His brief discussions of both Native Americans and modern women, two poles of emotional development between which modern man finds himself, illuminates the gendered nature of historical progress, which emerges as a movement from a hyper-masculine and rude age to a feminine and refined modernity.

In Smith's treatise on feeling, the Native American represents the first stage of social and economic development, "the age of hunters," and embodies the masculine virtue of self-command.[30] Concerned mainly with survival and subsistence, the "savage," according to Smith, is "too much occupied with [his] own wants to give much attention to those of another person."[31] He has neither time to feel for others nor to luxuriate in the favorite pastime of modern man, worrying about what others feel for him. In a famous passage, Smith describes a Native American's seeming insensibility to pain:

> While he is hung by the shoulders over a slow fire, he derides his tormentors, and tells them with how much more ingenuity he himself had tormented such of their countrymen as had fallen into his hands. After he has been scorched and burnt and lacerated in all the most tender and sensible parts of his body for several hours together, he is often allowed, in order to prolong his misery, a short respite, and is taken down from the stake; he employs this interval in talking upon all indifferent subjects, inquires after the news of his country, and seems indifferent about nothing but his own situation.[32]

Smith views the savage's impenetrability as both dangerous and admirable.[33] He worries that "[b]arbarians ... being obliged to conceal the appearance of every passion" readily cultivate "falsehood and dissimulation."[34] The savage becomes unreadable and his reactions cannot be anticipated. A seemingly calm exterior might disguise passions "mounted to the highest pitch of fury."[35] Yet he also attributes a "heroic and unconquerable firmness" to the savage and expresses, through his depiction of savage feeling, frustration with overly effusive moderns.[36]

Smith's ambivalence about modernity and commercial progress emerges from these comparisons of the emotions of the Native American to the modern European. He attempts to console himself for the lack of "masculine firmness" found in his modern world by attributing the savage's self-command to his necessary focus on subsistence, a focus that belongs to a separate world, even an earlier time. He finds that "[a]mong civilized nations, the virtues which are founded upon humanity are more cultivated than those which are founded upon self-denial and the command of the passions. Among rude and barbarous nations it is quite otherwise – the virtues of self-denial are more cultivated than those of humanity."[37] A humane and civilized society cannot help but look soft and feminine when compared to "rude and barbarous nations." He regrets the disappearance of Stoicism in the modern era, writing, "the weakness of love, which is so much indulged in ages of humanity and politeness, is regarded among savages as the most unpardonable effeminacy."[38] Smith returns to this comparison again and again, and each time modern man looks less and less like the developed specimen one would expect from the progressive schema of Smith's stadial history. He concludes his section on custom and fashion by reiterating the difference between "savage" and civilized man: "Hardiness is the character most suitable to the circumstances of a savage; sensibility to those of one who lives in a very civilized society. Even here, therefore, we cannot complain that the moral sentiments of men are very grossly perverted."[39] Ultimately, Smith's language suggests that, although excessive sentiment is proper to the modern age and not the "perversion" it may appear, the civilizing process results in an attenuation of society's masculine virtues.

Yet he also acknowledges the advantages to be found in his modern age of feeling. He describes "polished people" as "frank, open, and sincere,"[40] and finds they have a greater capacity for sympathy: "A humane and polished people, who have more sensibility to the passions of others, can more readily enter into an animated and passionate behavior."[41] He finds women best able to enter into the "passions of others" and describes humanity as "the virtue of a woman."[42] He goes on to explain that

> Humanity consists merely in the exquisite fellow-feeling which the spectator entertains with the sentiments of the persons principally concerned, so as to grieve for their sufferings, to resent their injuries, and to rejoice in their good fortune. The most humane actions require no self-denial, no self-command, no great exertion of the sense of propriety.[43]

Women's talent for "mere fellow feeling" without the ability to exercise "self-command" or even "propriety" contrasts sharply with the masculine savage's ability to suppress emotion and endure unimaginable pain. Yet the ability of women to enter into the suffering of others is nonetheless "exquisite" – in marked contrast to the "rude" emotions characteristic of an earlier age. Smith suggests that the sensibility of men bears a direct relationship to their treatment of women: "To talk to a woman as we would a man is improper: it is expected that their company should inspire us with more gaiety, more pleasantry, and more attention; and an entire insensibility to the fair sex renders a man contemptible in some measure even to men."[44] Despite Smith's comments on the ameliorative effects of cultivating feminine sentiments, he returns repeatedly to the dangerous consequences of overidentification with the object of suffering: "Women, and men of weak nerves, tremble and are overcome with fear, though sensible that themselves are not the objects of anger. They conceive fear, however, by putting themselves in the situation of the person who is so."[45] Interestingly, Smith turns to temporality to resolve the problem of overidentification. He writes, "time, the great and universal comforter, gradually composes the weak man."[46] He adds that "Time, however, in a longer or shorter period, never fails to compose the weakest woman to the same degree to tranquility as the strongest man."[47] Although no longer in a historical register, Smith continues to gender temporal difference. In this instance, nothing separates those of a weak feminine or strong masculine character but a "longer or shorter period" of time.

Smith's ambivalence about the masculine spirit of the earliest stages of human development as well as the feminine character of his own modern age invites a reconsideration of established narratives of development. Smith's stoic barbarians and emotive moderns provide an alternative to Norbert Elias's account in *The Civilizing Process* of humanity's movement from the freedom of emotional expression that he sees as prevalent in earlier ages to an increasing emphasis on the repressive forces of "social constraint."[48] Smith's account also raises questions about dominant narratives of the Enlightenment. Maureen Harkin sees Smith's account of the savage as reinforcing the rational Enlightenment subject: "Now it is polite society which evinces loss and a kind of poverty, and the savage begins to appear as the bearer of the kind of self-regulating rationality that is the dominant value not only in Smith's ethics but in the Enlightenment conception of the human subject."[49] In Harkin's assessment, the savage's self-command comes much closer to the "self-regulating rationality" of the ideal Enlightenment subject than the feeling and humane modern man Smith describes. Admittedly, this is one reading of Smith's reevaluation of the primitive, which reinforces traditional understandings of the Enlightenment as a movement toward reason and away from feeling. However, recent work by J. G. A. Pocock and others has moved scholars away from thinking about a singular Enlightenment narrative or set of ideas.[50] Attempts to think about multiple Enlightenments have been particularly productive for scholars of the Scottish Enlightenment, who have illuminated David Hume's and Smith's theories of feeling and sociability. This new scholarship suggests that Smith was not interested in producing a wholly rational Enlightenment subject or in recovering an unequivocal progress for modernity, but in understanding how emotions as well as reason influence behavior and are produced by larger economic and historical forces.

Historical Distance and Smith's Spectator

Smith's spectator has often been thought of as a means of negotiating distance, whether it be the distance between the spectator and the actor in David Marshall's account of the theatrical dimension of sympathetic identification or the geographical distance separating a victim of disaster and a spectator halfway across in the globe in Kwame Anthony Appiah's recent meditation on the responsibilities of a cosmopolitan.[51] Smith's attempt to trace a progress of feeling through ages or eras of human development also invites us to see his spectator as grappling with historical distance.[52] Smith's ideal spectator or moral observer searches for a balance between the overabundance of feminine sensibility in the modern age and the paucity of feeling he finds in the age of hunters. By mediating between stages of history, his ideal spectator takes on an androgynous quality and inhabits a position outside or between times.

As if to reflect his ambivalent nature, Smith's moral agent, who watches and reads about the events that unfold around him, has two parts. The spectator is wholly human, while the impartial spectator, who occupies the hearts of all humans, is both a part of the individual and a part of a larger universal human spirit. Smith's spectator observes and acts in the moment, but before the moment can become part of an overarching narrative it must be rehashed by the impartial spectator, to whom the spectator constantly appeals. The present moment emerges as incoherent and impenetrable, until it passes and can be rationally dealt with by the impartial spectator:

> But though man has . . . been rendered the immediate judge of mankind, he had been rendered so only in the first instance; and an appeal lies from his sentence to a much higher tribunal, to the tribunal of their own consciences, to that of the supposed impartial and well informed spectator, to that of the man within the breast, the great judge and arbiter of their conduct.[53]

While the mortal spectator is present in "the first instance," he always must "appeal" to the impartial spectator, recounting the present moment over which the "man within the breast" adjudicates. The "man within the breast, the abstract and ideal spectator of our sentiments" aids the mortal spectator in reimagining and redacting what has just occurred. In this sense, we can only ever know or experience the present moment at a temporal remove. The impartial spectator locates himself temporally both a step behind the victim and in the future as the arbiter of an event's outcome. Since we are all at times the sufferer and at other times making an "appeal" to the impartial spectator, we occupy two temporalities at once: as the sufferer, we exist wholly in the affect of the moment; as the impartial spectator, we experience a time delay, imagining the victim's initial pain and attempting to use reason to assimilate his or her past experience into our vision of the future. Smith frequently returns to this potential temporal gap when describing proper sympathetic identification: "The man whose sympathy keeps time to my grief, cannot but admit the reasonableness of my sorrow."[54] Yet to effectively "keep time," the impartial spectator must use the imagination as a time machine, traveling backwards in order to find fellowship with the sufferer toward whom he directs his sympathy.

The sympathetic agent Smith describes borrows from both the masculine and feminine poles of human development, making him difficult to locate on a historical or gender spectrum. At times, Smith's spectator seems to exist in two separate temporalities and two different places. Smith mixes elements of both the stoic savage and the "exquisite" productions of the feminine and modern age in his description of the ideally sympathetic subject. Smith's subject needs to restrain his feelings by calling on the impartial spectator, who teaches the agent the savage's self-command and aids him in tempering his emotions, instructing him to "flatten . . . the sharpness of [his passions'] natural tone, in order to reduce it to harmony and concord with the emotions of those who are about him."[55] This repression exists alongside Smith's desire for humanity "to feel much for others" because "to indulge our benevolent affections constitutes the perfection of human nature; and can alone produce among mankind that harmony of sentiments and the passions in which consists their whole grace and propriety."[56] The balance between masculine fortitude and feminine "indulgence" emerges in his description of the proper operation of sympathy. For example, before the observer can "heartily sympathize with the gratitude of one man towards another,"[57] there always seems to be an awkward prelude, where the spectator withholds his sympathy while the "man within the breast" exercises his self-command and adjudicates, deciding if an outpouring of emotion is warranted. As Smith writes, "Our heart must adopt the principles of the agent, and go along with all the affection which influenced his conduct before it can entirely sympathize with, and beat time to, the gratitude of the person who had been benefited by his action."[58] Smith's description of sympathetic identification emerges as a complicated weighing of masculine and feminine attributes.

Significantly, this gender difference also registers as a temporal one. If imagination and its vehicle, the impartial spectator, must both register and adjudicate on the event being described or observed, the ability of the subject to "keep time" must always be in question. To borrow Smith's orphic metaphor, the "harmony and concord" the impartial spectator seeks counter-intuitively requires him to miss a beat, "flatten ... his natural tone," satisfy himself with operating in a slightly off-beat and off-key fashion.[59] Smith summarizes the experience of living in this offbeat moment, the moment in which the spectator realizes he or she will never be able to "keep time" with the agent for whom he or she feels so deeply: "Though they will never be unisons, they may be concords, and this is all that is wanted or required."[60] In settling for concordance, Smith acknowledges "[t]hat imaginary change of situation, upon which sympathy is founded, is but momentary" and that "compassion can never be the same as original sorrow."[61] The time-lag experienced by Smith's spectator makes possible a number of readings that rely on postcolonial theories of time and subjectivity. For example, the failure of sustained synchronous feeling can be likened to what Homi Bhaba in *Location of Culture* calls the ambivalent "double-time" of the modern nation.[62] In Smith's theory of sympathy, the present moment of feeling from which the spectator must distance himself becomes what Bhaba describes as a "disruptive anterior" that "displaces the historical present – open[ing] it up to other histories and incommensurable narrative subjects."[63] Using a similar postcolonial theory of subjectivity, Luke Gibbons in *Edmund Burke and Ireland* reads Smith's spectator as a divided subject, attempting to straddle two histories and two nations. According to Gibbons, the immortal and disembodied spectator is free to benefit from the commercial advantages of the Union of 1707, while the mortal observer feels the cultural and physical wounds inflicted by the British before and after the Union.[64] What Gibbons' reading of the time of the spectator misses, however, is the gendered ambivalence that seems to complement the temporal confusion at the heart of *Theory of Moral Sentiments*. The Scottish Enlightenment historiographies that followed Smith's *Theory of Moral Sentiments* continued to struggle with this gendered trajectory of progress. As Silvia Sebastiani writes, "Gender confusion, concern for masculinity, and familiar complaints about feminization and commodification became integrated within the progressive historical scheme" of the Scottish Enlightenment.[65]

Smith's ideal subject balances self-command and humanity, the characteristics of the stoical savage and the delicate modern woman: "The man who, to all the soft, the amiable, and the gentle virtues, joins all the great, the awful, and the respectable, must surely be the natural and proper object of our highest love and admiration."[66] Unfortunately, this ideal balance is impossible to achieve because, as Smith explains,

> The situations in which the gentle virtue of humanity can be most happily cultivated, are by no means the same with those which are best fitted for forming the austere virtue of self-command. The man who is himself at ease can best attend to the distress of others. The man who is himself exposed to hardships is immediately called upon to attend to, and to control his own feelings ... It is upon this account, that we so frequently find in the world men of great humanity who have little self-command, but who are indolent and irresolute, and easily disheartened, either by difficulty or danger, from the most honourable pursuits; and, on the contrary, men of the most perfect self-command, whom no difficulty can discourage, no danger appall, and who are at all times ready for the most daring and desperate enterprises, but who, at the same time, seem to be hardened against all sense either of justice or humanity.[67]

Modernity produces the gentle and feminine "ease" man requires to feel for others, while the rude age and the "hardships" of subsistence living produce the necessary masculine "control" man requires to maintain the boundaries between the self and other that propriety and self-preservation demand. Ultimately, Smith's spectator mediates between gender and historical divides; yet, this spectator is an historical anomaly that joins the specific ages or temporalities that for Smith define our capacity for fellow feeling, or what Appiah has called the "limits of [our] moral imagination."[68]

Like Smith's ideal spectator, who impossibly spans historical and gender divides, many of the heroines and heroes of Ossian appear to challenge the terms of existing historical maps. James Macpherson's own theory of history, which he explicates in the dissertation he authored as an introduction to his final poem *Temora*, illustrates his argument with Smith:

> There are three stages in human society. The first is the result of consanguinity, and the natural affection of the members of a family to one another. The second begins when property is established, and men enter into associations for mutual defence against the invasions and injustice of neighbors. Mankind submit, in the third, to certain laws and subordinations of government, to which they trust the safety of their persons and property. As the first is formed on nature, so, of course, it is the most disinterested and noble. Men, in the last have leisure to cultivate the mind, and to restore it, with reflection, to a primaeval dignity of sentiment.[69]

Although Macpherson points to the shift in sentiment caused by changing economic and political structures, the final stage of human development merely restores the "dignity of sentiment" extant in the first stage. In Macpherson's account, any sense of progress is replaced by a more circular movement of restoration, which revives the ideal social conditions found in a "primaeval" society like the one Macpherson describes in Ossian. The remainder of this chapter examines the Ossian poems' intervention in this Enlightenment narrative of progress, arguing that the poems both examine the relationship between economic and social development and, ultimately, reject Smith's claim that delicate sentiments were manufactured by advanced commercial society. In doing so, the poems raise a number of questions about gender and progress and introduce a number of anomalous women, who, like the impartial spectator, trouble conventional understandings of gender and historical progress.

Undoing the Progress of Feeling

Perhaps the most famous poem of the Ossian series, *Fingal*, appeared in December of 1761. Published after the enthusiastic reception of *Fragments of Ancient Poetry* (1760), Macpherson's epic recounts the Irish chief Cuchullin's battle with the Scandinavian leader Swaran.[70] Faced with defeat, Cuchullin and the Irish people are saved by their Scottish allies, led by Fingal. From December 1761 until June of 1762, the *Scots Magazine* published an extensive review of *Fingal* which took issue with the poem's anachronistic depiction of ancient Caledonia. Significantly, the elements of *Fingal* that the reviewer understood as anachronistic were also moments when feminine sentiments or manners seemed to dominate Ossian's rude age. The reviewer promised to address the "beauties and blemishes" of this controversial poem;[71] as the months passed, the review became more and more acerbic and skeptical and the blemishes began to outweigh the beauties. In one instance, the reviewer takes issue with the authenticity of Macpherson's description of Cuchullin's famed chariot from Book 1 of the poem:[72] "Its sides are embossed with stones, and sparkle like the sea round the boat of night. Of polished yew is its beam, and its set of the smoothest bone. The sides are replenished with spears; and the bottom is the footstool of heroes."[73] The reviewer cannot imagine the manly Cuchullin stuffing himself into this jewel-encrusted vehicle, or the fear the chariot purportedly inspires in Cuchullin's enemies. He writes, "Indeed, the great object of the son of Arno's fear seems to be the finery of the chariot and prancing of the horses of Cuchullin; for in the description of the hero himself, there is nothing very martial."[74] The reviewer concludes that this vehicle should have led Cuchullin's enemy to ridicule instead of terror: "It had at least, been with much greater propriety; had the latter concluded that Cuchullin was weak and effeminate, from the magnificent foppery of his car; a foppery, by the way, little consistent with that penurious simplicity of manners described in other parts of the poem."[75] In the conclusion of his lengthy review, the author expresses frustration with the mounting paradoxes of the poem: "Cuchullin's car and harness are adorned with gems, and yet he has nothing better to drink out of than a shell."[76] The reviewer becomes so exasperated that he gives up, claiming "the puerilities and improprieties are too manifest to need pointing out, nor can we think that they justly reflect the real manners of the people and the times."[77] He reads the chariot's "effeminate" and "foppish" decoration, as well as its "prancing" horses, as anachronistic in the age of Ossian. The fact that "there is too manifest an incongruity in the representation of things, which could not hardly exist in the same time and place" leads to speculation about the authenticity of the poems as well as their representation of the sentiments and manners of ancient Caledonians.[78]

The reviewer concludes that Macpherson's ancient Highlanders behave in a manner that is incompatible with their level of development: "In regard to manners, the piece is equally defective . . . the manners of no age or people could be so inconsistent as they are represented in the poem."[79] Cuchullin's lack of "martial" character, as well as the tears shed by men and women alike, register not as a part of "primitive" societies where, as Smith demonstrates, self-command and stoic bravery dominate. The finer sensibilities enjoyed by Ossian and his peers are more appropriate to modern and cultivated societies. From the time of its initial publication, the debate surrounding Ossian and its historical significance coalesced around the issues of "manners," sentiment, and gender. The refined and feminine sentiments that characterized the

Ossianic age were a point of interest for both the poems' defenders and detractors, and generated a serious conversation about the gender of progress, which continued in a variety of genres including philosophical and historiographical treatises, poetry and fiction, and literary criticism.

Attention to the historical "improprieties," which were frequently also gender improprieties, in Ossian's poetry polarized the public and also motivated Hugh Blair's famous defense, which was published in subsequent editions of the poems from 1763 onwards. In his "Critical Dissertation on the Poems of Ossian," Hugh Blair, the first Professor of Rhetoric and Belles Lettres at the University of Edinburgh and a friend of both Smith and Macpherson,[80] defended the authenticity of Macpherson's poems and claimed, taking inspiration from Smith's stadial theory of history, that "of the four stages of history" the poems belonged to the first. Yet, because the poems "awake the tenderest sympathies, and inspire the most generous emotions," Blair spends a large part of the dissertation reconciling these fine feelings with the rude Ossianic age.[81] He acknowledges that "War and bloodshed reign through the Illiad . . . Whereas in Ossian . . . There is a finer mixture of war and heroism, with love and friendship."[82] He also admits that "We find tenderness, and even delicacy of sentiment, greatly predominant over fierceness and barbarity."[83] Ultimately, he finds the refined emotions within Ossian's verse and the prevalence of women in the plot, as warriors and huntresses, almost as disconcerting as the reviewer from the *Scots Magazine* found Cuchullin's jewel-box chariot: "A variety of personages of different ages, sexes, and conditions are introduced into his poems; and they speak and act with a propriety of sentiment and behavior, which it is surprising to find in so rude an age."[84]

Not willing to abandon the poems, as did the reviewer from the *Scots Magazine*, Blair attempts to explain their paradoxical nature by taking on the impossible task of dividing genuine affect from the affected performance of false feeling. He attributes to Ossian the ability to record and express delicate sentiments without the mannered affectation that characterizes the modern age: "His great art . . . lies in giving vent to the simple and natural emotions of the heart. We meet with no exaggerated declamation; no subtle refinements on sorrow; no substitution of description in place of passion."[85] Blair also works to protect the masculinity of the Highland warriors he describes: "The heroes show refinement of sentiment indeed on several occasions, but none of manners."[86] Despite his best efforts to separate the poems from the overwrought displays of emotion that Blair associated with modernity, there remains something curiously modern and feminine about Ossian and his verse:

> No poet knew better how to seize and melt the heart. With regard to dignity
> of sentiment, the pre-eminence must clearly be given to Ossian. This is indeed
> a surprising circumstance, that in point of humanity, magnanimity, virtuous
> feelings of every kind, our rude Celtic bard should be distinguished to such a
> degree that not only the heroes of Homer, but even those of the polished and
> refined Virgil, are left far behind those of Ossian.[87]

Ossian emerges as not only "surprising" in his "polish" and "refinement," but also feminine in his demonstrations of "humanity." Echoing
Smith's description of humanity, the most feminine and delicate sentiment, Blair describes the bard as possessed with "an exquisite sensibility
of heart" and "susceptible of strong and soft emotions."[88] Like Smith's
impartial spectator, the Ossian poet – who Blair describes as possessed
of refined sentiments and rude and unaffected manners – straddles the
boundaries between modern and premodern society, exhibiting masculine and feminine characteristics.

Other critics have explained the hybrid character of Ossian's verse
in various ways. Adam Potkay reads Ossianic sentiment as an extension of the larger project of the Scottish Enlightenment, arguing that
"Macpherson's cultural poetics do not treat the primitive and the
modern as mutually exclusive categories. Rather, it is impersonation
of an ancient Caledonian voice that makes the Scots' savage ancestors forbearers to the Scottish Enlightenment's most cherished ideas of
polity and manners."[89] More recently, Dafydd Moore has read Ossianic
poetry as an "attempt to bring about a union between polite manners
and martial heroism in order to forge a new sort of Sentimental ethos
of active citizenship," yet he finds that ultimately they "only encode the
culture's suspicions that these things remain antithetical."[90] What most
interests me about the paradoxical nature of Ossian's verse is not the
poem's effort to forward the psychic process of the Union of 1707 by
making the Ancient Scots avatars for modern and polite Britons; nor is it
the ways in which the poems attempt to reconcile contemporary Britons'
impossible desire to see themselves both as members of a powerful military force, active in Europe and on the imperial frontiers, and as sentimental agents proving their moral superiority through both sympathetic
and commercial exchanges. The heroes of Ossianic verse do appear as
historical anomalies, as Moore and Potkay suggest, and their anomalous condition made possible a revaluation of modern historiography's
gendered evolution and the feminine character of modernity. The female
heroines in the poems reinforce this reading, and supplement arguments
made about gender ambivalence and Ossianic historiography by Silvia
Sebastiani and others.[91] Although not central to most contemporaneous
reviews, Blair's analysis, or even modern Ossian scholarship, Ossianic

heroines embody the ways in which gender and historical anomalies dovetail in the poems and gesture toward alternative ways of understanding historical progress.

Like Cuchullin's chariot and Ossian's tears, Ossianic women also fit uneasily into Smith's theory of the progress of feeling and register as historical improprieties. They are modern in that they play an active role in cultivating feeling and developing the characteristics of "humanity" Smith claimed mark modern societies, yet they also exhibit the stoic and masculine characteristics associated in Smith with a primitive age. Women consistently engage in masculine behaviors, taking up the chase – often with a bow or dagger in hand – and joining in battle.[92] Women also act as bards, singing and playing much like Ossian, and their "songs of grief" show the "polish" and "humanity" Blair attributes to Ossian in his "Dissertation." By exhibiting a mixed character and borrowing from the feminine and masculine sentiments of different ages, the historically anomalous women of Ossian challenge the logic of linear history, which supports not only nationalistic narratives of unified and progressive development but also gender codes and norms that align feminine sentiments with commercial progress.

Although Ossianic heroines often die of grief, as do many of the women found in popular eighteenth-century sentimental fictions that were modeled after Samuel Richardson's heroine Clarissa, their emotions are often mixed with a masculine brand of self-command absent from these other narratives. In fragment XV, Morna learns that her lover Cadmor was killed by a rival for her affections, Duchommar. Returning from the hunt, Duchommar announces that he has both "slain a deer" and her lover. First, Morna expresses the depth of her feeling: "And is the son of Tarman fallen; the youth with the breast of snow! the first in the chace of the hill; the foe of the sons of the ocean! – Duchommar thou art gloomy indeed; cruel in thy arm to me."[93] After a moving speech such as this, a modern sentimental heroine would dissolve into tears. Instead, Morna asks to see the sword with Cadmor's blood on it. Before indulging in grief, she stabs Duchommar with his own sword. He fatally wounds Morna in return, but before she expires "she plucked a stone from the side of the cave, and placed it betwixt them, that his blood might not be mingled with hers."[94] Morna blends the modern's ability to express feeling with the command of Smith's stoic savage, who, instead of giving way to grief, refuses to show his emotions and mocks his tormentors. Like Morna, other Ossianic women also frequently take up arms to defend the memory of their spouse or betrothed. The epic *Fingal* includes the story of Degrena, the spouse of the Irish hero Crugal, who dies in battle against Scandinavian invaders. After witnessing the death of her spouse, Degrena rushes into battle. She "flies before the ranks of the foe . . . Her hair is on the wind behind. Her eye is red; her voice is shrill . . . But Degrena falls like a cloud of the morn; the sword of Lochlin is in her side."[95] Although her father Cairbar follows his daughter into battle to avenge her death, there is no discussion of the impropriety of the Scandinavian hero Lochlin engaging in battle with a woman, nor comment on Degrena's passionate flight into war. Despite their self-reflexive quality, neither the poems nor the poet comment on these anomalous representations of gender.

Further complicating the relationship between modern and rude ages, many of Ossian's heroines not only combine modern sensibilities with a primitive fondness for combat but also perform the gender ambivalence at the heart of the poems by donning armor in imitation of women familiar from medieval and early modern romances.[96] In *Fingal*, the bard Carryl relates the story of the two lovers Comal and Galvina, who enjoy typically masculine pursuits. Galvina's "dogs were taught to the chace. Her bow-string sounded on the winds of the forest. Her soul was fixed on Comal . . . Their course in the chace was one, and happy were their words in secret."[97] To test the depth of Comal's passion, Galvina puts on her lover's armor:

> She cloathed her white sides with his armour, and strode from the cave of Ronan. He thought it was his foe. His heart beat high. His colour changed, and darkness dimmed his eyes. He drew the bow. The arrow flew. Galvina fell in blood. He run [sic] with wildness in his steps and called the daughter of Conlach.[98]

In another of Macpherson's fragments, "Connal and Crimora," Crimora follows her lover into battle against his foe Dargo: "Crimora, bright in the armour of man; her hair loose behind, her bow in her hand. She followed the youth of the war, Connal her much-beloved. She drew the string; but erring pierced her Connal."[99] Crimora's faulty aim, which results in the death of the lover she was trying to protect, and Galvina's untimely demise might be read as warnings against women's participation in battle – a punishment for acting in a masculine realm; yet not all women are punished for their masculine behavior and attire.

Other armor-clad warrior princesses occupy esteemed positions in Ossianic lore and mark a historical space that resists being encoded as either masculine or feminine. For example, Sul-malla from Macpherson's final epic *Temora* follows the Irish chief Cathmor into battle with Fingal. She travels with the army and warns Cathmor of danger when Fingal announces his intention to engage the Irish hero in battle himself. Cathmor admits that he has long known of Sul-malla's presence:

"Daughter of strangers, he said; (she trembling turned away) long have I marked in her armour, the young pine of Inish-huma. – But my soul, I said is folded in a storm. Why should that beam arise, till my steps return in peace? Have I been pale in thy presence, when thou bidst me to fear the king?"[100] Sul-malla "trembles," exhibiting the feminine characteristics of fine feeling, but she does so paradoxically in full armor. The next day she witnesses Cathmor's death at the hands of Fingal and afterwards she sings of his bravery. Sul-malla remains as the keeper of Cathmor's memory, occupying masculine roles as both bard and warrior. Similarly, in "Darthula: A Poem," Darthula's father arms her after he discovers that his sons have died: "Take, Darthula, take that spear, that brazen shield, that burnished helmet: they are the spoils of a warrior: a son of early youth. – When the light rises on Selma, we go to meet the car-borne Caribar. – But keep thou near the arm of Colla; beneath the shadow of my shield."[101] Darthula enters battle "lifting her shining spear," but she eventually falls, "the last of Colla's race."[102] As the last of her race, Darthula occupies a position usually reserved for a son or a mourning father. Frequently referred to as the last of his race, Ossian, who loses his only son Oscar, became the prototype for disappearing native cultures, most often represented through an issueless father – perhaps most famously embodied by Chingachgook in James Fenimore Cooper's *The Last of the Mohicans*. The widowed and childless women within the Ossian poems emphasize the precarious future of the Highland culture and become potent symbols in their own right. With the exception of Evirallin, Oscar's mother and Ossian's wife, there is little mention of motherhood or childbearing in the poem. Children and infants are largely absent from Ossian's description of his world. The women of Ossian appear critical of a reproductive economy, where children ensure the future of not only their father's names but also their land and legacy. They gesture toward alternative modes of reproduction and non-biological affinities. Most prominent among these modes of reproduction are the songs the female bards in Ossian disseminate to future generations.

Although critics have noted the ways in which the Ossian poet blends masculine and feminine characteristics,[103] Celtic bards have been discussed as mainly a male phenomenon, with important exceptions like Sydney Owenson's Glorivina from *The Wild Irish Girl* (1806). According to Fiona Stafford, bardic poetry of the eighteenth century looked back to an earlier period when poetry served a more masculine and overtly political purpose. For example, in Thomas Gray's "The Bard" (1757), the last Welsh bard curses the English Edward I and his line for crushing Welsh independence and culture during the Welsh

Conquest of 1282. His song predicts an English future of tragedy and hardship, the result of Edward I's mistreatment of the Welsh people. Famously, the harp also became the symbol of Irish independence in the eighteenth century and was adopted by the United Irishmen, who led the Irish rebellion of 1798. In Stafford's view, Celtic bards "pose[d] a real political threat" and presented an alternative to contemporary poets and their poetry, which was "more suited to consumption at the tea-table than for inciting warriors on the battlefield."[104] The poems of Ossian serve to inspire warriors before and after a battle and record the history of a people, yet the bards – who would seem out of place at a tea table – are men and women. Many women take up the harp within the poems. Both Ossian and his wife Evirallin sing together. Carril, the bard of Cuchullin, remembers in *Fingal* all three performing together in their youth:

> Ossian king of swords, replied the bard, thou best raisest the song. Long has thou been known to Carril, thou ruler of battles. Often have I touched the harp to lovely Evirallin. Thou too hast often accompanied my voice in Branno's hall of generous shells. And often, amidst our voices, was heard the mildest Evirallin. One day she sung of Cormac's fall, the youth that died for her love. I saw the tears on her cheek, and on thine, thou chief of men. Her soul was touched for the unhappy, though she loved him not. How fair among a thousand maids was the daughter of the generous Branno![105]

Evirallin is the "mildest" of women, yet she sings alongside Ossian of the constant death and battle of their rude age, paradoxically eliciting the tearful sentiments that belong to a more refined era. Many women appear in a similar capacity. In the first book of *Fingal*, Cuchullin's bard Carril relates the battle of the Irish hero Cairbar with Grudar. After Grudar's defeat, he recounts Cairbar's sister Brassolis "rais[ing] the song of grief. She sung of the actions of Grudar, the youth of her secret soul. – She mourned him in the field of blood . . . Her voice was softer than the harp to raise the song of grief."[106] Sung completely by women, "Comala: A Dramatic Poem" tells the story of Comala, one of Fingal's lovers, who dies after being falsely informed that Fingal was slain in battle. The poem begins with Dersagrena asking her sisters to "lay down the bow and take the harp."[107]

Ossianic women act in a bardic fashion as guardians of a lost culture, particularly Malvina, who stands beside Ossian throughout the poems and seems to figure both the significance of women as the bearers of civilization within Scottish Enlightenment historiography and women's contributions to the development of Scottish Enlightenment thought. Malvina – the most recognizable of all the women in the Ossian poems, and the fiancée of Ossian's son Oscar – appears, like Darthula, as the last of her race, and like Evirallin as an accomplished bard in her own right. Ossian mourns Oscar throughout the poems, but the way in which he turns to Malvina after his son's death troubles typical understandings of Oscar's death, which, as Stafford writes, "robs Ossian of his natural insurance against oblivion, but also threatens the immortality of the forefathers, since in a non-literate society, history is a living tradition entirely dependent on communication from father to son."[108] Women, particularly Malvina, figure significantly in the transmission of Ossianic history. In "The War of Caros," he says to Malvina, "Be though near, to learn the song; and future times shall hear of Ossian."[109] In "The War of Inis-Thona," he claims that Malvina's voice was "like the harp."[110] He further invites her to play: "Daughter of Toscar, take the harp, and raise the lovely song of Selma; that sleep may overtake my soul in the midst of joy; that the dreams of my youth may return, and the days of the mighty Fingal."[111] Despite being younger than Ossian, Malvina dies before she can carry his song to "future times." Ossian's elegy to Malvina, "Berrathon," clarifies the place Malvina occupies in Ossian's world. Before he realizes Malvina has predeceased him, Ossian calls to her "O Malvina, with all thy music, come; lay Ossian in the plain of Lutha: let his tomb rise in the lovely field. – Malvina! Where art thou, with thy songs: with the soft sound of thy steps?"[112] He wants Malvina to memorialize him, and when he realizes that she has died, he says, "But thou has left us in darkness, first of the maids of Lutha! We sit, at the rock, and there is no voice; no light but the meteor of fire!"[113] Malvina's unsung song provides an alternative to Ossian's verse and gestures toward the importance of women within Scottish Enlightenment literature and philosophy as bearers of civilization, particularly in regards to history and the arts. Her working relationship with Ossian also prefigures the Bluestockings' collaboration with Scottish literati and the engagement of other women writers with the histories and historical methods that came out of Scotland during the late eighteenth century.

Bards such as Malvina also foreshadow later popular heroines who register as anachronisms, such as Glorvina of Sydney Owenson's *The Wild Irish Girl* and the titular heroine of Madame de Stael's *Corinne* (1807). Owenson and de Stael were both steeped in Ossian's lore and modeled their female bards after the figures found in Macpherson's popular poems.[114] Glorvina and Corinne, embodiments of Irish and Italian nationalism in turn, take up the harp, but their performances lead to radically different fates. Glorvina's songs charm an English tourist and teach him to appreciate Irish culture. Eventually they marry and Glorvina successfully assimilates into British society, echoing Ireland's union with Great Britain in 1800. Corinne, despite her devotion to the

Scottish Lord Nelvil, refuses to abandon her role as a public artist and adapt to the conservative expectations of her fiancé. Because of her inability to conform to Nelvil's expectation, Corinne dies in Italy. Like Corinne, the female bards of Ossian fail to meet the expectations of their gender and age.[115] They both feel in a curiously modern manner, but also possess a self-command and masculine strength characteristic of a more primitive era. Because of their awkward relationship to narratives of historical progress, the heroines of Ossian offered women writers like de Stael and Owenson a framework for investigating women's relationship to modernity and commercial society, as well as imperial expansion. These Ossianic predecessors from Morna to Malvina present an alternative to the ideal modern British woman, who could not be both delicate and tough, passionate and stoic. They also disrupt understandings of history that associate women's progress with commercial developments that create an "intensification of femininity" and a "surplus of sexuality," which, as Karen O'Brien argues, makes women "agents in the process of civilization," who "gain considerable influence as soon as the social conditions exist for them to excite and manipulate male desire ... play[ing] a key role in the formation and maintenance of morals, social norms, and 'manners.'"[116] The elevated social status women enjoyed in the Ossian poems depended on their ability to mix masculine and feminine traits, not on their ability to "excite and manipulate male desire." Behaving outside the official trajectory of history enables these female characters to question the progressive logic of development and the benefits it was thought to bestow on modern women.

The subsequent chapters of this book explore the ways in which women writers used the Ossian poems and Scottish historiography to explore alternative representations of women's relationship to history and commercial and imperial development. Women not only read *Theory of Moral Sentiments* and the Ossian poems, but also corresponded with Scottish literati and wrote their own Ossianic poetry. Malvina was a popular figure among the Bluestockings of Elizabeth Montagu's circle, and Anna Seward and the Ladies of Llangollen frequently referenced Ossian's "songs of grief." The phrase "tales of other times" was also adapted from Ossian by a number of eighteenth-century women writers.[117] The Bluestockings used the phrase repeatedly in their letters, Anna Seward in her poetry, Ann Radcliffe in her gothic novels, and Maria Edgeworth and Regina Maria Roche in their historical and gothic fiction. In their work, this phrase came to signify an alternative historical discourse that questioned women's relationship to the past and future and troubled existing understanding of progress and gender.

At first, the refrain "tales of other times" in the Ossian poems appears to have little to do with the concerns of women writers; yet the "other times" Ossianic poetry gestured toward seemed to preoccupy late eighteenth- and early nineteenth-century women writers. The phrase describes both the uncertainty of future events and a past that is in danger of being forgotten. In the poems, Ossian uses this phrase to describe his son Oscar's position within history. Before one of his final battles, Oscar finds himself distracted by the "feeble voices" of the ancestors who follow him into war. Finally, Oscar turns, draws his sword, and asks: "O ye ghosts of my fathers! ye that fought against the kings of the world! – Tell me the deeds of future times; and your discourse in your caves; when you talk together and behold your sons in the fields of the valiant."[118] Trenmor, the first king of Fingal's realm, appears in a ghostly "robe . . . of the mists of Lano," yet he carries an impossibly weighty weapon: "his sword is a meteor half-extinguished."[119] His words reinforce his incongruous appearance: "Many were his words to Oscar: but they only came by halves to our ears: they were dark as the tales of other times, before the light of the song arose."[120] Trenmor's words of "future times" come "by halves" and gesture to the uncomfortable and partially incomprehensible temporal position the past occupies in relation to the future. Although Smith's precise understanding of what it means to "keep time" in the modern age differs from Ossian's more cryptic insistence on "tales of other times" that point to uncertain futures and malleable pasts, both texts illustrate the difficulty of constructing linear histories in the 1760s. The "other times" Ossian gestures toward challenged the idea of universal history and refused the logic of stadial history. Uneven and multiple, temporality in both Smith and Macpherson creates a sense of unease that registers in Oscar, who feels sad and "alone . . . in the midst of a thousand foes."[121] Oscar's fear of being forgotten resembles the anxiety Smith's sufferer feels as he awaits the alleviating effects of sympathy, what Smith calls "this correspondence of the sentiments of others with our own [that] appears to be a cause of pleasure, and the want of it a cause of pain."[122] Just as Smith's spectator feared not corresponding with fellow humans on an individual level, Ossian and Oscar fear not finding their place in the universal history Smith introduced in his lectures at Glasgow.

Women writers adapted this phrase as a means of thinking through their own complex relationship to imperial and commercial development. The Ossian poems aided them in thinking through the moments and spaces where empire and commerce seemed to upset universal measures of development. More importantly, the poems worked as a wedge for prying apart linear temporalities that depended on a predictable unfolding of gender roles which linked women's progress and a greater appreciation of feminine sentiments to commercial and imperial development. The next chapter explores how these Ossianic "tales of other times" unfolded in the correspondence and poetry of first generation Bluestockings such as Elizabeth Montagu and Catherine Talbot.

Notes

1. For a discussion of the different editions of the Ossian poems, see Howard Gaskill (ed.), *The Poems of Ossian and Related Works*. All citations and subsequent references to the Ossian poems, including Macpherson's and Blair's defenses, will come from Gaskill's edition. For an additional discussion of Ossian's publication history as well as a discussion of its translation in Europe, see Gaskill, *The Reception of Ossian in Europe*; for a comparison of the first and subsequent editions of Adam Smith's *Theory of Moral Sentiments*, see Emma Rothschild, *Economic Sentiments*.

2. Ian Duncan in *Scott's Shadow* clarifies literature's role in mediating imperial expansion, arguing that the literature that followed the Jacobite rebellion, such as the Ossian poems and the fiction of Walter Scott and his contemporaries, attempted to "encode the formation of a distinctly modern kind of national subjectivity, in which the knowledge of our alienation from authentic cultural identities accompanies our privileged repossession of them as aesthetic effects" (p. 98); Ian Baucom in *Specters of the Atlantic* also includes a fascinating discussion of the *Theory of Moral Sentiments*. He argues that Smith's treatise on feeling theorized a "melancholy cosmopolitanism" that served to witness and testify to the horrors of imperial expansion and the transatlantic slave trade (p. 244).

3. For a discussion of the role the *Theory of Moral Sentiments* played in theorizing the Age of Sensibility, see William Reddy, *The Navigation of Feeling*; recently, Juliet Shields in *Sentimental Literature and Anglo-Scottish Identity, 1745–1820* has established Macpherson and Smith's centrality not just to the discourse of sensibility but also changing apprehensions of British national identity; Dafydd Moore in his essay "The Reception of the Poems of Ossian in England and Scotland" has also argued that the Ossian poems "might be seen as the apotheosis of eighteenth-century Sentimentalism" (Gaskill (ed.), *The Reception of Ossian in Europe*, p. 37).

4. Smith, *Theory of Moral Sentiments*, p. 245. All citations of *Theory of Moral Sentiments* will come from Ryan Hanley's recent edition, which uses the final 1790 edition of Smith's text. Although some of the women writers discussed in my study relied on earlier editions, particularly the first-generation Bluestockings, I chose to use the 1790 edition because it would have been available to many of the writers I discuss in the latter half of this book – and also because it reflects the influence of the work of Scottish literati who responded to the initial 1759 edition, and a deepening engagement with the stadial method.

5. Smith in his *Lectures on Rhetoric and Belles Lettres* uses Macpherson's "Erse poetry" as evidence of the "considerable perfection" of poetry in

"Rude and Barbarous nations" (pp. 136 and 137); Smith's citation of Ossian fits into a larger argument about prose's function as a motor of commerce in more developed societies and poetry's relationship to recreation and pleasure.

6. Gaskill, *Poems of Ossian*, pp. 35–6.
7. Ibid., p. 36.
8. Ibid., p. 36.
9. For the most recent example of this combative style of Ossian scholarship, see Thomas M. Curley, *Samuel Johnson, the Ossian Fraud, and the Celtic Revival in Great Britain and Ireland*. Although Curley's dismissive approach to the poems does seem anachronistic, his book evidences the persistence of this brand of Ossian scholarship.
10. For example, Joep Leerson in "Ossian and the Rise of Literary Historicism" argues that attention to issues of authenticity have led scholars to overlook the Ossian poems' contribution to "the rise of literary historicism," which included greater attention to national epics as well as the creation of the historical novel (Gaskill (ed.), *The Reception of Ossian in Europe*, p. 119).
11. See James Mulholland, *Sounding Imperial*, and Silvia Sebastiani, *The Scottish Enlightenment*.
12. For a recent discussion of the Scottish Enlightenment's role in creating modern disciplines see Clifford Siskin, *The Work of Writing*, and Colin Kidd, *Subverting Scotland's Past*.
13. Curley, for instance, adapting a Johnsonian perspective, finds that the Ossian poems "[offend] against morality but also . . . [violate] authentic history and the simple human trust that makes society possible" (*Samuel Johnson, the Ossian Fraud, and the Celtic Revival*, p. 2).
14. See J.G.A. Pocock's influential *Virtue, Commerce, and History* for a discussion of the role manners played in defining modern commercial society in the eighteenth century.
15. For discussions of Adam Smith's understanding of sociality as an inherent characteristic of humanity, see Karen O'Brien, *Women and Enlightenment in Eighteenth-Century Britain* and Dermot Ryan, "'The Beauty of That Arrangement.'"
16. Adam Smith, *Lectures on Jurisprudence*, p. 14.
17. Ibid., p. 239.
18. Rousseau and Locke also wrote conjectural histories, which imagine previous ages, but they did not write stadial histories, which equate material with social development. Unlike Smith, they also conjecture about a presocial state of nature. For a discussion of differences between conjectural and stadial history, see Ronald Meek, *Social Science and the Ignoble Savage* and Pocock, *Barbarism and Religion*, vol. 2.
19. Ibid., p. 292.
20. See James Chandler, *England in 1819*; Ian Duncan, *Scott's Shadow*; and Ian Duncan, "The Pathos of Abstraction," in Leith Davis et al. (eds), *Scotland and the Borders of Romanticism* (Cambridge: Cambridge University Press, 2004), pp. 38–56.
21. Chandler, *England in 1819*, p. 107.
22. Smith, *Wealth of Nations*, p. 95.

23. Ibid., p. 173.
24. Smith, *Theory of Moral Sentiments*, p. 239.
25. Smith, *Lectures on Jurisprudence*, p. 439.
26. Ibid., p. 439.
27. Ibid., p. 439.
28. O'Brien, *Women and Enlightenment*, p. 90.
29. In "Virtue and Commerce: Women in the Making of Adam Smith's Political Economy," Jane Rendall argues that the distinction Smith creates between the "gentle" and "those nobler qualities which stem from victory over one's own feelings . . . appears to be used metaphorically as a sexual one" (p. 58).
30. Smith's comments on "self-command" come primarily in Part VI of his treatise, which appeared for the first time in the sixth and final edition in 1790 and reflected a deepening interest in how cross-cultural comparisons might provide insight into the cultural and historical specificity of emotions and their relationship to economic progress. Emma Rothschild points out that as Smith revised the *Theory of Moral Sentiments*, his treatise took on a "strikingly less Christian" tone; not only did he remove most of his comments about deity, he replaced them with discussions of "conscience" and added a section on self-command that relies heavily on the type of cross-cultural comparisons familiar from his *Lectures on Jurisprudence* (p. 129).
31. Smith, *Theory of Moral Sentiments*, p. 240.
32. Ibid., p. 241.
33. For a discussion of the centrality of torture to Smith's theory of sympathy, see Lynn Hunt's *Inventing Human Rights*. Hunt views the modes of "imaginative identification" cultivated in readers by the novels of the period and theorized in texts such as Smith's *Theory of Moral Sentiments* as important moments in the history of human rights (p. 65).
34. Ibid., p. 243.
35. Ibid., pp. 243–4.
36. Ibid., p. 242.
37. Ibid., p. 239.
38. Ibid., p. 240.
39. Ibid., p. 245.
40. Ibid., p. 243.
41. Ibid., p. 242.
42. Ibid., p. 222.
43. Ibid., p. 222.
44. Ibid., p. 35.
45. Ibid., p. 46.
46. Ibid., p. 173.
47. Ibid., p. 174.
48. Norbert Elias, *The Civilizing Process*.
49. Maureen Harkin, "Adam Smith's Missing History," p. 439; see also Harkin, "Smith's Theory of Moral Sentiments: Sympathy, Women, and Emulation."
50. For a discussion of multiple Enlightenments, see Pocock, *Barbarism and Religion*, vol. 1, and Sankar Muthu, *Enlightenment Against Empire*.

51. David Marshall, *The Figure of Theater*; Kwame Anthony Appiah, *Cosmopolitanism*.
52. Baucom in *Specters of the Atlantic* argues that the two parts of Smith's spectator negotiate historical distance; however, instead of seeing this distance as spanning periods or ages, Baucom argues that Smith's spectator negotiates between a particular and an abstract understanding of history: "If the imagination allows us to enter into the historical world and to demonstrate some sympathy toward those who have suffered its violence, then it is also the imagination that, for Smith, abstracts the world, strips it of its historical specificity, allegorizes it" (p. 250).
53. Smith, *Theory of Moral Sentiments*, p. 152.
54. Ibid., p. 22.
55. Ibid., p. 28.
56. Ibid., p. 31.
57. Ibid., p. 88.
58. Ibid., pp. 88–9.
59. Ibid., p. 28.
60. Ibid., pp. 28–9.
61. Ibid., p. 28; in "Sympathy Time: Adam Smith, George Eliot, and the Realist Novel," Rae Greiner argues that the temporal disjunctions built into Smith's *Theory of Moral Sentiments* and the reflexivity of his feeling agent gives sympathy a narrative quality characteristic of realist novels.
62. Homi Bhaba, *Location of Culture*, p. 145.
63. Ibid., p. 167.
64. Gibbons makes a similar argument in "The Sympathetic Bond": "It is possible to read this as an allegory for the painful dilemma of Scottish culture in the mid-eighteenth century: it had to adjust itself and curb its excesses so as not to give offence to its urbane and self-possessed neighbor" (p. 279). He goes on to argue that Scottish Enlightenment historiography continually combined "progressivism with primitivism" (p. 284).
65. Silvia Sebastiani, "Race, Women, and Progress in the Late Scottish Enlightenment," p. 83.
66. Ibid., p. 175.
67. Ibid., pp. 176–7.
68. Appiah, *Cosmopolitanism*, p. 156.
69. Gaskill, *Poems of Ossian*, p. 211.
70. As other critics have noted, the epic framework of *Fingal* was influenced by Macpherson's study of the classics at the University of Aberdeen.
71. Review of *Fingal, an Ancient Epic Poem*, *Scots Magazine* 24 (February 1762), p. 86.
72. In Derick S. Thomson's classic study of Ossian's Gaelic sources *The Gaelic Sources of Macpherson's Ossian*, he finds the description of Cuchullin's chariot to be one of Macpherson's more faithful translations.
73. Review of *Fingal*, *Scots Magazine* 24 (February 1762), p. 204.
74. Ibid., p. 204.
75. Ibid., p. 204.
76. Review of *Fingal*, *Scots Magazine* 24 (June 1762), p. 320.
77. Review of *Fingal*, *Scots Magazine* 24 (May 1762), p. 261.
78. Ibid., p. 261.

79. Review of *Fingal*, *Scots Magazine* 24 (June 1762), p. 320.
80. Blair has been widely acknowledged as the first professor of English litera-
    ture at any institution. For a discussion of the Scottish contribution to the
    making of English literature, see Siskin, *The Work of Writing*.
81. Gaskill, *Poems of Ossian*, p. 399.
82. Ibid., p. 361.
83. Ibid., p. 349.
84. Ibid., p. 394.
85. Ibid., p. 396.
86. Ibid., p. 354.
87. Ibid., p. 358.
88. Ibid., p. 352.
89. See Adam Potkay, *The Fate of Eloquence in the Age of Hume*, p. 206.
90. Dafydd Moore, *Enlightenment and Romance in James Macpherson's The
    Poems of Ossian*, p. 113.
91. Although published in English after the majority of this study was com-
    pleted, Silvia Sebastiani's excellent *The Scottish Enlightenment: Race,
    Gender, and the Limits of Progress* explores Scots literati's interest in the
    relationship between gender and progress in ways that complement and
    complicate my own study. Sebastiani's focus on Macpherson as an histo-
    rian uncovers some of the potentially racist implications of Caledonian
    exceptionalism. Kames's and Macpherson's polygenetic understandings
    of race certainly fed into dangerous nineteenth-century understandings of
    racial difference. Sebastiani's study invites a greater consideration of the
    differences and similarities between stadial history's parsing of race and
    empire.
92. For a discussion of the women in Ossian's verse and Burke's gendered
    discourse of the sublime and the beautiful, see Lisa Kozlowski, "Terrible
    Women and Tender Men: A Study of Gender in Macpherson's Ossian,"
    in Howard Gaskill and Fiona Strafford (eds), *From Gaelic to Romantic
    Ossianic Translations* (Amsterdam: Rodopi, 1998), pp. 119–35.
93. Gaskill, *Poems of Ossian*, p. 30.
94. Ibid., p. 30.
95. Ibid., p. 67.
96. Dafydd Moore argues convincingly in *Enlightenment and Romance* that
    the Ossian poems are more appropriately placed in the tradition of the
    medieval romance. Ossianic women's donning of arms seems to borrow
    from the medieval romances to which Moore sees the poems as indebted.
    Moore views the contradictions and inconsistencies of the Ossian poems
    as a function of their engagement with romance: "Conflict and ambiva-
    lence, an undermining of the values which are otherwise being promoted,
    a compensatory world elsewhere hedged and haunted by the world it
    seeks to escape, these are then the defining characteristics of the romance
    mode" (p. 72).
97. Gaskill, *Poems of Ossian*, p. 70.
98. Ibid., p. 70.
99. Ibid., p. 13.
100. Ibid., p. 280.
101. Ibid., p. 142.

102. Ibid., p. 146 and p. 142.
103. Potkay, *The Fate of Eloquence*, pp. 201–3.
104. Fiona Stafford, *The Last of the Race*, p. 97.
105. Gaskill, *Poems of Ossian*, p. 96.
106. Ibid., pp. 61–2.
107. Ibid., p. 105.
108. Stafford, *Last of the Race*, p. 104.
109. Gaskill, *Poems of Ossian*, p. 114.
110. Ibid., p. 117.
111. Ibid., p. 117.
112. Ibid., p. 193.
113. Ibid., p. 193.
114. Although outside the scope of this book, the primitive self-command and modern sensibilities of Ossianic women also foreshadow popular figures from Walter Scott's fiction, particularly Rob Roy's wife Helen MacGregor, who leads the warriors of her Highland clan in her husband's absence against British troops. MacGregor defends a pastoral mode of Highland life under attack by the modernizing forces of the British Empire. Frank Osbaldistone describes her as an "Amazon" and a fierce "Chieftainess," who leads her clan against the English troops and afterwards appears with "specks of blood on her brow, her hands and naked arms, as well as on the blade of the sword, which she continued to hold." After seeing Helen MacGregor's masculine comportment in battle, Osbaldistone finds it remarkable that she appears the next day dressed in "a more feminine taste" and speaking "with the manners of a princess." Osbaldistone describes her English as "graceful, flowing, and declamatory." Like the women of Ossian, Helen MacGregor's polished manners are difficult to reconcile with her rude environment. See Walter Scott, *Rob Roy*, ed. Ian Duncan (Oxford: Oxford University Press, 1998), p. 411.
115. The heroines of Ossian closely resemble Madame de Stael's Corinne, who refuses to put down her harp and become Oswald's wife. De Stael was an Ossian enthusiast and Macpherson's poems clearly influenced her feminist narrative of Italian national sentiment. Madame de Stael, *Corinne, or Italy*, trans. Sylvia Raphael (New York: Oxford University Press, 2008).
116. O'Brien, *Women and Enlightenment*, p. 89.
117. For a discussion of the popularity of the phrase "tales of other times" in late eighteenth-century gothic and historical novels, see Anne Stevens, "'Tales of other times.'"
118. Gaskill, *Poems of Ossian*, p. 112.
119. Ibid., p. 112.
120. Ibid., p. 113.
121. Ibid., p. 113.
122. Smith, *Theory of Moral Sentiments*, p. 11.

Chapter 2

Ossianic History and Bluestocking Feminism

Although filled with references to James Macpherson and his Ossian poems, the correspondence of Elizabeth Montagu, the Queen of the Bluestockings, rarely mentions the debates over the poems' provenance, an issue that preoccupied Montagu's contemporaries such as Samuel Johnson, Thomas Percy, and David Hume. In a letter to Lord Lyttelton from 1760, Montagu responds playfully to the forgery accusations leveled at Macpherson soon after the initial publication of the *Fragments of Ancient Poetry*: "The Bishop of Ossory tells me Mr. Macpherson receives 100 per annum subscription while he stays in the Highlands to translate the poems; if he is writing them, he should have a thousand at least."[1] In another letter, she offered a more measured and thoughtful response:[2] "the poems cannot be as ancient as pretended. It seems to me possible, that some great bard might from uncertain and broken tradition, and from the scattered songs of former bards, form an epic poem, which might not agree with history."[3] When pressed, she acknowledges the anachronisms within the poems but refuses to take sides in the raging debates over their historical legitimacy, concluding that she finds "great difficulty in believing or disbelieving the authenticity of these poems."[4] Despite this ambivalence, she remained a passionate devotee of Ossianic poetry and a close friend of Macpherson and his advocates, Hugh Blair and Lord Kames. The poems' real or pretended third-century origins became for nineteenth- and twentieth-century readers the defining factor in the poems' placement within literary history;[5] Montagu's response to the Ossian debate suggests that eighteenth-century readers' interest in the poems extended far beyond Macpherson's dubious translating practices. Largely uninterested in verifying the poems' author or their precise date of origin, Montagu and her fellow Bluestockings were fascinated by the questions the poems raised about history and progress. The poems, which featured men and women singing and often fighting alongside one another in a clearly premodern world, raised important questions for the Bluestockings about the relationship between women's social progress and economic development.

In many ways the Ossian poems provided a template for Bluestocking salons, where both sexes debated issues of literary, social, and political interest. Although the term Bluestocking conjures the image of a socially awkward and often masculine woman, whose devotion to study and the betterment of the female condition make her poorly suited for her domestic duties, this understanding did not emerge until the late eighteenth century. Montagu self-consciously set herself and her fellow Bluestockings apart from stereotypical portrayals of the learned lady. In a letter to Elizabeth Carter, the famous translator of *Epictetus*, Montagu separates Bluestockings from the stock figure of the learned lady:

> As to the prejudice against learned Women, it has arisen from some ungainly uncouth kind of animals, who finding themselves destitute of feminine softness and graces and incapable of the economical arts, did therefore fancy, that not being fine women could by help of hard words become wise and learned men, and so in greasy nightcaps they sat down to study and at last became the kind of academical monsters called a pedant, and they are as unlike Minerva in a Museum as at the loom and with these monsters my dear sister, must you and I and every women who loves reading be often classed.[6]

Stereotypical accounts of learned women excluded them from a polished and modern age and relegated them to an "uncouth" and bestial stage of development. Montagu and her fellow Bluestockings attempted to undo this narrative: to be a Bluestocking, one had to be full of "feminine softness and grace" as well as knowledge. Although Montagu's critique of masculine women expresses her own deep conservatism and gender biases, her alignment of femininity with wisdom reflects her belief that learned women marked a polished and refined society.

Among first-generation Bluestockings like Montagu, Elizabeth Vesey, Catherine Talbot, and Carter, the term Bluestocking signified the men and women who attended the salons of Montagu and Vesey and were committed to cultivating their intellectual powers and sentiments through conversation instead of isolated study in "greasy nightcaps."[7] With the exception of their military exploits, popular heroines from the Ossian poems such as Malvina and Darthula acted remarkably like these first-generation Bluestockings. Ossian's heroines sang alongside male bards and feasted afterwards with their male companions, all the while softening the manners of the opposite sex and inspiring a compassion and polish absent from other early societies, particularly the ancient civilizations of Greece and Rome. By hosting frequent Ossian-inspired gatherings that she dubbed "the feast of shells," Montagu made the connection between Ossianic and Bluestocking societies concrete. Significantly, these Ossianic feasts included male and female Bluestockings, and reenacted the equivalent social relations that she found in the poems. Montagu's correspondence, which includes detailed accounts of these feasts, and the poetry of her fellow Bluestockings suggests that the Ossian poems were an important part of a larger mid-eighteenth-century movement, set in motion by the Bluestockings and the philosophers, historians, and poets of the Scottish Enlightenment, to track the development of manners and the role of women in civil society. The history, philosophy, and literature that arose out of this context valued manners, or the polish and grace women were supposed to inspire in a nation's civil society, in contrast to the more traditionally masculine attributes of a nation's civic culture. Connecting the civility of Ossianic heroes to the Scottish Enlightenment's interest in developing a feminist history of manners, Adam Potkay has concluded that "the poems reconcile the age's nostalgia for the ancient polis ideal with a modern taste for civility. In so doing, they also bridge the gap separating the emerging 'feminism' of polite society from the male 'chauvinism' of both the ancient polis and its modern apologists."[8] Silvia Sebastiani also sees the poems as intervening in history, yet instead of healing historical rifts, the poems in her view create a particularly Scottish history. She argues that the "significant social importance" of women in the distant past represented by the Ossian poems uncovered for Scots literati a "Caledonian exceptionalism."[9] The Bluestockings built on the Ossianic exception in surprising and sometimes paradoxical ways, and the poems played a key part in the development of Bluestocking feminism, what Gary Kelly has called a "cultural revolution" of manners and a revaluation of women's contribution to civil society.[10] The Ossianic exception drew the attention of not only the Bluestockings but also Scottish literati, who made women's progress and the development of manners gauges of historical development. Pinpointing the precise origins of the poems was less of an issue for the Bluestockings than the space they opened up for historians, philosophers, and writers to explore women's relationship to historical development and the progress of civil society.

After examining the Bluestockings' interest in and contributions to Scottish Enlightenment historiography as well as Ossianic poetry, this chapter explores the responses of two different first-generation Bluestockings, Montagu and Catherine Talbot, to the Ossian poems.[11] Montagu's response to the Ossian poems was shaped in part by her own exceptional status as a colliery owner and manager who oversaw a vast business with numerous employees for decades after her husband's death. Montagu's letters reveal that she embraced her role as a civilizing force, responsible for feminizing commerce and industry, for example, by improving working conditions and establishing schools for her miners' children.[12] The Ossian poems and the extensive correspondence she conducted with several Scots literati provided her with an opportunity to explore the function of feminine sentiment in Britain's ever-expanding commercial society. Working from a slightly different vantage than Montagu, the more reclusive Catherine Talbot was more critical of women's role in the civilizing process. She adapted the ghostly Celt in her imitations of Ossian to theorize women's ambivalent placement in progressive narratives of history and explore the tension between imperial development and the refinement of social sentiments. Written to document the coronation of George III, her Ossianic poetry makes visible the feminine and colonial histories the English center – in its efforts to represent a homogeneous body politic – often elided. Her position as a dependent of the Archbishop of Canterbury, Thomas Secker, who voluntarily maintained her and her mother after her father's early death, sets her apart from the financially independent and powerful Montagu. Talbot's more precarious economic status may have given her a different perspective on the poems' placement of refined sensibilities in a pre-commercial and Celtic past. In her imitations, she adapts Ossian's voice and his position outside commercial society to question women's position as an ornament in what she calls Britain's "imperial diadem."[13] The temporally remote landscape of the Ossian poems provided both Talbot and Montagu with a place to conjecture about the relationship between the past and the present, and a site to investigate the gendered differences that marked modern and premodern economies and social systems.

An Ossianic Women's History

By mapping the development of manners from the earliest "savage" state to the development of advanced commercial culture, Scots intellectuals made women central to the study of human development.[14] Lord Kames, in *Sketches of the History of Man* (1774), pronounced "the history of the female sex, a capital branch of the history of man, comprehend[ing] great variety of matter, curious and interesting."[15] Borrowing heavily from Kames, the Scots physician William Alexander published his three-volume *The History of Women from the Earliest Antiquity to the Present Time* in 1779.[16] The first and longest chapter of John Millar's *The Origin of the Distinction of Ranks* (1771), "Of the Rank and Condition of Women in Different Ages," suggests that before the development of civil society can be understood, women's contribution to its progress must be considered.[17]

Not only did these texts give women a central role, but they also invited a female audience. Although Lord Kames dedicated his *Sketches* to middle-class men who he described as neither "learned" nor "vulgar,"[18] he translated all the quotations into English with women and, perhaps, his less "learned" male readers in mind: "As one great object of the Editor is to make this a popular work, he had chiefly with a view to the female sex, subjoined English translations of all quotations from other languages."[19] In fact, Kames addressed an actual as well as an ideal female audience; he corresponded with Montagu throughout the composition of *Sketches*, periodically sending her drafts of various sections. At one point in their correspondence, he toyed with including one of her letters in a chapter of the *Sketches* entitled "the Progress of Morality and Manners," claiming her comments would make "an excellent Appendix, if it prove not an embroidery too fine for the Cloth."[20] In this moment Kames likens the process of writing history to the feminine practice of embroidery and suggests that Montagu's delicate contribution would best his rude approach. Although he chose not to include Montagu's discussion of manners, he did include her comments on taste in a later edition of his more famous work, *The Elements of Criticism*. On the Bluestockings' side, the contents of Vesey's library make it almost certain that Kames's *Sketches* as well as the histories of his fellow Scotsmen were a topic of conversation. According to an auction catalogue from 1926, Vesey's library included copies of all four volumes of Kames's *Sketches*, Millar's *Origin of the Distinction of Ranks*, and the conjectural histories that preceded them, including Adam Ferguson's *Essay on the History of Civil Society* (1767), David Hume's *Essays and Treatises on Several Subjects* (1758), and William Robertson's essay "A View of the Progress of Society in Europe," which introduced his *History of Charles V* (1769).[21]

Recently scholars have reintroduced conjectural history as an important part of the development of eighteenth-century feminism.[22] Adopting Hannah Arendt's definition of the social as the modern breakdown of the private and public realms, Mary Catherine Moran has argued that conjectural history, by theorizing the development of society, made women and sociability central to mapping historical change.[23] Harriet Guest has noted that, as the growth of British commercial culture became a marker of national achievement and identity, women of fashion "acquired significance not just as the embodiment of the corruptions of commercial luxury, but as a sign of the polished politeness that is the fruit of commercial prosperity."[24] Many of the Bluestockings participated in the attempt to redefine commercial prosperity as a sign not of corruption and degeneration, an endpoint or harbinger of the nation's collapse, but of national achievement compatible with morality and continued progress.[25] Montagu's efforts to build schools for the children of the workers in her coal mines stand as one example of a benevolent and feminine capitalism. Although women like Montagu provided the polish and compassion necessary to recode the potentially corrosive commercial exchanges central to the modern experience as beneficial and progressive, the taint of commerce was difficult to remove completely. The Bluestockings' interest in the rude economy and developed manners of Ossianic women and men suggests that they themselves might have also sought an alternative to the dangerous equation of women's advancement with commercial progress – an equation that, as Laura Brown argues, could potentially make British women the "scapegoats" for the unsavory byproducts of excessive consumption, such as "imperial violence" and "capitalist alienation."[26]

Ancient Caledonia emerged as a viable alternative because, historically speaking, eighteenth-century British women and the Celtic warriors of the Ossian poems could be viewed as living in parallel dimensions. According to Mark Salber Philips, "classically conceived historical narrative," which concerns itself with the documented realm of political action, excludes both women and the "primitive Briton," who are both "creatures governed by passions and swayed by the extremes of sensibility."[27] Whereas histories concerned solely with the political realm repressed women and the ancient Celts of the British Isles, conjectural histories cast them as central by making manners instead of politics their dominant concern. Catherine Talbot's engagement with Ossian exemplifies the parallels between modern women and the ancient Celts. By aligning herself with Ossian in her letters and poetry, she disrupted the relationship between women and commerce, suggesting feminine polish and sentiment might be compatible with the simple living conditions of economically undeveloped societies. In fact, Talbot's Ossianic and feminist rhetoric anticipated Kames's, Alexander's, and Millar's histories, all of which explored the potential for an alternative British women's history located in the distant Scottish past.

The Bluestockings and their Scottish contemporaries used conjectural history to explore two competing stories of Britain's past and present: a universal history, which privileged economic development, and an Ossianic history, which stressed feeling. Proceeding through four stages, the introduction to Millar's *Origin of the Distinction of Ranks*, for instance, outlined a universal narrative of human development, tracing the gradual transformation of rude savages in hunting and gathering cultures into refined citizens of advanced commercial societies. Millar argued that as survival becomes less of an issue, men are less absorbed by the "attainment of bare necessaries."[28] Their focus shifts to the "several conveniences of life" that cultivate "the various branches of manufacture, together with commerce," the arts and sciences, as well as "feelings of humanity."[29] Millar marked this final stage of human development not just through an identification of the society's means of production, but also through an assessment of the status of feeling. In a developed society, women, as the disseminators of sentiment, occupy a central position and are valued because of their contribution to the development of manners: "The influence of such manners must be extremely favourable to the rank and dignity of women; who are deprived of that consideration and respect which, in a polished nation, they are accustomed to derive from the passion between the sexes."[30] In "savage nations," where the necessities of life are much more difficult to come by, feeling takes a back seat to survival, and female virtues are forgotten: "From the extreme insensibility, observable in the character of all savage nations: it is no wonder they should entertain very gross ideas concerning those female virtues which, in a polished nation, are supposed to constitute the honour and dignity of the sex."[31] This narrative of development provided an economic and ethical justification for empire: theoretically, the spread of British commerce corresponded to the loosening of the cultural bonds oppressing women worldwide. As the developmental ideal, Britain was responsible for cultivating the economies and sentiments of those territories that inhabited an earlier stage of development, including the remote Scottish Highlands.

Although a logic of universal development dominated in these histories, conjectural history also suggested that different stages of economic progress exist in different places at a single time, allowing for the spatial and temporal comparisons recently described by James Chandler and J. G. A. Pocock.[32] The constant comparisons within these histories exacerbated inconsistencies within the universal model, raising questions about the superiority of the developed commercial culture of Great Britain, its imperial practices, as well as the status of women within a society ruled by complex relationships between property owners. Reason dictates that women in more advanced societies should have greater access to power because, as Millar writes, "the paternal jurisdiction has been reduced within narrower bounds, in proportion to the ordinary improvements of society."[33] Yet as the diverse examples of the treatment of women throughout history from ancient Caledonia, Germany, Rome, and Greece to contemporary Africa, America, and Great Britain accrued within these histories, Millar's general principle grows more and more distorted. What looked like a universal law at a distance disappeared under the weight of specific and contradictory examples.

Celtic women in particular distorted this map of human develop-ment. Although these historiographers were obviously troubled by, for instance, the matrilineal societies of the Iroquois and the polygamous women Millar found in the ancient Median Empire of Iran,[34] they assim-ilated these non-European exceptions into their universal logic. After recounting the extraordinary status of women in some North American cultures, Millar writes, "the women of North America do not arrive at this influence and dignity till after a certain age, and after their children are in a condition to procure them respect; that before this period they are commonly treated as the slaves of men; and that there is no country in the world where the female sex is in general more neglected and despised."[35] Finding female slavery within societies that practice matrilineal inheritance and overlooking contradictory evidence in order to ensure women's "neglected and despised" status, Scottish philoso-phers attempted to negate non-European exceptions. But, unlike the exceptions from non-European cultures, those found in Celtic cultures remained unchecked, creating a gap that troubled the notion of progress and decentered the developing historical narrative of Great Britain.

Using the Ossian poems as evidence, conjectural histories often depicted the Highlands in the time of Ossian as an idyllic space where relative gender equality led to a refined sociability that eliminated the rough treatment of women they found in Homer's ancient Greece. Both Millar and Kames discussed and quoted from Ossian extensively in making an argument similar to the one found in Blair's "Critical Dissertation on the Poems of Ossian." Like Blair, they established the Ossian poems as a possible origin for a national literary tradition that, unlike the verse of classical Rome and Greece cited by British neoclassi-cal writers, originated in the British Isles and anticipated modern British sensibilities. In Sketch VII, "The Progress of Manners," Kames used the Ossian poems as historical evidence of the Celt's potential contribution to the development of British identity:

> Hitherto there appears as great a uniformity in the progress of manners, as can reasonably be expected among so many different nations. There is one exception, extraordinary indeed if true, which is, the manners of the Caledonians described by Ossian, manners so pure and refined as scarce to be equaled in the first age of society, acquainted with no arts but hunting and making war.[36]

Although only shepherds, and therefore at the second of four stages of economic development, Ossian's Highlanders feel and act as do modern and "refined" Englishmen. Millar's citation of Ossian similarly undermined the modern Englishman's monopoly on refined feeling: "In the compositions of Ossian, which describe the manners of people acquainted with pasturage, there is often a degree of tenderness and delicacy of sentiment which can hardly be equaled in the most refined productions of a civilized age."[37] "Delicacy of sentiment" thrives without the presence of commerce in Ossian, troubling the rationale for British imperialism. As a result, the exceptional status of the Highlands weakened the representational power of the English center and undermined the imperial narrative of Britain.[38]

Although the Ossian poems were later discounted as historical evidence of an early Celtic age, they provided a laboratory for these influential historiographers to argue for the separation of commerce and refined feeling; they introduced the possibility that an "inferior" economy dominated by pasturage does not necessarily result in the oppression of women. As Kames noted:

> Had the Caledonians made slaves of their women, and thought as meanly of them as savages commonly do, it could never have entered the imagination of Ossian, to ascribe to them those numberless graces that exalt the female sex, and render many of them objects of pure and elevated affection.[39]

Collapsing distinctions between literature and history, Kames argued that the "numberless graces" of Ossian's heroines evidenced the elevated status of women in his era. Objects of "pure and elevated affection," they were untainted by commerce. Likewise, William Alexander, influenced by "the daughters of the North . . . the first to inspire men with sentimental feeling,"[40] dismissed economic development as an accurate gauge of "progress" altogether:

> The rank, therefore, and condition in which we find women in any country, mark out to us with the greatest precision, the exact point in the scale of civil society, to which the people of such a country have arrived; and were their history entirely silent on every other subject, and only mentioned the manner in which they treated their women, we should, from thence, be enabled to form a tolerable judgment of their barbarity, or culture from their manners.[41]

For Alexander, the presence or absence of commerce in a society was far less important than the treatment of women in appraising the pace and level of cultural development. Women, their treatment, and the quality of their lives could be counted as the most important indicator of a society's degree of civilization and its corresponding distance from "barbarity."

As they questioned the value of economic evidence and introduced the possibility that the "numberless graces" of the female sex could occupy an elevated position in an otherwise "rude" society, conjectural historians raised serious questions about Britain's imperial project. Did the Celtic case prove that the development of sentiment and the rise of commerce could be independent of each other? Did the spread of commerce really produce refined sentiments and elevate the human condition, particularly the female condition? Although these questions went unanswered and continue to do so today, they remain an early example of the complexities associated with gauging women's status in modern commercial society.

By challenging the connection between commerce and feeling, the Ossian poems created a space in which women could become bearers of sentiment without running the risk of being portrayed as part of a compromised commercial system, one that spawns not only refined feeling but also luxury and decay. As Millar wrote, "The growth and decay of society have, in some respects, a resemblance to each other; which, independent of imitation, is naturally productive of similar manners and customs."[42] The Ossianic histories of the Scottish Enlightenment transformed the elevated exchanges that occurred in Bluestocking salons from signs of commercial achievement and portents of the British Empire's decay into a revival of the native traditions of the British Isles forgotten or suppressed by a purely English history.

Elizabeth Montagu's Feasts of Ossian

Soon after the publication of Macpherson's *Fragments* in 1760, Elizabeth Montagu began holding eccentric Ossianic dinner parties called "the feasts of shells," during which guests "had the feast of shells and drank out of a nautilus shell to the immortal memory of Ossian."[43] In honor of Ossian, the recently rediscovered Highland bard, Montagu recreated – down to the unconventional stemware – the ceremonial meals of the Highland warriors described by Ossian's self-proclaimed translator, the controversial James Macpherson.[44] Montagu even counted "the Bard Macpherson" among the "tuneful train" who attended her Highland feasts held throughout the 1760s and 1770s.[45] In a letter to Elizabeth Carter from 1761, Montagu includes a nearly identical account of another feast: "I had a quadrille table last night; and last week the Bard Macpherson, many others of the tuneful train and we had the feast of shells and drank out of a nautilus shell to the immortal memory of Ossian."[46] During 1761–62, Macpherson and the artist Allan Ramsay, who was painting Montagu's portrait, frequented Montagu's and the Earl of Bath's London residences and honored Ossian at many of Montagu's parties. In an invitation to Elizabeth Vesey, a close friend and fellow Bluestocking, Montagu anticipates a Caledonian feast from this period:

> Mr. Macpherson the translator of the Highland poems, with some other Bards, are to dine here tomorrow, if you will be of the party, you will certainly improve and I hope enjoy it ... [I]f you have not read the highland poems you will think I mean a dinner of cockles, oysters, and muscles [sic], but if you have dined with the sons of Morven/a gallant race/you will understand me. Let me have your answer tonight.[47]

Besides Vesey, who became a devotee of Ossian, other frequenters of Montagu's feasts included Edmund Burke, James Macdonald, Lord Lyttelton, Bath, Ramsay, Elizabeth Carter, and Benjamin Stillingfleet (from whose blue-worsted stockings the Bluestockings purportedly got their name). These Ossianic gatherings extended at least throughout the 1770s, long after the poems' initial success. In 1772, Montagu describes for Vesey another "feast of shells" more than ten years later, attended by Macpherson (who seems to have been a regular), Sir Joshua Reynolds, Lord Lyttelton, and the playwrights Richard Cumberland and Alexander Dow.[48] Montagu's Ossianic feasts provide a new vantage on the philosophical and aesthetic underpinnings of Bluestocking feminism, which – as Montagu's correspondence with Lord Kames and Hugh Blair demonstrates – developed alongside Scottish Enlightenment historiography.

By the mid-1760s, "the feast of shells" in Montagu's correspondence had become a shibboleth for her salon meetings and "the sound of the harp" a shorthand for the elevated and "tuneful" conversation that marked these occasions. In writing to her husband about a brief sojourn in Tunbridge Wells, Montagu celebrates the "tuneful tribe" she encounters there.[49] She also compares Carter to Ossian and invites her to "raise the song" in response to a sublime landscape they encounter on one of their tours of the English countryside.[50] Malvina, Ossian's female counterpart in the poems, also came to occupy an important place in Bluestocking rhetoric. While traveling with Carter in Germany in July of 1763, Montagu longs for the company of her London friends and writes to Vesey, "Dedicate to our spirits two chairs in the cave of Malvina."[51] By 1763, Vesey had begun to designate some of her salons as the Cave of Malvina or the Bower of Malvina, and Montagu, in turn, begins to refer to Vesey as "our Malvina" in letters to Carter, Bath, and Lyttelton.[52] Like Ossian, Malvina "raises the harp" in many of the Ossian poems, including "Croma," and survives along with Ossian the fall of their race.

Malvina served as an important symbol within Bluestocking feminism because of her contribution to the cultivation of the arts and social discourse in the poems.

Montagu's feasts and Ossianic rhetoric also served the less lofty purpose of procuring subscribers for Macpherson's epics *Fingal* in 1762 and *Temora* in 1763. Montagu's correspondence evidences that she used her vast network of powerful friends to ensure the poems' success and acted as an important patron for Macpherson. Although in the Advertisement of the 1762 edition of *Fingal* Macpherson refused to list the subscribers, he admitted that they were numerous and powerful:

> The translator thanks the public for the more than ordinary encouragement given him, for executing this work. The number of his subscribers does him honour. He could have presented to the public the first names in the nation; but, though more have come to his hands, than have appeared before the works of authors of established reputations, yet many more have subscribed; and he chooses to print none at all rather than an imperfect list. Deeply sensible of the generosity of a certain noble person, the translator yet avoids to name him, as his exalted station as well as merit has raised him above the panegyric of one so little known.[53]

The "certain noble person" mentioned by Macpherson is certainly, as Howard Gaskill notes, the Earl of Bute; however, "the first names of the nation," according to Montagu's correspondence, included Englishmen and women such as Lord Lyttelton, the Earl of Bath, and the Duchess of Portland.

The nation's "first names" found their way onto *Fingal*'s subscription list – due, at least in part, to the enthusiasm of Montagu, who helped define aesthetic and literary merit in late eighteenth-century Britain.[54] In a letter to Bath from 1761, Montagu writes:

> I have taken the liberty to enclose Mr. Macpherson's proposals, and if your Lordship designs to subscribe to the work, and have not already done so, I should be very glad to have the honour of your name on *my list*. I have read the first canto, which far exceeds my expectations . . . The original Ersh is to be seen at Mr. Millar's. I have also enclosed a letter from Edinburgh which gives an account of these poems.[55]

In addition to the Earl of Bath, she sent the poems to the Bishop of London, who rejected the poems as forgeries, and to Charles Morton, the antiquarian and manuscript librarian for the British Museum.[56] She also sent them to her husband, Edward Montagu, as well as Elizabeth Carter. In a letter from 1761, she writes to her sister Sarah Scott, the author of *Millennium Hall*, "I have subscribed to the Epic Highland poem for you of which I was shown one entire canto and a great part of another and think it may stand on the shelf with the great epic poems."[57] In addition to establishing Montagu's efforts to popularize the Ossian poems, this letter also suggests that Macpherson or his Scottish advocates were sending drafts of *Fingal* to Montagu and soliciting her feedback. Testifying to Montagu's power and influence in the world of arts and letters, a guest list to one of Montagu's Ossianic feasts included in a letter to Elizabeth Carter from 1763 mentions literary powerbrokers from Great Britain and France, "Last night I had a very agreeable party. Lady Harriet Ropes, Mrs. Vesey, Mrs. Harris, James Macdonald, Col Drumgold, Hermes Thismoedothes, Mr. Stillingfleet, and Mr. Macpherson and Mr. De Clor secretary to the academy of belles letters at Paris and author of the life of Louis . . . You see my friend I live at the feast of shells, in the sound of the harp."[58]

By circulating manuscripts of the poems before they were published, Montagu also influenced Macpherson's revision process and helped foster Malvina's central role as Ossian's main interlocutor. In doing so, she also helped create a historical precedent for her own Bluestocking salons. In October of 1760, Lyttelton sent Montagu four of the Ossian poems in manuscript, writing, "I am glad to hear we shall have another volume of Highland Poems. To stay your stomach (for, as I know, your appetite is eager towards them), I send you a copy of four of a later date than the others now printed, and not much inferior to them in the Natural Beauty and Force of Description, tho' not, I think, so bold and sublime."[59] Of the four poems Lyttelton mentions, only a manuscript copy of "Croma" survives in the Huntington Library's Montagu Collection. Substantially different from the final version printed in the 1762 version of *Fingal*, Montagu's copy of "Croma" was circulated to the Earl of Bath and probably to Carter, both of whom mention the five bards of the poem in their letters. Montagu also met with Macpherson several times before the poems' publication in 1762, and the difference between the manuscript copy of "Croma" and the final version suggests that he incorporated the comments of Montagu and her salon into the final version. Although similar to the five bard section of "Croma," the manuscript version of the poem includes frequent line breaks and, most significantly, does not include the published version's long preface, which situates the songs of "Croma's" five bards in the context of a discussion between Ossian and Malvina. The preface in the manuscript version merely describes the poem as "of [a] much later date than the foregoing fragments" and announces that the five bards and their chief will "make their observations on the Night."[60] Without the published preface, the poems lose their connection to a mixed-sex Bluestocking mode of sociability and stand alone as scattered Scots songs that figure the poetic qualities of night.

In contrast to the manuscript version, the preface of the published version of "Croma" begins with a description of Malvina mourning the loss of Oscar. Ossian describes her song as "lovely" but worries that "sorrow wastes the mournful."[61] To distract her from her grief, Ossian "remembers the days of his youth."[62] He recounts a war he waged on behalf of an Irish king, Crothar, to avenge the death of his son. After Ossian defeats Crothar's enemy, the Irish king holds a feast during which the five bards sing the songs of night which are included in the manuscript version. In the context of Macpherson's involvement with the Bluestocking circle, the additional preface of the poem, which begins with the exchange of songs between a man and woman, Ossian and Malvina, and concludes with a feast that features the performances of a variety of bards, reads as a homage to Macpherson's time within Bluestocking society and showcases the connections between Montagu's modern world and the Ossianic past in which she was so invested.

Although Montagu's interest in Scotland began with her love of Ossianic poetry, her devotion to Macpherson fostered philosophical and aesthetic bridges between the Bluestockings and the literati of the Scottish Enlightenment. For example, before David Hume withdrew his support of Macpherson and the Ossian project, he attempted to use Montagu's influence to pressure his friend Hugh Blair into providing clearer evidence of the poems' authenticity. He writes in 1763, "I have been in company with Mrs. Montague, a lady of great distinction in this place, and a zealous partisan of Ossian. I told her of your intention, and even used the freedom to read your letter to her. She was extremely pleased with your project ... You see, then, that you are upon a great stage in this inquiry, and that many people have their eyes upon you. This is a new motive for rendering your proofs as complete as possible."[63] Although Montagu tirelessly promoted the poems and helped create the Ossian vogue, her Scottish friends never convinced her that it was important or necessary for the poems to be precisely and accurately dated. Despite this, her interest in the Ossian poems initiated relationships between her and many of the leading figures of the Scottish Enlightenment that endured for several decades. Blair began a lasting correspondence with Montagu, in which they discussed not just the merits of the Ossian poems, but also her *Essay on Shakespeare*, which he taught regularly to his students at the University of Edinburgh. Montagu decided to educate her nephew and heir at the University of Edinburgh under the tutelage of Blair, who eagerly sought out Montagu's responses to the philosophical productions of his friends and colleagues.[64] When Adam Smith published *The Wealth of Nations* in 1776, Blair wrote to Montagu:

> It gives me a very sensible pleasure to have my own opinion of Dr. Smith's book confirmed by your judgment. I am not in the least surprised at the careful perusal that you have bestowed upon a work so much beyond the reach, and uncongenial to the taste of modern fine ladies . . . I heartily join in your wish, and would even convert it into a prayer, that the rulers of nations would listen to many of his wise and salutary counsels: and am not without some hope that the views which he has opened may gradually conduce to the general benefit.[65]

Notwithstanding his belief that Montagu's abilities were exceptional compared to most "modern fine ladies," Blair's investment in her approval demonstrates the shaping influence she exerted on the work of her Scottish contemporaries.

With the exception of Dr. John Gregory, the author of *A Father's Legacy to his Daughters*, with whom Montagu maintained a close relationship until his death (even taking his daughter Dorothea into her household),[66] Montagu's closest friend in Scotland was Lord Kames. She met Kames on her first trip to Scotland in 1766 and confessed in her letters to engaging in "much critical coquetry" with the Scotsman.[67] After this initial meeting, they conducted a correspondence that lasted until Kames's death in 1782. Not only did Kames invite Montagu to contribute an essay on the proper use of ornaments to the second edition of his *Elements of Criticism*, he also sent her drafts of various sections of his *Sketches*. His letters report that he received comments from Montagu on a section of the *Sketches* that he referred to as "the historical Essay on Ossian." This draft section of the *Sketches* explains in an account of the "progress of the fine arts" the disappearance of the bard, who wed historical analysis to a passion for poetry. Kames laments that as "subjects of writing multiplied . . . people began to reason" instead of feel. This results in the disappearance of the bard, the dissociation of history from feeling, and history's descent into "humble prose."[68] Kames references Montagu in this draft and suggests that her comments have led him to the conclusion that the spread of literacy corresponded with the disappearance of the bard. In a later letter he thanks Montagu for her help with his manuscript and writes, "In the capacity of an author, I have no reason to be disgusted at the world – but to have all my readers like Mrs. Montagu! It would be too great a luxury, it would be above crowns and scepters."[69] Montagu's exchanges with Blair and Kames place her Bluestocking philosophy in direct conversation with Scottish philosophy and historiography and reveal a complex network that proves these two discourses, which are often studied in isolation, to be mutually informing. The Bluestockings served as living examples of the principles of the new historiography Scottish philosophers were inventing; likewise, Scottish historiography and literature provided a historical context for Bluestocking feminism and a means through which these literary women could imagine their relationship to historical and commercial development.

While shaping and commenting on the work done by her Scottish counterparts, Montagu also incorporated many of the tenets of Scottish philosophy into her own worldview. As in Scottish philosophy, manners functioned as a key category in her understanding of historical development. In a letter to Lyttelton from 1762, she anticipates Kames's discussion of history, feeling, and the disappearance of the bard in his *Sketches*:

> I think we neglect too much that part of our history which gives the manners of the different ages. As in an ignorant and credulous age fables obtain belief as facts, so in a refined and skeptical one facts are in danger of passing for fables. Modern witts have taught the daughters of memory to reason when they should relate. Deep historians like modest travelers are afraid to tell the wonders of the countries they have seen, and customs widely differing from our own.[70]

In this passage, Montagu argues that factual reporting and "reason" have their limits when it comes to historical analysis, which often examines customs and beliefs "widely differing from our own" that can seem more like "fable" than historical narrative. She emphasizes the importance of feeling to historical analysis and transforms historiography into a feminine enterprise, worrying that "modern witts" have taught the "daughters of memory" to "reason when they should relate." Montagu also incorporated an emphasis on the "manners of different ages" into her *Essay on the Writings and Genius of Shakespeare*, which was universally celebrated after its publication in 1768. She conceived and wrote her defense of Shakespeare during the 1760s and drew on her discussions of Ossian and Scottish philosophy in shaping her defense.[71] In a letter to her husband Edward from 1764, she requested Lord Kames's *British Antiquities* as well as Adam Smith's *Theory of Moral Sentiments*. The letter suggests that Smith informed her defense of Shakespeare. She writes, "I also want Smith on moral sentiments, this book relates in some chapters to a subject at present under my particular consideration."[72] Smith, famously, contrasted the manners of different ages in his treatise, thinking through the gains and losses of modernity in gendered terms, as described in the last chapter.

Adapting Smith's comparative and culturally relativist approach into her *Essay*, Montagu both praises Shakespeare for accurately representing the crude manners of his age and argues that the English bard's greatness – like Ossian's – rests in his ability to convey lofty sentiments that challenge the relationship between historical development and refined feeling. She begins by glossing Shakespeare's crude humor, which Voltaire disparaged, as an accurate reflection of the earlier time in which he lived. She takes issue with Voltaire's attack on Shakespeare for "want of delicacy and politeness in his pieces," and asks how Shakespeare, living in an unrefined era, could match Voltaire's modern tastes.[73] According to Montagu, Voltaire possesses a facile understanding of the relationship between historical progress and the development of manners. She argues that all writers are at least a partial product of their age and admits that Shakespeare "bears the marks of the unpolished times in which he wrote" and "falls sometimes into the fashionable mode of writing" popular in Renaissance England.[74] She argues that the "paltry tavern[s]" in which Shakespeare staged his plays required him to pander to an "unlettered audience, just emerging from barbarity."[75] She turns what Voltaire sees as Shakespeare's weakness into a strength, suggesting that a good tragic poet will "represent men such as they were; and, indeed, when the fable and manners do not agree, great improprieties and perfect incredulity ensue."[76] She turns the tables again on Voltaire and faults "the French Tragedians" not only for "deviat[ing] from the character of the Individual represented, but even from the general character of the Age and Country."[77] Alternatively, Shakespeare's genius in his historical plays lies in his ability to "represent" his characters "with sentiments and manners agreeable to their historical characters."[78] Echoing Smith's discussion of sympathetic identification in his *Theory of Moral Sentiments*, she claims that this accurate historical representation "must have engaged the attention of the Spectator, and assisted in that delusion of his Imagination from whence his sympathy with the story must arise."[79]

According to Montagu, Shakespeare's popularity rested in his ability to represent his age but at the same time transcend historically determined factors to produce refined sentiments in an unpolished age: "Such is his merit, that the more just and refined the taste of the nation is become, the more he has increased in reputation. He was approved by his own age, admired by the next, and is revered, and almost adored by the present."[80] Like Ossian, many of Shakespeare's refined sentiments are more appropriate to the modern era and justly celebrated in the present. A reader must forgive Shakespeare's crude jokes, as they forgave Ossian's paganism, and appreciate the "refined" feelings expressed by each writer. She concludes that Shakespeare, because of his ability both to represent the manners of a particular time and place and convey feelings that were beyond his age, should be considered not just a great poet, but also "one of the greatest moral Philosophers that ever lived."[81]

As in her reflections on literature, Montagu's discussions of economic and commercial growth in her correspondence employ and even refine the philosophical methods of her Scottish contemporaries. As a business-woman, she was invested in examining the consequences of commercial development. In a letter to her husband from 1764, she writes, "Indeed industry tames and ease and prosperity soften; so that to introduce arts and manufactures is introducing the sweet civilities of life and banishing ferocity and brutality."[82] Her condescending frustration with the "pittmen" in her coal mines stems, in part, from what she perceives as their inability to assimilate into the modern economy and grow beyond subsistence-level thinking: "they earn much more than labourers, their children get a shilling a day at 9 or 10 years old, but they are so barbarous and uncultivated they know no use of money but to buy meat and liquor with it."[83] According to Montagu, her pittmen would do well to invest in luxuries, such as books, theater, or even household goods that might bestow upon them the polish Montagu believes they should cultivate. Her pittmen act like hunters and gatherers, who can only think of their basic needs, and refuse to let their excess earnings act as an improving influence. As well as seeing commerce as a civilizing force, Montagu also betrays an awareness of Adam Ferguson's critique of commercial development and his less sanguine view of the modernity commerce creates. In a discussion with Carter on the differences between French and English character, she writes, "I wish I could think with my dear antigallican friend that the English are less self interested than the French. I fear the commercial character of our nation makes us rather more sordid."[84] These two contrasting representations of Britain's "commercial character" demonstrate her complex understanding of commerce as a civilizing force, as well as a potentially corrupting influence.

Montagu's reservations about the civilizing powers of commerce come through most clearly in the observations on life in the Highlands that she makes during her first trip to Scotland in 1766. Since her impression of the Highlands was shaped by the Ossian poems, it should not be surprising that her report on Highland life unsettles the equation of commercial and historical progress. In fact, she discovers that the civil institutions that develop out of commercial progress can distort feeling:

The mistress of a miserable hovel at Glencairn tells all passengers that her name is Campbell and she is related to the Duke of Argyll. This inspires a nobler kind of pride than a pair of laced shoes could do and I assure you *the barefooted noblesse of the Highlands are wonderfully courteous*. There is a certain spirit and ardour of mind, encouraged by the independence they live in, the fresh air they breathe and the great object they behold. It is true they are in subjection to their Chief, but they feel as much pride in his greatness as fear of his power. They consider him as their relation as well as their master, so render obedience without that humiliation that usually attends it. I think therefore we should find some assurance from seeing human nature civilized and enobled by some social ideas without being intimidated by civil laws and institutions or mortified by poverty continually compared to riches.[85]

The Highland woman or "noblesse" Montagu describes possesses a "courteous[ness]" and "independence" that seems impossible to cultivate in a complex civil society. In fact, she evidences a "human nature civilized" in the absence of a developed civil society. Montagu's assessment was shared by many contemporaries. Despite his antipathy for Montagu and the Ossian poems, Samuel Johnson, in his *Journey to the Western Islands* (1775), includes a complimentary account of Highland women. Early on in his tour, he describes an encounter in a rude hut with the daughter of one of his hosts: "We knew that the girls of the Highlands are all gentlewomen, and treated her with great respect, which she received as customary and due, and was neither elated by it, nor confused."[86] In Johnson and Montagu's tours, the possibility emerges that the "prosperity" of commercial society might only superficially elevate the status of women. Sentiments inspired by an empty "pair of laced shoes" or a modern house pale when set against the noble feelings that grow organically out of the bonds of community and mutual affection enjoyed by women in Highland society.

Montagu's critique of commercial development takes on an even sharper edge when she applies it to imperial expansion. Interestingly, she uses the Ossianic phrase "tale of other times" to articulate her response to the British presence in India. In a letter to Carter from 1774, she applies Ossianic rhetoric to her analysis of the British East India Company:

> The tale of times past is wonderful, it is horrid, may not the tale of times to come be as wonderfull and as horrid? Indeed the tale of the present times is most marvellous. A set of citizens establish a trading corporation for spice and tea and things for their wives breakfasts and their children's ginger bread, and they get a bit of land in the East to build warehouses, and what do my citizens [do] then, but take it in their heads to dispose of the Empire of Indostans, and they do dispose of it. They sit crosslegged in Leadenhall street and decide the fate of mighty Princes. Read their list of directors, then look at the map of the East Indies, and you will never again wonder that Pismires have desolated fertile regions. I should like to see the instructions of our directors to their commanders abroad. (In town a stiled) Gent: of the fishmongers or saddlers company, do order you John o'nokes Lieutenant of such a regiment, to dethrone Shaw [Shah] such a thing stiled light of the world, commander of the nations, emperor of etc., etc., etc., etc. these things are for wise

reasons ordered by him who [illegible] by worldly weak, subduing worldly strong, gives us daily lessons how vain and frivolous are all things that relate to the transitory condition of humanity.[87]

The Ossianic rhetoric of this paragraph functions to challenge conventional understandings of historical progress. Instead of a clear sense of teleological development, the "tale of the present" she relates gestures toward a desperate future that may be more "horrid" than the past. If the past was "horrid," the present overseen by the male directors or the "pismires" of the British East India Company, who "dethrone Shaw such a thing styled light of the world" to provide "spice and tea and things for their wives breakfasts and their children's ginger bread," emerges as even more dreadful. Montagu's distaste for the middle-class merchants of the British East India Company can be explained, at least in part, by her desire to uphold a class hierarchy that retained the majority of a nation's wealth in the hands of the aristocracy to which she belonged. The threat the British nobility – including Montagu – feel from encroaching merchants is transposed onto the indignities suffered by the "mighty Princes" of the East. Despite the obvious class bias at work in her description, her Ossianic critique of Empire still remains a startling appraisal of imperial expansion. From one perspective, commercial and imperial development could look like a civilizing force, but seen through the lens of the Ossian poems it often looked like a "horrid" cycle of attempts to "subdue" great cultures in an effort to forward the mundane commercial and imperial interests of the British Empire. Montagu's fellow Bluestocking Catherine Talbot develops this critique of the British Empire in her imitations of Ossian.

Catherine Talbot in Ancient Caledonia

Catherine Talbot's three imitations of Ossian, written between the publication of James Macpherson's *Fragments of Ancient Poetry* in 1760 and the close of the Seven Years War in 1763, are some of the earliest examples of Ossianic imitation. In these poems, she extends the Bluestockings' interest in Malvina and voices another female bard, whom she calls Therina. Like Montagu's commentary on Ossian in her letters, Talbot uses Therina to comment on women's complex relationship to British imperialism and commerce. Her imitations, which were published posthumously and in all likelihood circulated within Bluestocking salons in manuscript, forward a dialectical view of history that uses Ossianic time as an alternative way of thinking about the relationship between the past, present, and future.

Although Talbot certainly knew of Montagu's feasts, she probably never attended one, and her exposure to the poems came mostly through her correspondence and conversation with other Bluestockings, particularly Elizabeth Carter. The reclusive Talbot published little during her lifetime and is perhaps best known for her friendship with Carter and their correspondence, which Carter's nephew the Reverend Montagu Pennington published in 1808.[88] After Talbot's death in 1770, Carter published *Essays on Various Subjects* (1772), a collection of Talbot's essays and poetry, which included her imitations of Ossian. These imitations develop the Bluestocking personas of Therina and Carthona, who figure Talbot and Carter and embody the shared features of Bluestocking and Ossianic sociability. She uses these Ossianic personas to reflect on the Seven Years War, George III's coronation, and even Montagu's Ossianic feasts, giving Ossian's ancient Caledonia a strikingly modern character. By integrating Ossianic sentiment into the present, she explores its utility as an active and disruptive historical force within her world.

Talbot's imitations attempt to resolve the central dilemma posed by the Ossian poems, which, as Dafydd Moore has argued, work at cross purposes, "stak[ing] a claim for Celtic superiority" by "locating civic sentiment within the Celtic past," while framing these bold claims for Celtic culture with an "apocalyptic tone and sense of inevitable doom." The effect of this approach, Moore explains, is to depict Celtic culture, however admirable, as an antiquarian relic, an inactive part of Britain's remote past.[89] Talbot's imitations solve this problem by making the Ossianic past into an active part of the present. According to Robert Griffin, early modern writers understood imitation not as "slavish adherence to a prior model, but rather as a species of invention . . . The source text, or more often texts, are evoked precisely in order to trope, translate, transplant, or graft them into a new context."[90] By incorporating Ossian and his ancient Caledonia into her experience of the present, Talbot creates a "new context" for understanding contemporary events, a context that critiques both Britain's imperial project and the unmarked English, masculine perspective through which contemporary events were often filtered. This attention to temporality is present in the structure of Talbot's text. Although her history begins in the first poem by reproducing the defeat and the temporal dislocation of Ossian as a description of Therina's alienation from British politics and culture, the second and third poems criticize the hopelessness of the first poem and transform Ossianic sentiment into an active part of the present. These final poems use an Ossianic voice to "blast" (in the spirit of Walter Benjamin) a hole in universalizing narratives of commercial expansion, especially those that cited the progress of women as a justification for imperialism.

Talbot's imitations read like a journal of contemporary political events encrypted in a Celtic code. They include two long prose poems, one beginning in Ossian's voice and one addressed to Ossian, as well as a dialogue between Therina and Carthona.[91] The highly self-referential nature of Talbot's imitations makes it likely that Therina and Carthona are Ossianic figures for Talbot and Carter. Yet in the landscape of ancient Caledonia, the political concerns and national events the two Bluestockings often mention as asides in their letters become central. Talbot develops these dramatic Ossianic personae to think about how women figure in and complicate progressive accounts of British history.

Although many of Talbot and Carter's letters are taken up with descriptions of their health and domestic responsibilities, in addition to their literary and scholarly pursuits, they frequently reach out to the wider world by commenting on the Jacobite rebellion of 1745, the Seven Years War, and other national events. The Archbishop's relationship with George III gave Talbot access to detailed accounts of high-profile events such as the King's coronation, and her letters record a more than passing interest in the details of the ceremony and George III's behavior. During the Seven Years War as well as the Jacobite Rebellion, her correspondence with Carter, who lived on the Kentish coast in Deal, also betrayed a pressing awareness of the potential for French invasion and the horrific consequences, both personal and national, that could ensue. Often, the personal and the national crossed paths, as when, early in the Seven Years War, Talbot held "national prospects" responsible for one of her frequent depressions.[92] Although Carter attempted to convince Talbot that "people in private life" have no need to think about global politics, Talbot seemed unable to shake her concerns.[93] Talbot's imitations of Ossian appear to be an extension of moments like this. The secluded caves in which Ossian dwells and the isolation of which he sings, "sad, forlorn, and blind; and no more the companion of heroes,"[94] resonate with her own experience as a reclusive woman writer, distraught by but powerless in the face of violent British imperial expansion.

Reinforcing the kinship between Talbot and Ossian, the setting of the first imitation shifts, almost imperceptibly, from ancient Caledonia to a faux Celtic retreat that, oddly enough, appears to be a stand-in for her quarters in the Archbishop's palace just outside of London. Frequently, when London is mentioned in her letters to Carter, Talbot describes the metropolis not as bustling or exciting but rather as "the most forlorn and joyless of all desarts," a place of "desolateness" where she experiences an alienation similar to that expressed by Ossian.[95] The first imitation does not introduce Therina until the middle of the poem. The three-paragraph prose poem begins with a bard who, at first, appears to be Ossian in solitude, wondering why the "Daughter of the Gentle Smile" does not visit.[96] The situation mirrors one in Macpherson's "Berrathon," which was published along with *Fingal* in December of 1761. In "Berrathon," Ossian waits in vain for his son's betrothed Malvina. Eventually, he discovers that Malvina, the only other surviving member of his family, has died. Alone, he imagines Malvina living "among the spirits of thy friends" in the "dwelling of Fingal" where Fingal and Ossian's "friends sit around the king, on mist; and hear the songs of Ullin."[97] Talbot's Ossian-like bard guesses that the missing woman for whom she waits has suffered a similar fate, visiting "thy hall of Joy [where] The Feast of Shells is spread: the Bards are assembled around. Sad I sit alone, and listen to the beating Rain."[98] The second paragraph supports a reading of this first imitation as a version of "Berrathon," with Ossian as the speaker. It begins with the bard wondering who will memorialize his death, since all his friends have preceded him into the afterlife: "When I go to the narrow House, Silence shall rest upon my Memory."[99] Here, the unnamed bard echoes Ossian, who fears going to his grave without anyone to celebrate his fame and wishes that Malvina had lived long enough to "lay Ossian in the plain of Lutha: let his tomb rise in the lovely field."[100] Abruptly in the same paragraph, however, the speaker's voice jumps from the first person and the present tense to the third person and the past, revealing the speaker to be not Ossian but a woman, Therina.

Therina's tendency to shift tense and number mirrors Ossian's own erratic style. At the end of "Berrathon," after jumping between the present and a story about his long-past adventures with Malvina's father Toscar, Ossian thinks about joining the dead: "I am alone at Lutha: my voice is like the last sound of the wind, when it forsakes the wood. But Ossian shall not be long alone, he sees the mist that shall receive his ghost."[101] His jump between the first and the third person makes him simultaneously a part of the present and a relic from a lost age whose actions can only be discussed at an awkward remove. Talbot's bard, Therina, struggles in a similar fashion, shifting between persons and tenses:

> For lonely I sit all the Day, and listen to the dashing Rain. The keen Wind whistles at my Gate, and drives away the timid Guest. Dark Boats pass by on the swift Stream, but no Passenger lands at my Hall. Thou too, O sweet Daughter of the Smile, didst sail over the blue Wave, when the Voice of Joy was in the Hall of Kings. But Therina past the Day silent and solitary.

When a thousand Oaks flamed beyond the Stream, she saw the distant Blaze, like the red Streaks of the setting Sun. She heard the Murmur of the distant Shouts, and at last through the dark Air, she saw the approaching Torch, that lighted back her Friends, from the Feast of empty Shells. She ran to meet them through the lonely Hall: and the Wind lifted her Cloke.[102]

The revelation that it is not Ossian, but Therina, who "past [sic] the day solitary and silent" and "saw" and "heard" the actions of those around her, transforms the poem from a reflection on a lost Scottish past to a meditation on Talbot's own sense of herself as a female writer, who, like Ossian, straddles the past and the present, existing in a space between times. She is a first-person observer and commentator on contemporary events, and yet she is located at an insurmountable remove, in a feminine periphery that causes her to slip in and out of the present tense. Ossian's purposelessness and detachment reflect Talbot's sense of herself as an upper-class Englishwoman. In a letter to Carter from 1765, Talbot reflects on her frustration with daily life:

> Because I have little to do, I do nothing with spirit . . . If Dr. Franklin would come over, and order me to clean the house with my own hands, I should be as happy as he made the Paris ladies by such sort of prescriptions . . . Or, if his Majesty would make me Secretary of State. In short any thing (one excepted) that would take me from the appearance, without the reality, of being quite at my own liberty to do just what I please. I should sing like a gay French peasant, instead of growling like a free-born English woman.[103]

Talbot's discontentment with her apparently privileged position as an upper-class woman of leisure finds expression in her imitations of Ossian. Without a Benjamin Franklin to prescribe a common-sense treatment for her languor, the liberty she enjoyed as an upper-class English woman translated not into the ability to participate in the domestic as well as political concerns of the day, but rather into ennui and alienation from matters of present importance. Far from celebrating herself as a feminine sign of progress and civilization, Talbot feels like Ossian – an addled relic from a distant age.

In the final two paragraphs of the first imitation, Talbot's present and Ossian's past become almost indistinguishable. Therina's appearance, in the middle of the second paragraph, forces readers to revisit the "Feast of empty Shells." In this second reading, the feast from which Therina's friend returns appears to be not a gathering of Celtic heroes in the afterlife, but a Montagu-inspired theme party. In this reading, "the bards" who "are assembled round" become the members of Montagu's Bluestocking salon, which included male and female poets.[104] Although Talbot's extensive correspondence with Carter suggests that she was keenly aware of Montagu's frequent gatherings, her status as the Archbishop's ward compelled Talbot to limit the frequency of her appearances at gatherings like Montagu's feasts and, even more so than her fellow Bluestockings, to suppress her contributions to the public sphere. She relegated her writings, for the most part, to her "considering drawer," an interstitial space between the public and private that Talbot and Carter mention several times as a place where Talbot stored items she was considering for publication.[105] Sylvia Harcstack Myers confirms this view of Talbot's characteristic reticence and her wariness about venturing into the public realm: "Of all the Bluestockings she seems to be the one whose cleverness and talent were the most dampened by her own discomfort at being known as a person who wrote."[106] In her letters, Talbot describes a sense of mental and physical paralysis similar to that of the displaced and isolated Ossian. Lingering beside the tombs of his long-gone companions, completely shut off from the outside world, Ossian describes himself in "Connal and Crimora," from the *Fragments of Ancient Poetry* (1760) as without direction: "Sightless I sit by thy tomb. I hear the wind in the wood, but no more I hear my friend."[107] If she was not consciously imitating Ossian in a 1760 letter to Carter, in which she confesses to feeling often like "a stupid piece of petrification,"[108] certainly she conveyed a distinctly Ossianic sense of immobility and temporal dislocation.

With Therina's emergence, Fingal's Hall of Kings also undergoes a dizzying renovation and becomes the site of George III's coronation. This transformation has been long recognized by Talbot's editors, from Elizabeth Carter to, most recently, Rhoda Zuk, who have glossed "the Voice of Joy in the Hall of Kings" as an allusion to the coronation. Archbishop Secker performed the coronation of George III and must have shared the details with Talbot, who described the ceremony in a letter to Carter from 1760. In the letter, she presents herself as a peripheral figure, interested in events of national importance, yet barred because of her status as Secker's ward: "I would have given an ear to have been at chapel yesterday, to see the graceful figure, the unaffected seriousness, and awful attention . . . and here live poor I in a cloyster, and can only dream over at night the busy scenes I have heard of in the day."[109] Talbot's account complements Therina's description of the invisible barriers that prevent her from interacting with the world around her: "The keen Wind whistles at my Gate, and drives away the timid Guest. Dark Boats pass by on the swift Stream, but no Passenger lands at my hall. Thou too, O sweet Daughter of the Gentle Smile, didst sail by over the Blue Wave, when the Voice of Joy was in the Hall of Kings."[110] This first imitation creates a female variant of Ossian, who at first appears largely indistinguishable from the ghostly bard, languishing outside contemporary literary and political circles as she wonders, "Will no Voice reply to my Song? I too have a Harp, which the Wind sweeps with its Wings."[111] The Scottish periphery and the literary and political margins to which Talbot felt banished because of her gender begin to resemble one another: both belong to a previous age and a distant world that, like the ancient Caledonia of conjectural history, appear peculiarly modern. By adopting Ossian's archaic Caledonian address, Talbot creates a female bard out of place and out of step with the cultural and political events that pass before her.

While the first poem accepts dislocation and defeat, the second and third poems in the series recuperate Ossian's lost world. Instead of bemoaning their position outside of a linear or progressive history, they employ the uneven temporality of the first imitation to critique the progress of the British Empire as well as women's status within this universalizing narrative.

Talbot's second imitation takes the form of a dialogue between Therina and her female friend Carthona. Initially, Therina responds to Carthona's concerns about her mental well-being by resisting the Ossianic register that gave her voice, persuading Carthona that the first imitation was a performance: "Partial is thine eye, kind Daughter of Harmony, and idly fictitious was my plaintive strain. My expectations look beyond the narrow house, and the view terminates in splendour."[112] Therina reveals the gloom and doom of the first poem to be "idly fictitious," a disconnected aesthetic indulgence that merely revisits and replicates Ossian's self-pitying strains. Instead of continuing to produce these maudlin and idle fictions, she launches a critique of Ossian's atheism and solipsism, what she calls "the reverse of my plaintive strains."[113] Through a "reversal" of the first imitation, Therina transforms the periphery she describes in the first imitation as a territory of dislocation and invisibility, rendering it visible within the context of the larger nation. In so doing, she transforms women from signs of progress to critics of universalizing narratives of development: the same narratives that dismiss the Ossianic world as irrelevant or exceptional and suture female progress too tightly to commercialism and imperial expansion.

Talbot's discussion of the "splendour" that waits beyond the grave appears to be a direct criticism of Ossian's paganism and rejection of Christianity. Such a revisionist approach includes an attack on Ossian's desire to view himself as part of a lost culture, an anachronism from a pre-Christian world. Ossian's refusal to convert to Christianity, a refusal mentioned briefly by Macpherson,[114] would have been significant to

Talbot. Her most popular work, "Reflections on the Seven Days of the Week,"[115] consists of a series of essays written to prompt daily religious reflection. Talbot's religiosity and her close relationship with her ecclesiastical guardian made her an unlikely fan of the notably irreligious Ossian. Indeed, in the second and third imitations she directly criticizes Ossian for his atheism. Her piety did not eliminate the possibility, however, that she also recuperated his voice as a means of representing her own relationship to Great Britain. Harriet Guest and Emma Major have argued separately that religion sanctioned the Bluestockings' participation in the public sphere. Guest has suggested that religion makes public participation an "obligation" for women, because "if they think profoundly about religion, as their rational and moral nature requires that they should, then they will be unable to think superficially about anything, because nothing is irrelevant to religion."[116] Relying mainly on evidence drawn from Montagu's correspondence, Major has examined the Bluestockings' particularly Anglican faith and argued that their religious devotion gave them a special responsibility to the British nation. As the embodiments of Anglican piety, the Bluestockings were responsible for cultivating high-minded sentiments that could stave off imperial decay and transform "George III's Britain into an earthly paradise of divinely blessed progress."[117]

Talbot's insistence on looking "beyond the narrow house" did allow her to imagine the public as well as the national appeal of her poetry. Yet, instead of ensuring the progress of the British Empire, Talbot's religion aided her in redeeming Ossian and transforming his narrative into a conduit that allowed her to see beyond a one-dimensional history of economic progress. She used her religion to interpret Ossian's tense-shifting temporal acrobatics and to reinscribe in her own poems the temporal leaps and connections denied by secular time. Challenging the homogeneous time of the nation, Talbot creates what Benjamin would call a mystical constellation between her "own era" and "a definite earlier one."[118] At first, aligning Talbot with the twentieth-century Benjamin might seem forced, but in her imitations she undoubtedly uses the Ossianic past to disturb the progressive flow of history, "blasting" the Ossianic era into her own present experience of the nation. In doing so, Talbot disrupted – as did the Ossianic histories of the Scottish philosophers – universal history, the mode of historiography preferred by what Benjamin has called historicism. Practitioners of historicism, according to him, record the history of the victor in which "the present ruler steps over those who are lying prostrate."[119] It is no stretch to include in the category of the prostrate those like Ossian, who are relegated to a lost past and suppressed by the dominant English culture of

Great Britain. Talbot's poetic historiography resembles what Benjamin has described as the "weak messianism" of historical materialism, reflecting her desire to redeem the Ossianic past and "blast open the continuum of history."[120] It suggests that the universal story of human development, which aligns economic progress with the progress of women and the cultivation of feeling, can be halted by resurrecting the "prostrate" and temporally remote Ossian and relocating him to the present. The Ossian poems provided a historical field in which Talbot could separate women and commerce and unsettle universal history.[121] By transferring Ossian's lament into the present, Therina transforms his bereft descriptions of isolation and transplants the severed periphery he describes into the larger, if spatially and temporally discontinuous, British social whole, which contains ancient Caledonia as well as the experience of British women.

Armed with Ossian and with her religious sensibilities, Talbot moves to challenge the equation of women's elevated status with the nation's commercial achievements. The crown that Therina and Carthona argue over in the second imitation recalls the earlier description of the coronation and returns us to Therina's meditation on her own place in the national landscape. Carthona, anxious about the depressed strains sung by Therina in the first imitation, confronts Therina about her perception of herself as, like Ossian, already entombed in a lost world: "Thy melancholy strain pierced my heart. I view thee already as in the narrow house, where all is silence and darkness. I look upon thee as a diamond buried deep in the rock, when it ought to be flaming on an imperial diadem."[122] Carthona recognizes Therina's potential as a national symbol "flaming" in the "imperial diadem" central to the representation of the nation. Instead of mourning her outsider status, as in the first imitation, Therina corrects Carthona's appraisal of the center's importance: "Yet I am not a Diamond, O Carthona, but a feeble Glowworm of the Earth, whose sickly Lustre would go out in open Day, and . . . is beheld to Advantage, only from being judiciously placed amidst Obscurity."[123] Therina appears suspicious of the central place occupied by the gem, preferring instead the obscurity of the peripheries. In retreat, Therina transforms into something more practical, if less visible: a glowworm of "low estate," but "useful sometimes . . . direct[ing] the Steps of the benighted Traveller."[124] By rejecting her place as the gem or ornament in the imperial crown, Therina challenges, as did Montagu and the conjectural histories of Kames, Millar, and Alexander in the 1770s and 1780s, the troubling imperial logic of universal history that links women, luxury, commercial expansion, and national achievement. The Ossianic periphery, as in the conjectural histories discussed earlier, becomes an environment in which feeling can thrive without the commercial trappings.

Therina continues to revive the periphery, contrasting the utility of her placement in obscurity with Ossian's understanding of his peripheral position as outside time, always already lifeless, and buried in the concerns of "the narrow house." Unlike Ossian, she "look[s] beyond the narrow house."[125] This phrase can be read as an invitation to look toward God, and as an attempt to project herself from the grave of the Ossianic past she identifies with so closely and into a future anticipated by the Ossian poems and their egalitarian treatment of women. In spite of her debt to Ossian, at the end of the dialogue Therina separates herself from Malvina and Ossian, relegating them to the past:

> Yet what is the fame of Malvina? And what was the merit of Ossian? The threads of my life, O Carthona, though homely, are woven amid others of inestimable tincture. The ties of indissoluble friendship have mingled them among threads of purest gold, the richest purple, and the brightest silver. Such are the durable textures, which heaven has framed in the loom of civilized society: While the scattered threads of Fingal's days are like autumnal cobwebs, tost by winds from thorn to thorn: whence some few of peculiar whiteness are collected by the musing bard, when solitary he roams amid the pathless wild.[126]

Therina reads Ossian's and Malvina's redactions of the past as without "merit" and outside the "loom of civilized society." They are "cobwebs," lost strands of time, easily brushed away. She concludes by defining herself in opposition to them, claiming that she is essential to the creation of the "durable textures" of "civilized society," yoked by "indissoluble friendships" to a living and vibrant social matrix. In this contradictory moment, Therina speaks in an Ossianic register from the peripheries to incorporate the periphery back into the national fabric. While performing this rhetorical feat she brushes away her Celtic ally and predecessor like an "autumnal cobweb." Ossian's ability to embody the particular Scots history Kames and Millar were so invested in retaining recedes behind the women-centered history Therina struggles to uncover.

Yet, in the third imitation, preserving the dialectical movement of the series, Talbot retreats from the complete disavowal of the second poem. In this final poem of the series, she once again connects ancient Caledonia to the global and political present of Britain and recovers the Ossian poems' contemporary relevance, which even Ossian seems to deny. Therina addresses Ossian directly and admits to loving his verse, but worries over what she sees as its lack of application to the physical, living world: "True Ossian, I delight in Songs: Harmony sooths my Soul.

It sooths it O Ossian, but it raises it far above these grassy Clods, and rocky Hills."[127] She invites Ossian to be silent and reconsider the objective of his songs:

> Harp of Ossian be still. Why dost thou sound in the blast, and wake my sleeping fancy? Deep and long had been its repose. Solid are the walls that surround me. The idle laugh enters not here: why then should the idler tear? Yet Ossian I would weep for thee: I would weep for thee, Malvina. – But my days are as the flight of an arrow. Shall the arrow turn aside from its mark?[128]

Therina chastises Ossian for distracting her and critiques the content of his work, which, in her view, simply "retrace[s] the War and Bloodshed, of the Days that are past." Although Therina sings in an Ossianic register, unlike Ossian she refuses to "remainest by choice an orphan in an orphan world" performing exclusively for "a cloudy Fingal."[129] Therina, instead, recognizes the present import of Ossian's verse:

> While thou sittest gloomy on the storm-beaten hill, and repeating to the angry blast, the boast of human pride: the tales of devastation of war, the deeds of other times. *Far other times are these* – Ah would they were! For still destruction spreads: still human pride rises with the tigers of the desert, and makes its horrid boast![130]

Talbot's imitations of Ossian, written during the Seven Years War, call attention to the potential for critique in the Ossian poems, especially the possibility that his songs might not be just the songs of "other times," but a viable appraisal of contemporary imperial contests. Replacing the native deer of Ossian's verse with "tigers of the desert" confuses and links ancient Caledonia with India, large portions of which Britain gained at the end of the Seven Years War. Through this substitution, Therina acknowledges the contemporaneity of Ossian's lament over the disappearance of ancient Caledonia with the destruction wrought by modern Britain's imperial expansion and pleads with Ossian to extend his gaze from the "storm-beaten hill" and into contemporary life. Through Ossian's poetry, Talbot created a new but familiar context for her own experience of the British present, arguing that the present may be an uncanny repetition of "other times" instead of a developmental endpoint, the conclusion of a teleological narrative that justifies and explains Britain's imperial project.

By embracing and cultivating Ossian's voice and ancient Caledonian culture, Talbot, Montagu, and their fellow Bluestockings did more than indulge in a mid-century craze for shells, harps, and all things Scottish. The Bluestockings and the Scottish Enlightenment historiographers and writers with whom they corresponded and feasted used ancient Caledonia to register women's complex relationship to the progress of the British state. In their different ways, both Montagu and Talbot adapted Ossian's voice and perspective to explore women's representation in progressive accounts of British history. In so doing, they sometimes reinforced, as in Montagu's comments on the pittmen in her coalmines, the progressive course of history. More often, as in Montagu and Talbot's meditations on India, they replaced progressive historiography with an uneven, repetitive, and, in Talbot's case, a potentially redemptive temporality. The "other times" that emerge from their work make distant ages and places continuous with the present, and the British present often indistinguishable from foreign temporalities and spaces. This new historiography introduced the possibility that aligning the present with a forgotten age might make room for an unanticipated future, a future that would nurture feminine virtues without linking them to the vices fostered by commerce and empire. The next chapter explores the second-generation Bluestocking Anna Seward's vision of the alternative temporality theorized in Montagu's correspondence and Talbot's poetry.

Notes

1. Elizabeth Montagu to Lord Lyttelton, 31 October 1760, in Emily Climenson (ed.), *The Queen of the Bluestockings*, p. 211.
2. In the twentieth century, Thomson concluded that Macpherson's poems were neither wholly forged nor traceable to any clear oral or written origin. He found that Macpherson most likely altered Gaelic oral sources to meet the generic expectations of the epic and appeal to the more refined emotions produced by eighteenth-century sensibilities. See Derick S. Thomson, *Gaelic Sources of Macpherson's "Ossian."*
3. Montagu to Lord Lyttelton, 31 October 1760, MO1404, Montagu Collection, Huntington Library; although Climenson's excerpts of Montagu's letters are useful, I will also rely heavily on Montagu's unexcerpted and unpublished correspondence, which is held at the Huntington Library. The originals Climenson worked from contain many references to Ossian and the Scottish Enlightenment that she chose not to include in her 1906 edition. MO is an abbreviation for the Huntington's Montagu Collection.
4. Ibid., MO 1404.
5. Soon after the publication of the Ossian poems, leading figures in eighteenth-century British literary culture – most notably Samuel Johnson – accused James Macpherson of forgery. Initially, most Scottish literati, such as Hugh Blair, Adam Ferguson, and David Hume, vehemently

defended the poems' authenticity; however, the skepticism of the British establishment led to an official inquiry into the poems' authenticity. Despite the 1805 Report of the Highland Society of Scotland, which argued that the poems were derived from the sources Macpherson collected on his journeys to the Highlands, the poems retained their reputation as forgeries. Useful discussions of the Ossian poems' contribution to eighteenth-century debates over originality as well as their status as a gauge of the changing relationship between Scotland and England include Richard Sher, *Church and University in the Scottish Enlightenment*; Katie Trumpener, *Bardic Nationalism*; and Kathryn Temple, *Scandal Nation*.

6. Montagu to Elizabeth Carter, 13 October 1767, MO 5862.
7. On the origins of the term Bluestocking, see Gary Kelly, "Bluestocking Feminism and Writing in Context," in Elizabeth Eger (ed.), *Bluestocking Feminism: Elizabeth Montagu*, vol. 1, pp. ix–liv; Nicole Pohl and Betty Schellenberg, "Introduction: A Bluestocking Historiography," in their *Reconsidering the Bluestockings*, pp. 1–19; and Deidre Lynch, "Bluestockings," *The Oxford Encyclopedia of British Literature*, pp. 214–19.
8. Adam Potkay, "Virtue and Manners in Macpherson's Poems of Ossian," p. 121.
9. Silvia Sebastiani, "Race, Women, and Progress in the Late Scottish Enlightenment," pp. 86–7; see also Jane Rendall, "Tacitus Engendered," pp. 57–74. In this essay, Rendall argues that the eighteenth-century interest in Macpherson's Ossian poems as well as Tacitus's history of Germania were key to shaping Whig historiography and making women and manners central to understandings of British identity.
10. Gary Kelly, "Bluestocking Feminism," in Elizabeth Eger et al. (eds), *Women, Writing, and the Public Sphere*, p. 164.
11. See Emma Major, *Madam Britannia*, for a relevant discussion of the ways in which Montagu and Talbot linked British national virtue to femininity.
12. Elizabeth Child, "Elizabeth Montagu, Bluestocking Businesswoman," in Pohl and Schellenberg (eds), *Reconsidering the Bluestockings*, p. 154.
13. Catherine Talbot, "Imitations of Ossian," in Rhoda Zuk (ed.), *Bluestocking Feminism: Catherine Talbot and Hester Chapone*, vol. 3, p. 140.
14. See, for example, Harriet Guest, *Small Change*; and E. J. Clery, *The Feminization Debate in Eighteenth-Century England*.
15. Lord Kames, *Sketches of the History of Man*, p. 168.
16. William Alexander, *The History of Women*.
17. John Millar, *Origin of the Distinction of Ranks*, pp. 14–108.
18. Kames, *Sketches*, p. v.
19. Ibid., p. vii.
20. Kames to Montagu, 25 December 1768, in Helen Whitcomb Randall, *The Critical Theory of Lord Kames*, p. 110.
21. *The Library of Mrs. Elizabeth Vesey 1715–1791* (Newcastle-on-Tyne: William H. Robinson, 1926).
22. See Mary Catherine Moran, "The Commerce of the Sexes," and Mark Salber Philips, *Society and Sentiment*.
23. Unlike Arendt, Moran sees the entrance of the private into the public

as a positive development, especially because it provided women with a more visible role (Moran, "The Commerce of the Sexes," p. 69). See also Hannah Arendt, *On the Human Condition*.

24. Guest, *Small Change*, p. 85.
25. On the changing relationship between luxury and women, see Elizabeth Eger, "Luxury, Industry and Charity: Bluestocking Culture Displayed," in Maxine Berg and Elizabeth Eger (eds), *Luxury in the Eighteenth Century*.
26. Laura Brown, *Ends of Empire*, p. 19.
27. Philips, *Society and Sentiment*, p. 113.
28. Millar, *Origin of the Distinction of Ranks*, p. 3.
29. Ibid., pp. 3–4.
30. Ibid., p. 32.
31. Ibid., p. 23.
32. See Chandler's discussion of uneven development and stadial history in his *England in 1819*; see also Pocock, *Barbarism and Religion*, vol. 2: "Nor is it suggested that the four stages necessarily occurred in a fixed order, so that a condition of society governed by one mode of sustenance gave way to one governed by another; the original desert island was a heuristic device leaving it perfectly possible that the several modes of sustenance may have overlapped and existed concurrently" (p. 322).
33. Millar, *Origin of the Distinction of Ranks*, p. 131.
34. Ibid., p. 54.
35. Ibid., pp. 51–2.
36. Kames, *Sketches*, p. 281.
37. Ibid., pp. 62–3.
38. In her recent *Scottish Enlightenment*, Silvia Sebastiani explores the role gender played in the Scottish Enlightenment's understanding of race. She identifies a tension between thinkers such as Kames and Macpherson, who understood Celtic cultures as exceptional among "savage" peoples, and Gilbert Stuart, William Robertson, and Adam Ferguson, who viewed ancient Celtic communities as "one of many examples of the better condition of women among peoples living closer to nature" (p. 160). Although Kames's and Macpherson's arguments for polygenesis played a role in the "evolution of modern racism" (p. 155), the Ossianic poems raised many questions about imperial progress both within and outside the British Isles that complicated as well as contributed to essentialist ideas about race. This chapter draws on the work of Scottish literati from both sides of the divide Sebastiani explores in order to survey the different modes of cultural comparisons that the Ossian poems made possible.
39. Ibid., p. 301.
40. Alexander, *The History of Women*, p. 172.
41. Ibid., p. 107.
42. Millar, *Origin of the Distinction of Ranks*, p. 219.
43. Montagu to Lyttelton, 17 November 1761, in Climenson, *The Queen of the Bluestockings*, vol. 2, p. 268.
44. The standard account of Macpherson's life and work is Fiona J. Stafford's *The Sublime Savage*.

45. Montagu to Lyttelton, 17 November 1761, in Climenson, *The Queen of the Bluestockings*, vol. 2, p. 268.
46. Montagu to Elizabeth Carter, 18 December 1761, MO 3077.
47. Montagu to Vesey, c.1761 (this letter is an undated fragment, but its contents suggest 1761), MO 6377.
48. Montagu to Vesey, 13 February 1772, in *Mrs. Montagu, "Queen of the Blues": her Letters and Friendships from 1762–1800*, ed. Reginald Blunt (London: Constable and Company Limited, 1923), pp. 257–8. See also Rothschild, *The Inner Life of Empire*, which provides an important perspective on James Macpherson's connections not only to London society, but also to the larger British Empire in America and India.
49. Montagu to Edward Montagu, 5 July 1771, MO 2758.
50. Montagu to Carter, 10 August 1765, MO 3150.
51. Montagu to Vesey, 14 July 1763, MO 6370.
52. Montagu to Carter, 17 October 1756, MO 3158.
53. James Macpherson (trans.), *Fingal, an ancient epic poem.*
54. See Elizabeth Eger, *Bluestockings* for an important recent discussion of the Bluestockings' role as powerful patrons and critics of the arts in mid and late eighteenth-century Britain.
55. Montagu to Lord Bath, c.1761, MO 4511 (emphasis mine).
56. Charles Morton to Montagu, August 1761, MO 4005.
57. Montagu to Sarah Scott, 26 June 1761, MO 5784.
58. Montagu to Carter, 6 May 1763, MO 3098.
59. Lyttelton to Montagu, 18 October 1760, MO 1291.
60. James Macpherson, "Croma," c.1760, MO 1505.
61. James Macpherson, "Croma," in Howard Gaskill (ed.), *The Poems of Ossian and Related Works*, p. 187.
62. Ibid., p. 187.
63. David Hume to Hugh Blair, 6 October 1763, in Dafydd Moore (ed.), *Ossian and Ossianisms*, vol. 1, p. 131.
64. For a discussion of Montagu and Blair's correspondence, see also Eger, *Bluestockings*, p. 146.
65. Hugh Blair to Montagu, 8 June 1776, MO 489.
66. For more on Montagu's tutelage of Dorothea Gregory, see Betty Rizzo, *Companions without Vows*, pp. 112–41; Gregory frequently solicited advice from Montagu, and the epistolary advice Montagu offered Gregory on the rearing of his daughters influenced the composition of his famous *Father's Legacy to his Daughters*. See my "A Delicate Debate."
67. Montagu to Carter, 18 August 1776, MO 3181.
68. Kames to Montagu, 26 February 1772, MO 1171.
69. Kames to Montagu, 12 August 1771, MO 1172.
70. Montagu to Lyttelton, 12 September 1762, MO 1419.
71. See Eger, *Bluestockings*, pp. 129–47, for a discussion of Montagu's *Essay* in the context of British women writers' responses to Shakespeare.
72. Montagu to Edward Montagu, 16 August 1764, MO 2524.
73. Elizabeth Montagu, *An Essay on the Writings and Genius of Shakespear*, p. 5.
74. Ibid., pp. 5 and 10.

75. Ibid., p. 13.
76. Ibid., p. 48.
77. Ibid., p. 44.
78. Ibid., p. 57.
79. Ibid., p. 57.
80. Ibid., p. 10.
81. Ibid., p. 57.
82. Montagu to Edward Montagu, 28 January 1764, MO 2484.
83. Montagu to Carter, 31 May 1766, MO 3171.
84. Montagu to Carter, 24 December 1764, MO 3141.
85. Montagu to Carter, 28 August 1766, MO 3180.
86. Samuel Johnson and James Boswell, *A Journey to the Western Islands of Scotland (1775) and The Journal of a Tour to the Hebrides (1786)*, ed. Peter Levi (New York: Penguin, 1984), p. 58. Although many of the chieftains' wives they encounter spent considerable time in Edinburgh or London, Johnson and Boswell continually comment on the pleasing contrast they create with their rude surroundings. After a discussion of the Lady of Rasay and her family, Johnson writes, "a more pleasing appearance of domestic society is not to be found in the most polished countries" (p. 75). Boswell also comments on Johnson's pleasure at meeting Lady Macleod at Dunvegan. Despite their surroundings, Boswell notes that he no longer hears of Johnson's "impatience to be in civilized life; though indeed I should beg pardon – he found it here" (p. 282). Johnson does not spend much time on his encounter with Lady Macleod except to say that at "Dunvegan I had tasted lotus, and was in danger of forgetting that I was ever to depart, till Mr. Boswell sagely reproached me for my sluggishness and softness" (p. 83).
87. Montagu to Carter, 5 September 1774, MO 3341.
88. Catherine Talbot, in Rev. Montagu Pennington (ed.), *Letters between Elizabeth Carter and Catherine Talbot, from the Year 1741–1770*.
89. Dafydd Moore, "Heroic Incoherence in James Macpherson's *The Poems of Ossian*," pp. 55 and 56.
90. Robert J. Griffin, *Wordsworth's Pope*, p. 50.
91. Talbot may have borrowed from a male character in the Ossian poems named Carthon, but Carthona remains Talbot's invention.
92. Pennington, *Letters between Elizabeth Carter and Catherine Talbot*, vol. 1, p. 408.
93. Ibid., p. 411.
94. Gaskill, *Poems of Ossian*, p. 87.
95. Pennington, *Letters between Elizabeth Carter and Catherine Talbot*, vol. 1, pp. 183 and 541.
96. Zuk, *Bluestocking Feminism: Catherine Talbot and Hester Chapone*, p. 139.
97. Ibid., p. 193.
98. Ibid., p. 139.
99. Ibid., p. 139.
100. Ibid., p. 193.
101. Ibid., p. 197.

102. Ibid., p. 139.
103. Pennington, *Letters between Elizabeth Carter and Catherine Talbot*, vol. 2, p. 23; Talbot's Dr. Franklin appears to be Benjamin Franklin, whose Bluestocking sympathies are clear in publications such as his *Reflections on Courtship and Marriage* (1746), which was published throughout the later half of the eighteenth century.
104. Zuk, *Bluestocking Feminism: Catherine Talbot and Hester Chapone*, p. 139.
105. Pennington, *Letters between Elizabeth Carter and Catherine Talbot*, vol. 1, p. 250.
106. Sylvia Harcstack Myers, *The Bluestocking Circle*, p. 227.
107. "Connal and Crimora," in Gaskill, *Poems of Ossian*, p. 18.
108. Pennington, *Letters between Elizabeth Carter and Catherine Talbot*, vol. 1, p. 481.
109. Ibid., p. 482.
110. Zuk, *Bluestocking Feminism: Catherine Talbot and Hester Chapone*, p. 139.
111. Ibid., p. 139.
112. Ibid., p. 140.
113. Ibid., p. 141.
114. Macpherson describes Ossian as only encountering a Christian missionary and the tenets of this new religion in "his extreme old age," claiming Ossian's rejection of Christianity is still preserved in the oral culture of the Highlands (Gaskill, *Poems of Ossian*, p. 46).
115. Catherine Talbot, *Reflections on the Seven Days of the Week*.
116. Harriet Guest, *Small Change*, p. 139.
117. Emma Major, "The Politics of Sociability: Public Dimensions of the Bluestocking Millennium," in Pohl and Schellenberg (eds), *Reconsidering the Bluestockings*, p. 192.
118. Walter Benjamin, "Theses on the Philosophy of History," in *Illuminations*, p. 263.
119. Ibid., p. 256.
120. Ibid., p. 262.
121. The Ossianic challenge to stadial histories of economic progress can also be read as anticipating Benjamin's desire to use "weak Messianism" to ward against historicism and its tendency to produce universal history. Fleshing out this relationship requires tracing a genealogy of historical materialism that begins with the Scottish stadial histories, which influenced Karl Marx. Over the last fifty years, the connection between stadial history and Marxist analysis has been established by several scholars. See, for example, Ronald Meek, "The Scottish Contribution to Marxist Sociology," in *Economics and Ideology and Other Essays* (London: Chapman Hall, 1967), pp. 34–50; and Ian Duncan, "Primitive Inventions."
122. Zuk, *Bluestocking Feminism: Catherine Talbot and Hester Chapone*, p. 140.
123. Ibid., p. 140.
124. Ibid., p. 140.
125. Ibid., p. 140.

126. Ibid., p. 141.
127. Ibid., p. 142.
128. Ibid., p. 142.
129. Ibid., p. 142.
130. Ibid., p. 143.

Chapter 3

Queering Progress: Anna Seward and *Llangollen Vale*

In his introduction to the *Poetical Works* (1809) of the eighteenth-century provincial poet and literary critic Anna Seward, Walter Scott claimed that her "peculiarities of taste" might not stand the test of time.[1] In a sense, he was right. Seward occupies an anomalous place in literary history between the neoclassical and the Romantic periods. Her love of balanced heroic couplets and elaborate diction register as dated by the 1780s, while her favorite poetic topics, the natural world and local culture, lead some to describe her as a precursor of the Romantics. In the late eighteenth century, before the barriers between these literary periods were constructed, Seward was a respected poet and literary critic whose essays appeared frequently in *The Gentleman's Magazine*. Her contemporaries attributed to her the invention of two new genres: the "poetical novel" with *Louisa* (1784) and the "epic elegy" exemplified in her *Monody on Major Andre* (1781);[2] wildly popular, these poems went through multiple editions.[3] Today, her generic innovations read like literary artifacts. Seward's popularity, like her experiments with genre, faded quickly. At the turn of the century, the acclaim she garnered for her poetry as well as the dramatic readings she undertook in the salons of Lady Anna Miller of Batheaston during the 1770s and 1780s disappeared. She became an anachronism. Her taste for ornate language, complex verse forms, and public readings were judged to be outmoded affectations. Although she was a great friend and promoter of Robert Southey, her more sociable brand of poetic practice drew his derision. He recounts the poetess greeting him in 1808 with an extemporaneous and "theatrical" reading of an encomium she had just written to his verse.[4] He describes the whole meeting as "tragic-comic or comico-tragic" and confesses that he was almost unable to stifle his laughter during Seward's performance.[5] Seward's taste for artifice and verbal complexity, which was inherited, according to Scott, from her friend the poet and doctor Erasmus Darwin, also came under attack.[6] Scott took issue with her preference for "florid description . . . lofty metaphor . . . bold personification . . . [and] diction which inversion and the use of compound epithets rendered as remote as possible from the tone of ordinary language . . . too remote from common life, and natural expression, to retain its popularity."[7]

Seward's curious place in literary history has drawn the attention of critics interested in theorizing a long eighteenth century that encompasses the Romantic and neoclassical periods. Most recently, Claudia Thomas Kairoff has labeled Seward an "ultimate eighteenth-century poet" and productively uses Seward's work to "trace the century's evolving trends."[8] Although Kairoff's important work does much to reestablish Seward's centrality to eighteenth-century literary history, my chapter resists the impulse to restore Seward to the canon. Instead of situating Seward as the "daughter" of Samuel Johnson or Erasmus Darwin or a "mother" of Romanticism,[9] this chapter understands her critical and poetic production as forging a new historical framework for literary study that rejects conventional understandings of the nation and family. Seward's desire to trouble teleological and linear narratives of literary history, including her intervention in the ancient versus modern debate as well as her rejection of the formal experiments of the Romantics, suffuses her writing, from her early praise of the Ossian poems to the composition near the end of her life of her famous long poem *Llangollen Vale* (1796).

Seward, like the first-generation Bluestockings discussed in the previous chapter, used the Ossian poems and the principles of Scottish Enlightenment historiography to explore gender as a gauge of historical progress. Unlike Elizabeth Montagu and Catherine Talbot, Seward did more than just critique the Scottish Enlightenment's tendency to align femininity with modernity and the "civilizing" impulses of imperial development. Seward's criticism, which can be found mainly in her published correspondence, develops the ambivalence toward progress and empire found in the Ossian poems' suggestion that refined and feminine sentiments could exist in a rude age, and uses this Ossianic temporality to trouble conventional understandings of literary development. Her *Llangollen Vale*, which describes the picturesque Welsh valley and celebrates its famous occupants – from the Welsh national hero Owen of Glendower to Seward's contemporaries and close friends Sarah Ponsonby and Eleanor Butler, the poem's dedicatees – practices the approach to history she theorizes in her correspondence and breaks the connection between economic and imperial development and the progress of women. An uneven Ossianic temporality shapes *Llangollen Vale*, which draws on a range of literary and historical methodologies to create connections between Welsh rebellions of an earlier age and the eighteenth-century tale of Butler and Ponsonby, members of the Irish gentry who ran away from Ireland and their families to live in exile in the Welsh countryside. Her poem explores alternatives to progressive accounts of economic development as well as normative temporalities of nation, reproduction, and inheritance.[10]

By mixing her account of the ladies' life in Wales with antiquarian, bardic, and Ossianic histories, Seward creates a historical method that, to borrow from Heather Love's recent account of queer history, can be characterized as "backwards." Queer history, as described in the work of Love, Judith Halberstam, and Carolyn Dinshaw, offers a productive way of understanding both Seward's attachment to the past and the new relationships to temporality made possible by her reading of Ossian. By challenging progressive narratives of the nation and the family, queer history provides a larger framework for the distaste Seward expressed for marriage (she claims in an early letter that "I have not seen the Man, with whom I did not prefer the idea of a *distant* to that of a near union") and her intense "romantic friendship" with Honora Sneyd, whom she lost when Sneyd died from consumption a few years after her marriage to Richard Lovell Edgeworth.[11] Although Teresa Barnard in her recent biography has importantly warned against reading Seward's sexuality in twenty-first-century terms,[12] Seward's attachment to Honora resonates with recent accounts of queer history that do not depend upon transparent accounts of sexual practice or explicitly stated desires. Whether as a sister or a lover, Seward simultaneously mourned and memorialized Sneyd in poetry and letters for the last thirty years of her life. Instead of looking toward potential futures, Seward "turns backwards" and mourns perpetually and often joyfully. Similarly in *Llangollen Vale*, she idealizes the ladies' exile, isolation, and obscurity in a Welsh valley that appears anachronistically in the poem to belong to an earlier pastoral period. In *Feeling Backwards*, Love defines "backwardness" as a refusal of the future and a longing to live "disconnected from any larger historical continuum."[13] The anti-progressive temporality Seward creates in the poem and the ladies' desire to live in an earlier age, marked by the strange neogothic renovations they conducted on their estate, Plas Newydd, and their noted collection of antiquities, suggests a longing to escape the inevitability of historical progress and conventional understandings of women's contribution to the development, refinement, and even the reproduction of humankind.

Seward's and the ladies' "backward turn" also explains their desire to align themselves with a discontinuous figure like Ossian, who, as the "last of his race," stands outside linear narratives of progress and traditional forward-looking accounts of reproduction. Childless and isolated, yet able to indulge in the peculiar pleasures of sentimental verse that mourns an earlier age, Ossian's circumstances resembled those of Butler and Ponsonby. Ossian was an even more important figure for Seward, who mourned a series of companions, including her sister Sarah, Honora, her father, and later in life the married vicar choral of Lichfield Cathedral, John Saville. Toward the end of her life, she writes to her friend Mrs. Powys about her fears of losing her remaining friends and remembers those, including Honora, "who now, though slumbering in the dark and narrow house, render pleasant the tale of other times, by the power of those indelible images of their persons, their talents, and their kindness, which they have left in our hearts."[14] To describe her backward thoughts and feelings, she lifts phrases from the Ossian poems such as "the dark and narrow house" and the "tales of other times" in an effort to resist hegemonic maps of progress and development.

The two major sections of this chapter explore Seward as both a critic and a poet. The first section reads Seward's epistolary criticism, particularly her discussions of Macpherson, Scottish literature, and the Ossian poems, as an essential context for interpreting her *Llangollen Vale*. Before writing *Llangollen Vale*, Seward spent years experimenting with narratives of historical and literary development in her published and unpublished correspondence as well as her poetry. Ossian looms large in her account of British literary history, which can be found largely in the six volumes of her letters published by Archibald Constable in 1810. The distinctly Anglophone canon she develops includes provincial and Celtic authors largely excluded by more canonical critics such as Samuel Johnson, and creates an uneven map of literary development that echoes the unevenness found in the Ossian poems and to a lesser extent Scottish historiography – the subject of the previous chapter of this book. The Ossian poems also figure in her attempts to step outside abstract and progressive historical narratives and recount the private and embodied effects of Britain's wars abroad in the Americas and India. These experiments with literary history act as a preface to her composition of *Llangollen Vale*. Through her critical practice, Seward developed an alternative account of national and imperial development and a historical method that allowed her to rethink the relationship between larger narratives of improvement and the "progress of women" in *Llangollen Vale*.

The second section of this chapter looks at Seward as a poet. In addition to focusing on Seward's understanding of the poet as historian and the reception of *Llangollen Vale*, this section examines Seward's use of her source texts and the ways in which she manipulated poetic and historical genres to integrate Butler and Ponsonby's friendship into her celebration of Welsh resistance to English political and cultural power. I argue that her desire to highlight the discontinuities and gaps in dominant histories and look "backwards" not only makes her approach to history queer but also complements her reliance on bardic and antiquarian histories which often describe minor actors, events, and cultural practices that, as Marilyn Butler argues, allowed for the existence of "national imperative[s]" that were at odds with the "present of the nation-state."[15] The portions of Seward's poem that describe her visit to the ladies and their home, Plas Newydd, have dominated recent interpretations of the poem,[16] while the stanzas devoted to Welsh history have been largely overlooked. Both Paula Backscheider and Stuart Curran see Seward's poetry as grappling with the difficulty of representing same-sex desire. This chapter builds on their work, but instead of focusing exclusively on Seward's figuring of same-sex desire, it examines Seward's placement of queer relationships in the historical record. By looking at the various historical contexts Seward offers for the ladies' friendship, it becomes possible to uncover not just a queer relationship but also a queer history. Seward, like the filmmakers and artists Halberstam analyzes, attempts to capture "strange temporalities, imaginative life schedules, and eccentric economic practices" and to narrativize – even historicize – an alternative "way of life."[17]

Seward as Critic: Decentering British Literature

In an essay on the importance of Seward's letters to studies of the developing British literary canon,[18] Norma Clarke has argued that Seward saw herself more as a literary critic than a poet. Walter Scott reinforced this view in his introduction to Seward's *Poetical Works*. In his discussion of Seward's critical practice, Scott quotes from one of Seward's letters, which elevates a vernacular and feminine education above a masculine and classical one and invests literary women with critical powers not available to more scholarly men:

> Many, excel me in the power of writing verse; perhaps scarcely one in the vivid and strong sensibility of its excellence, or in the ability to estimate its claims – ability arising from a fifty years sedulous and discriminating study of the best English poets, and of the best translations from the Greek, Roman, and Italian. A masculine education cannot spare from professional study, and the necessary acquisition of languages, the time and attention which I have bestowed on the compositions of my countrymen.[19]

According to Seward, masculine "professional study" requires an immersion in Latin and Greek that impedes men from fully appreciating the productions of their own "countrymen." Seward, unlike her male counterparts, has had time to cultivate the "sensibility" necessary to appreciate vernacular literature. Notably, Seward supplemented her knowledge of the "best English" poets with a close study of Celtic bards and provincial poets to forge a distinctly Anglophone rather than English canon. In an age of imperial development, and during a time when most literature is understood as consolidating a coherent British identity,[20] Seward instead took what John Kerrigan has called an "archipelagic approach" that acknowledged the uneven territory of the British isles, which contained different ethnicities, language communities, and cultural groups.[21] Seward's canon recognized that "rude" dialects might exist beside more polished diction, and her preference for local and elegiac poetry reflects a desire to resist narratives that build toward homogenization or project imperial greatness. Her own account of British literature, like her status in literary history, seems anomalous, mixing periods, places, and poets in ways that resist simple equations of the progress of civilization with the development of literary tastes. Seward's uneven literary history emerges most clearly in her resistance to Johnson's account of British literature and his attacks on Ossian as well as her placement of Ossian in her canon of contemporary "classics" that were detached from any notion of literary progress and development.

Seward's distinctly Anglophone canon can be traced back to her early love of Ossian. When Seward first encountered the Ossian poems as a young woman in 1762, she defended their authenticity, citing the Bluestocking Lord Lyttelton's belief that "these fragments, are not the composition of modern genius, though it may have drawn out, enlarged, blended, and connected them."[22] She maintained this unpopular position long after others had abandoned their defense of the poems' provenance, only reconsidering the issue in the early nineteenth century when Walter Scott persuaded her to concede that "those yet adored volumes, are the fruit of Macpherson's genius."[23] Like Elizabeth Montagu before her, she transferred her adoration without reservation from Ossian to James Macpherson, stating that, "Henceforth, therefore, I shall consider him as one of the greatest poets which the late century, so rich in great poets, had produced."[24] Seward continually read, reread, and – like the first-generation Bluestockings who were the subject of the previous chapter – even rewrote the Ossian poems.[25]

In a letter to one of her girlhood companions, she writes that the Ossian poems have become an object of "study" for her and her sister Sarah:

We have been lately engaged in exploring the inestimable treasure which had, during so many ages, lain concealed in the darkness of the Erse language. Macpherson has kindly and ably drawn aside the curtain, and the venerable bards, the mighty heroes, the maids of Caledonia and Ierne, with the spirits of the airy halls, come forward, and, with just and graceful dignity, assert their claims to ancient honours, and to an high station on classic ground.[26]

In the same letter, she dismisses "fastidious people" who "affect to question the originality of Ossian" and asserts that the "daring spirit in this work resembl[es] that of the sacred writings"; the poems contain "a great blaze of imagination, but it is the random fire of the ruder ages." She concludes her letter with a 43-line poem detailing the aesthetic merits of Ossian. In her typically good-humored fashion, she admits that the poems are repetitious and imagines that some might "pronounce them cloying," but finds the poet's power in the "new lights" he sheds on familiar images and argues that the "picturesque effect" they leave in the reader's mind make the repetition pleasurable.[27]

Seward's lifelong passion for Ossian put her at odds with Samuel Johnson, who she knew through her acquaintance with his stepdaughter Lucy Porter, an important member of the Lichfield community. Johnson's own tastes and eccentricities have long been used to define the eighteenth century; conversely, Seward's own "peculiar" tastes have transformed her into a footnote or anecdote in studies of Johnson. Much attention has been given to their personal relationship, which was marked by Johnson's withering comments about Seward's stern grandfather, who was Johnson's schoolmaster when he was a boy in Lichfield. Although Seward's attractiveness was well known, even prompting Boswell to boldly request a lock of her hair,[28] Johnson frequently remarked on Seward's terrifying resemblance to her ancestor and his boyhood instructor. The dislike was mutual. In a letter written just before Johnson's death, Seward recounts visiting him in Lichfield. During their visit, he requested that she return often, and she attributes his kindness (a bit uncharitably) to his willingness to "fain escape, for a time, in any society, from the terrible idea of his approaching death."[29] She claims that he "never did feel much regard for" her because she "never would be awed by his sarcasms, or his frowns, into acquiescence with his general injustice to the merits of other writers; with his national, or party aversions."[30] After Johnson's death, Seward critiqued Boswell's hyperbolic adoration and instead presented a more measured portrait of Johnson. She respected and celebrated Johnson as an essayist, but found his poor manners and volatile temper less charming than the obsequious Boswell. She was most troubled by his literary criticism, particularly his *Lives of the Poets*, calling his portrait of Thomas Gray, one of her favorite poets, "the absurd . . . sophistry. . of [an] arrogant decider."[31] In a letter to her friend Hester Piozzi from 1788, she writes, "Greatly as I admired Johnson's talents, and revered his knowledge, and formidable as I felt the powers to be of his witty sophistry, yet did a certain quickness of spirit, and zeal for the reputation of my favourite authors, irresistibly urge me to defend them against his spleenful injustice."[32] Unfortunately, Seward's own project as a literary critic has been subordinated to the back-and-forth between Boswell and Seward over Johnson's character.[33]

Unlike Johnson, Seward was not invested in a canon that emphasized English national identity at the expense of the other nations of the British archipelago. While Seward admired Celtic and regional poetry, Johnson's literary tastes were more urban and Anglocentric. In addition to defending Ossian, Seward in her letters promoted local poets, such as Francis Mundy, whose *Needwood Forest* attempted to save an ancient woodland in Staffordshire from enclosure and deforestation, and William Newton, who Seward names as the voice of the Peak District. In contrast, Johnson in his *Lives of the Poets* elevates Alexander Pope and John Dryden at the expense of Thomas Gray, whose Welsh poem "The Bard" he criticized for attempting to "swell" a "singular event . . . to a giant's bulk."[34] He admires Pope's and Dryden's attempts to find universal systems and patterns but finds Gray's poem, which recreates the suicide of a Welsh bard during Edward I's conquest of Wales, unable to support "any truth, moral or political."[35] Johnson's critique of Gray suggests an inability to reconcile English and Celtic histories and can be linked to his well-documented attacks on the merit and authenticity of the Ossian poems. Seward interpreted Johnson's hostility toward both Macpherson and his verse as a product of Johnson's national chauvinism. In a letter to Walter Scott from 1806, Seward discredits Johnson's *Journey to the Western Islands of Scotland* (1775) and his well-known assessment of Ossian's merit: "Dr. Johnson's scornful assertions on this subject, have no weight with me; believing, as I have ever done, that his impatient jealousy of a new classic, of such high antiquity, emerging from the mists of time, and in the land of his detestation, was the motive of his journey to Scotland."[36] Seward ascribes Johnson's contempt for the Ossian poems and Scotland to a "jealous" desire to evade the threat posed by Scotland's rival literary and cultural history. By dismissing Ossian, Johnson ensures the superiority and dominance of the English literary and cultural tradition within the emerging British canon. Seward's defense of Ossian played a major part in her effort to create a more inclusive Anglophone canon that included voices from the peripheries such as Scotland and the provinces, including her native Lichfield and its environs.

Unlike Johnson and Boswell, Seward also seems unconcerned with the effect of Scotticisms and dialect on the English language. Although she rejects informal usage, scolding Hester Piozzi at one point for the inordinate amount of "dids," "does," "thoughs," and "toos" in her published writing, she celebrates poetry written in Scots.[37] In a letter to Walter Scott, she acknowledges the relationship between Scots language and culture: "I hope it [Scots] will not be lost amongst you; that your men of genius, yet unborn, will have the patriotism to preserve it by frequently making it the vehicle of their inspirations."[38] Seward even experiments with Scots in her own verse. After the publication of her poem "Rich Auld Willie" in the third volume of Walter Scott's *Border Minstrelsy*, she explains that her facility with what Scott dubs her "theoretical Scotch" (Seward's attempt to approximate Scots dialect in the poem) is a result of her provincial roots and her proximity to Scotland:

I was born 50 miles nearer Scotland than in Lichfield, and passed the first seven years of my existence in my native village, amidst the eminences of the Peak of Derbyshire. Hence the first scenery which stuck upon my infant perceptions, with wonder and transport, is brought back by poetic pictures of wild, uncultivated, lonely nature.[39]

Seward's proximity to the Peak District, her regional version of the Scottish Border, contributes to the ease with which she can adopt the Scots tongue and replicate a "theoretical" version of Scots in her poetry. Her contribution to the *Border Minstrelsy*, "Rich Auld Willie," allows her to associate her provincial world with the romantic Scottish Border and herself with the Celtic bards she so admired, from Scott and Burns to Ossian himself.[40]

In many ways, Seward's and Johnson's clashing perspectives on the Ossian poems and Scotland mirrored their different relationships to their native Lichfield. Johnson saw Lichfield as part of the British past. Johnson's notation on Lichfield in his *Dictionary of the English Language* (1756) creates a sense of the city as a less than vital community: "LICH. A dead carcass; whence *lichwake*, the time or act of watching by the dead; *lichgate*, the gate through which the dead are carried to the grave; *Lichfield*, the field of the dead, a city in Staffordshire, so name for martyred Christians."[41] Although Johnson at times honored and celebrated his birthplace, his descriptions did much to establish it as a retrograde space, part of the British past, and of little importance to the present. Suggestively in the *Life*, Johnson establishes Lichfield's backwardness by aligning it not only with Britain's Roman past but also with what he characterizes as a lifeless and backward Scotland. At one point, Johnson confesses to suffering from restlessness and ennui during long visits to Lichfield. In response, Boswell remarks, "I wonder at that, Sir; it is your native place," and Johnson answers, "Why, so is Scotland *your* native place."[42] The boredom Johnson suffered from while in Lichfield as well as his noted distaste for Seward's close friend Erasmus Darwin, a leader of Lichfield intellectual life, contributed to his devaluation of his provincial home.[43] In Johnson's assessment, Lichfield and Scotland are places to be visited infrequently and subordinated to London, the measure of English cultural and intellectual life, the standard against which peripheral territories were judged and, ultimately, found lacking.

Scotland and Lichfield become closely tied to Seward's unconventional sense of what makes a classic; throughout her letters, she attempts to break the concept's connection with ancient Greece and Rome. In a letter to Walter Scott, she prepares him for his upcoming visit to Lichfield by establishing its literary and artistic credentials:

> Our little city is classic ground by many more claims than that of having given birth to the greatest and most eloquent moralist this nation boasts, seated on the tribunal of its language; – by its being the nursery of David Garrick's youth, – and by the thirty-three years residence of the celebrated Darwin, together with that of several other distinguished, though perhaps less distinguished inhabitations.[44]

By applying the term "classic" to her contemporaries Garrick, Johnson (the "eloquent moralist"), and Erasmus Darwin, she develops a sense of the classic as peculiarly modern and British. Lichfield, in Seward's estimation, is a "classic ground" not because of its historical connections to ancient Rome or Greece, but because of its "distinguished inhabitants."[45] By using the term "classic" to describe modern authors, Seward dispenses with linear understandings of literature's development and illustrates what David Duff has called in a different context her "revolutionary attitude" to established modes of literary classification.[46] "Classic" becomes a purely aesthetic category detached from any particular age, location, or even style. Seward deconstructs the ancients versus moderns debate and makes the conventional application of these terms to literature superfluous.

When writing to Scott, she also designates Scotland as a "classic ground, which I could at no time have trodden without the liveliest enthusiasm."[47] She continues to discuss the literary roots of her "love and veneration [for] the Caledonian scenery, Lowland and Highland," beginning with Walter Scott, Ossian, and including Allan Ramsay, who authored the popular *Tea Table Miscellany*, a collection of Scots poetry and ballads. Throughout her correspondence, Seward reinforces the connection between Scottish and provincial literary culture. During a trip to the nearby Buxton Spa, which neighbors the Peak District, she finds herself in the company of "a constellation of Scottish talents," including the historian and philosopher Adam Ferguson, author of one of the inaugural texts in the conjectural history tradition, *Essay on the History of Civil Society*. As a way of securing her own credentials among these notable Scots, she circulates two poems written by her favorite local poet, William Newton or the Peak Minstrel, "that prodigy of self-cultivated genius ... the minstrel of my native mountains."[48] Through the Peak Minstrel, she attempts to impress these notable Scots with her discovery of the next Ossian. Seward conflates the wilds of ancient Caledonia with the nearby Peak District and blurs the temporal and geographic boundaries separating Scotland and England as well as the classical and modern. Rhetorically, she denies the literary canon a progressive structure and an English orientation.

Seward creates an analogy between her provincial surroundings and Scotland and positions them as native "classic grounds" capable of anchoring and sustaining a canon that includes English as well as Celtic languages. As Harriet Guest and John Brewer claim in their accounts of "the Swan of Lichfield," her work was central in the shift of national feeling from London to the provinces. Brewer describes Seward's vision of the constituent parts of the nation as equal partners, each capable of representing the larger nation: "While a London artist or critic saw the nation as a cultural hierarchy with London as its pinnacle, the provincials saw it as a collection of roughly comparable places, comprising a more egalitarian nation."[49] Seward's canon unsettles hierarchical relationships: the relationship between the provinces and London, and by association, Scotland and England, the relationship between male critics like Johnson and feminine and provincial voices such as her own, and also the relationship between the past and the present. The new British canon that emerges from Seward's writing loses all sense of direction and fixity. She creates Milton, Pope, Ossian, Shakespeare, Scott, and Beattie as equals and even includes lesser-known provincial poets. She dispenses with the idea of linear development in her literary history and chooses to create a decentered and uneven British canon; she elevates women as experts in vernacular literature, and sets Celtic dialects alongside standard English. She creates a British literature where classic and modern authors coexist and even collapse into one another, placing authors such as Walter Scott alongside ancient poets such as Homer and the more historically suspect Ossian. Seward's literary history lacks coherence or what we might think of as a plot – but it forwards a way of thinking about literature that, instead of valuing literary progress or a centralized national identity, adopts shared aesthetic experiences or sentiments as a mode of adducing literary value.

Traces of Seward's theory of history, which she articulates most fully in her *Llangollen Vale*, appear not just in her literary criticism but also in her imitations of Ossian, which in attempting to extract the poems' essential literary and historical value act as critical commentary. In her imitations, Seward demonstrates a desire to use what Susan Manning has called Ossianic rhetoric to reveal the gaps and lacunae passed over in progressive or teleologically oriented histories.[50] Seward creates what Manning calls a "sentimental experience" that is "simultaneously a connected and a disconnected one" through her use of Ossianic fragments. Like the Ossian poems, Seward's imitations and epistolary allusions to the poems "bring readers and participants together in a momentary community of feeling, but that moment is emotionally and narratively disconnected from the next focal point of sentiment. The union which sympathy offers is syntactically paratactic, and without diachronic extension."[51] If possible, Seward's imitations of Ossian are even more fragmentary and disconnected than the originals. Published posthumously in her *Poetical Works*, her imitations include a brief scene from *Fingal*, entitled "Crugal's Ghost," and an even shorter segment from *Temora* called "Cuchullin's Ghost." In reducing Macpherson's two epics, *Fingal* to 110 lines and *Temora* to a mere 16, she disregards the plot of each poem altogether, making Ossian more portable and applicable to a range of experiences. In a footnote to "Crugal's Ghost," she explains her reduction of these epics into "detached" fragments: "The passages very well bear being detached, and form in themselves a perfect whole."[52] When recommending the poems to a friend, who has admitted not enjoying them, Seward suggests reading them in pieces and ignoring the narrative:

> I confess, however, that inevitable weariness attends a long perusal of Ossian. We should not attempt to read him regularly, but to contemplate him in detached passages . . . Could I persuade you to take up Ossian, at intervals, I am persuaded you would grow accustomed to his manner, and feel the truth of the poet Gray's assertion respecting these poems, that "imagination resided, in all her pomp, many centuries ago, upon the bleak and barren mountains of Scotland."[53]

The feeling of traumatic history and affective experience the Ossian poems capture trumps any sort of narrative progression or coherence. Seward's fragmented imitations of Ossian build on these reading directives and contribute to the sense of her British canon and perhaps British history as detached from a progressive narrative or a coherent national identity.

In contrast to the first-generation Bluestocking Catherine Talbot's imitations, Seward manipulates the form of the poems instead of their content. In doing so, she transforms rude fragments into polished pieces, challenging Enlightenment ideas about the relationship between refinement, modernity, and historical development. Rather than peppering her imitations with contemporary references to coronations or imperial tigers as does Talbot, she reproduces the poems' content and diction almost exactly. For example, Crugal's ghost appears as he does in Macpherson's poems with a "livid wound," and Connal, the hero to whom Crugal appears, addresses the ghost, "As a mortal visitant, with life-blood warm."[54] Crugal acts as he does in *Fingal*, warning Connal of the destruction to be wrought by Swaran on the too-small Irish army and pleading with him to await the arrival of Fingal and the Scottish reinforcements. Crugal's ghost, as in *Fingal*, invites Cuchullin's wrath: Cuchullin, incensed by the ghost's suggestion of retreat, threatens to "penetrate its dark retreat, / And force his knowledge from its secret seat."[55] Seward follows her brief redaction of *Fingal* with the even shorter story of Cuchullin's specter, who appears briefly in *Temora* and manifests himself physically in the destruction wrought by a violent storm. Cuchullin's ghost lurks ominously in the clouds and thunder of the storm:

> One ample cloud a sable curtain rear'd
> And faint, behind its edge, a red star peer'd
> And in its shade a tall, unreal form
> Stalk'd though the air, and mourn'd amid the storm.[56]

Although she sticks to the content of the poems, Seward transposes the free verse of the Ossian poems into English heroic couplets. By imposing a clear formal structure in her imitations, she closes the poems off in a way denied by the free verse of the originals. Seward's Ossianic fragments become sealed and detached felt experiences – outside of a larger narrative or historical continuum.

Seward also polishes and refines these ancient poems by adding an elaborate and markedly English rhyme scheme and using modern diction to express ancient themes. When she encapsulates fragments of a "rude" culture in a polished and modern form, she invites questions about the dependence of civility and refined feelings on the economic structures of advanced commercial culture. Whereas Macpherson's awkward diction and open prose style attempted to replicate the archaic speech patterns of ancient Celts, Seward's rhyming couplets aim for an elevated, writerly sophistication. In effect, Seward adds a feminine and modern British polish to the "rude" verse of Ossian. For example, in the lines from *Fingal* describing the ghost of Crugal's appearance to Connal, Macpherson utilizes a dash to reproduce actual pauses in speech: "The stars dim-twinkled through his form; and his voice was like the sound of a distant stream. – He is a messenger of death."[57] Seward's imitation forces these lines into a sing-songy rhyming couplet: "He spoke to us of death's impending storm, / Though stars dim twinkled thro' his misty form!"[58] In a footnote, Seward invites readers to consider her decision to render Ossian's verse into heroic couplets in the context of Alexander Pope's translation of the *Iliad*, explaining that her imitations attempt to achieve "the effect of that, in which Pope had given us of a still more ancient Bard than Ossian."[59] Johnson's assessment of Pope's decision to render the *Iliad* into heroic couplets illuminates Seward's thinking about the Ossian poems: "Pope wrote for his own age and his own nation: he knew that it was necessary to colour the images and point the sentiments of his author; he therefore made him graceful, but lost him some of his sublimity."[60] Like Pope, Seward takes an ancient poem that provided evidence of a lost "classical" world and revived it, eliminating its masculine sublimity but adding a feminine "grace" and polish. Ironically, Seward's effort to modernize Ossian through the adaptation of rhyming couplets made her seem anachronistic to twentieth-century critics, who faulted her for being unable to appreciate the formal innovations of the Romantics;[61] however, in the context of her other writings about Ossian, these imitations can be understood as troubling the connection between historical progress and feminine refinement, demonstrating that sophisticated feelings and poetic practices could be compatible with a rude age.

The surprising value of these little-read and largely forgotten imitations to Seward's theory of development becomes clearer in the context of Seward's correspondence. In her letters, she grafts the Ossian poems into a larger and heterogeneous British framework and uses them to disrupt any sense of a linear or progressive British history. For example, when Seward welcomes back her dear friend Colonel Hastings, who lost an arm in the Napoleonic Wars, she describes their meeting in an Ossianic register: "Never were joy and grief so mingled in my soul; they shook my whole frame and deluged my eyes."[62] Here, Seward cites the Ossianic lament of "joy of grief," identified by Hugh Blair as the emotion or desire that prefaces a call for a bard's performance and his song of loss due to war or love.[63] In this passage, Seward joins Ossian's retellings of cultural and personal loss with the maimed Hastings's recent experience in Britain's seemingly never-ending global war with France. Hastings's experience becomes a repetition of an ancient past and an effect of imperial progress. "Joy of grief" becomes a tag for the peculiar pleasure Seward takes in remembering what once was, looking backwards (to borrow from Heather Love), and feeling a past that can only be partially recovered and understood. Years earlier, while vacationing in Buxton, she quotes from the "old Bard of the North" when thinking about her beloved and departed friends Honora Sneyd and her famous lover Major Andre, who was executed as a spy by the Americans during the Revolutionary War and memorialized by Seward in her *Monody on Major Andre*.[64] In another phrase lifted directly from Ossian's description of departed friends, Seward describes the memory of Honora and Major Andre as "rising, like an exhalation, in my memory."[65] By persistently associating Ossian with contemporary historical events, Seward creates a portrait of Great Britain that produces jarring analogies between contemporary history and Scotland's distant past. In Seward's adaptations, the Ossianic fragment become a means of "sketching ... a genre that had not yet come into being, or of a performance of which a full performance was not yet possible"; her Ossianic fragments were a way of representing new potential histories, "a foundation stone rather than a ruin."[66] Far from being a seamless English history, Seward's Great Britain becomes an uneven and fragmented territory populated by Ancient Scots, provincial voices, and women such as herself. Likewise, Seward replaces a clear narrative of British literary development with the repetitions, discontinuities, fragments, and backward glances that she develops into a historical method in her *Llangollen Vale*.

Seward as Poet: Llangollen Historiography and the Vale's "Peerless Twain"

Although stylistically Seward's poetry has been read as outmoded and belonging to an earlier age, the content of her poems has often been understood as predating and anticipating the environmental concerns of her Romantic successors or ahead of its time in its willingness to engage with same-sex desire, particularly in her elegies to Honora Sneyd. Sharon Setzer argues that Seward's account in "Colebrook Dale" of the impact of the iron industry on the picturesque landscape of rural Shropshire "predates Wordsworth's more oblique response to that threat a few miles above Tintern Abbey"; Donna Coffey finds Seward's comments in the same poem "unique ... [for] the depth of their concern for the impact of industrialization on nature."[67] These critics have made possible a new understanding of Seward's relationship to the early industrialists of the Lunar Society, which was composed of philosophers, scientists, and inventors living near Birmingham. The society included Matthew

Boulton, James Watt, Joseph Priestley, and a number of Seward's close friends, acquaintances, and correspondents, including Erasmus Darwin, Thomas Day, Richard Lovell Edgeworth, and Josiah Wedgwood. Seward's relationship with these proponents of industry and commercial expansion provides a rich context for reading her poems. Seward's "Colebrook Dale," which Setzer has argued rests on an analogy between industrialization and rape, links feminist and environmental critique; in addition, her frequent apostrophes to "Hygeia," which she makes in many of her poems including *Llangollen Vale*, express a concern for the impact of nearby Birmingham's smoke stacks on Lichfield's air quality.[68] Seward's nature poetry troubles conventional notions of literary progress: she anticipates the critiques of industrialization made by the major Romantic poets who followed her, yet the verse forms and formal diction she favored associate her with an eighteenth-century tradition of poetry that preceded her.

Curran's recent analysis of the aesthetics of romantic female friendship in Seward's Honora poems and her *Llangollen Vale* demonstrates how tricky Seward's poetry can be to locate on existing maps of literary history and development. He acknowledges Seward's verse as "highly significant for the history of an emerging feminism," yet he argues that this "somehow pales before the remarkable interiority of Seward's exploration of the dynamics of female friendship. There she confronts a love that will not allow displacement, a second self that hovers over her as a ghostly, almost demonic, spectre, and a muse who is most forcefully a presence in her unrecoverable absence."[69] Curran's reading both positions Seward's poetry as a part of an "emerging" discourse and as steeped in a "spectral" or "backwards" temporality that refuses to be displaced by heteronormative desires. As a result of readings such as Curran's, much attention has been given to Seward's biography, particularly her relationship with her companion, Honora Sneyd. Honora lived with Anna, her sister Sarah, and her parents from an early age. After Sarah's death in 1764, Honora became Seward's constant companion, but their friendship ended soon after Honora became the second wife of Richard Lovell Edgeworth in 1773. She figures largely in Seward's elegies and as the object of John Andre's affection in her *Monody on Major Andre*. In her letters, Seward writes to Butler and Ponsonby about Sneyd, referring to her as "my constant companion," "the sun of my youthful horizon," and "my lost Honora."[70] Many, including Curran and Backscheider, have used this biographical context to interpret Seward's poetry, including *Llangollen Vale*, as explorations of alternatives to heteronormative relationships in the eighteenth century. *Llangollen Vale*, which celebrates the romantic friendship of the ladies of Llangollen and the pristine Welsh countryside, joins the concerns surrounding progress of both environmental and feminist critics, and I would argue that these concerns benefit from being aligned with Seward's passion for bardic poetry, particularly Scottish and Ossianic verse.

Reading Seward's poem as a product of Ossianic poetry and Scottish historiography provides a new context for theorizing Seward's explorations of industrialization, progress, and the refined feelings produced by the female friendships she so valued. These issues combine in *Llangollen Vale* to raise questions about women's contributions to the progress of civilization as well as civilization's impact on relationships between women. Seward experiments with eighteenth-century discourses of historiography in *Llangollen Vale* and, in doing so, troubles narratives that attempt to align economic development with the progress of women and challenges heteronormative understandings of temporality that rely on women civilizing their male counterparts. As Curran and Backscheider argue, the same-sex attachment expressed in Seward's meditations on romantic female friendship cannot simply be equated with modern lesbian identity, yet the strange poetic historiography Seward employs in *Llangollen Vale* resonates with Halberstam's and Love's accounts of queer histories that attempt to trouble progressive narratives and to rethink the place of gender and sexuality within teleological and linear understandings of historical development. Queer history also explains Seward's investment in the strange temporality of the Ossian poems, providing another means of understanding what critics have labeled the "unique," "remarkable," and "emergent" quality of her verse and the "eccentricities" and "peculiarities" of the poet.

Poetry for Seward was the raw material of history, and her experiments in *Llangollen Vale* with poetic genre should be understood as an attempt to experiment with historical method or, at least, expose the gaps within existing methodologies. Along with many other eighteenth-century writers including Macpherson, Montagu, and Kames, Seward understood, as Maureen McLane makes plain, that "poetry not only precedes the discourse of history: it was historical discourse, or rather it was the hegemonic discourse of the past, as numerous eighteenth-century conjectural historians observed."[71] Poetry and historiography during the eighteenth century enjoyed a chiasmatic relationship that Seward exploits in her *Llangollen Vale*. She was acutely aware, as were Adam Smith, Kames, and Montagu before her, that poetic forms and language might be used as a measure of progress. Although Seward's account of the progress of poetry does not derive directly from any one source, she does seem to be in dialogue with Adam Smith's "Considerations Concerning the First Formation of Languages" in which he argues that as language develops it "becomes more simple in its rudiments and principles . . . as it grows more complex in its composition."[72] He associates "this simplification of the principles of language" with language becoming "less agreeable to the ear" and discusses the problems translators have when rendering ancient poetry into a modern form.[73] Seward also mentions Lord Kames's discussion of the relationship between poetry and history in her letters. When commenting on her own attempt at imitating an Arabian ode, she mentions a series of Lapland poems that Lord Kames includes in his *Sketches on the History of Man* (1778) and claims that they are superior to the translations that appeared years earlier in the *Spectator*. According to Seward, Kames's translations are "ruder and faithful translations" and "exquisitely in keeping with the Lapland character, soil, and climate."[74] Seward's attention to the relationship between national development and environment, as well as her recognition of "ruder" forms as more authentic, reflects a familiarity with the larger tradition of conjectural history as well as Kames and his discussion in *Sketches* of the relationship between poetic form and historical development. He writes that "bards were the only historians before writing was introduced."[75] He goes on to argue, although in a slightly different vein than Smith, that poetry changes as the arts progress: "when an language, in its progress to maturity, is enriched with variety of phrases fit to express the most elevated thoughts, men of genius aspire to the higher strains of poetry, leaving music and song to the bards."[76]

A 1796 letter to Seward's friend Mrs. Stokes links Seward's literary concerns to the Scottish historical method. The letter describes poetry as arising after a change in material conditions. According to Seward, poetry originates "from the instant that the social compact gives to man a surplus of time from that which is employed in providing for his natural wants, together with liberation from that anxiety about obtaining such provision, which is generally incompatible with those abstracted ideas from which poetry results."[77] In her account of the rise of poetry, she claims that, "As this leisure, and freedom of thought, arises with the progress of subordination and inequality of rank, men become poets, and this long before their language attains its copiousness and elegance."[78] Here, Seward's argument about the rise of poetry echoes John Millar's claim in his *Origin of the Distinction of Ranks* (1774) that economic progress allows time for the arts to flourish. Seward continues in this letter to link the progress of poetry to a stadial and progressive schema of history:

> The writers of such [uncultivated] periods, therefore, present poetic ideas in coarse and shapeless ingenuity. In the unskilled attempt to refine them, they

become in the next stage of the progress, an odd mixture of quaintness and simplicity; but it is reserved for genius, learning, and judgment in combination, supported by the ample resources of a various, mature, and complete language, to elevate, polish, and give the last perfection to the rudiments of poetry, – first so coarse and abortive, – afterwards so quaint, and so shredded out into wearisome redundance.[79]

Poetry moves from a "coarse" age to the "quaintness and simplicity" of perhaps a pastoral period, and, finally, reaches maturity with the modern "polish" that marks poetry in a commercial age. In a letter from later in the same year to Miss Wingfield, Seward describes how the Ossian poems trouble this stadial schema: "The morals of the benign heroes and of their mistresses, the daughters of the aged warriors, have a purity and greatness beyond what history or poetry have ascribed to those of more civilized nations: while their manners have unrivalled dignity, sentiment, and grace."[80] Seward's poetic practice builds on the lessons she learned from Ossian.

Not surprisingly, eighteenth-century readers of Seward's *Llangollen Vale* also used Ossian as a context for interpreting Seward's poem. Seward acknowledges this connection by including an epistle linking *Llangollen Vale* to the Ossianic tradition in her collected letters from an admirer of her poetry, the antiquarian Thomas Park.[81] In his letter to Seward, Park recounts his efforts to save the *Llangollen* manuscript from a London printer. Park claims to have found Seward's manuscript "much sullied and defaced."[82] For producing a clean and more usable copy of the manuscript, the printer rewarded him with the damaged original. Not only does Park use this act as a means of introducing himself to the famous Swan of Lichfield, but he also includes in his letter a poem describing his efforts to save the *Llangollen* manuscript from a "touch impure." Drawing the phrases "sons of song" and "tuneful throng" directly from Ossian's poetry, this poem celebrates Seward's verse and associates *Llangollen Vale* with an Ossianic tradition:

> . . . Fondly dear
> To me have ever risen the sons of song.
> Seward I honoured their bright compeer,
> The syren-sister of the tuneful throng;
> And hence my ardency of zeal sincere
> To wrest her sibyl-leaves from senseless wrong.[83]

Seward appears in Park's poem as the "bright compeer" or "sister" of the Celtic bards found in *Fingal* and *Temora*. Seward obviously relished the comparison. She not only included Park's letter in the body of correspondence that she instructed Constable to publish after her death, but also responded to his letter and continued her correspondence with him until the end of her life. Park's depiction of Seward as "the syren-sister" of the "son of songs" signals her larger interest in the project of the Ossian poems, which offered readers a new and non-linear way of thinking through their relationship to British history and imperial development. Building on Ossian's unconventional treatment of history, *Llangollen Vale* mixes the public and the private, the personal and the political, the past and the present, and allows the particular histories of the periphery to stand in for a more abstract British story. Instead of looking outward at the progress of the British Empire and into the future, Seward turns inward to a piece of the British archipelago and a contested history of the British Isles that draws readers "backwards" and fits awkwardly into larger narratives of development.

Inspired by an antiquarian account of the region, Thomas Pennant's *A Tour in Wales* (1778–83), Seward's *Llangollen Vale* joins his account of Welsh history to the experiences of Sarah Ponsonby and Eleanor Butler. Butler, a daughter of an Irish aristocrat whose ancestor had been stripped of his title after the Jacobite rebellion of 1715, rejected several potential husbands who were supposed to aid her family in recovering their fortunes and reputation. After more than a decade of refusing to assist her family through a financially advantageous marriage, she met the much younger Sarah Ponsonby, with whom she developed an intimate friendship. After a forced separation and a failed attempt to escape from their guardians, the two were finally allowed to leave Ireland.[84] They lived the rest of their lives in exile in Wales and formed what Ann Cvetkovich calls a "new culture," reflected in the name of their home, Plas Newydd, which means new mansion. Despite the name of their residence, however, they renovated in a neogothic style that created a fictional past instead of a recognizable present or anticipated future. Although Plas Newydd was a site of exile and "dislocation" from the national and familial histories that limited their possibilities in Ireland, it also gave them a freedom to create a new time and place and rewrite conventional histories.[85] Seward's source text, Pennant's *Tour* – which, like the ladies' story, revolves around failed rebellions, thwarted relationships, and ruined dynasties – allowed Seward to find new possibilities in the ladies' dislocation from nation, family, and history. The fragments of Welsh history recounted by Pennant and the ladies' unique experiences should not be understood as equivalents; yet, by putting the ladies' "private" story in dialogue with a larger Welsh history, Seward suggests that the ladies' personal rebellion might be connected to the exclusions that structure the British nation-state.

In the introduction to his *Tour*, Pennant presents his history in antiquarian fashion as an account of the proud but conquered Welsh people who, with the exception of a brief period when they were forced to submit to Roman rule, were able to maintain their independence against great odds:

> The hardy Saxons, for above three centuries, could not make an impression even on our low lands. Ossa was the first; who extended his kingdom . . . His conquest was but temporary; for we possessed Chester, the capital of Cornwall, til the year 883, when it was wrested from us by the united force of the Heptarchy beneath the able Egbert. This indeed reduced our confines but did not subdue our spirit. With obdurate valour we sustained our independency for another four centuries, against the power of a kingdom more than twelve times larger than itself: and at length had the glory of falling, when a divided country, beneath the arms of the most wise, and more warlike of English monarchs.[86]

From Pennant's larger account of the "obdurate valour" of the Welsh, Seward focuses on his description of Llangollen Vale and adopts three notable parts of the Vale's history: Owen of Glendower's occupancy of the Vale and his role in the final and most serious rebellion of Wales against England; the late fourteenth-century story of Lady Mifanwy Vechan and her spurned and lovelorn admirer, the Bard Hoel; and the experiences of cloistered nuns who lived in the valley's Abbey of Valle Crucis. To Pennant's account, she adds a description of the ladies and their house, Plas Newydd. In doing so, Seward explicitly associates the ladies' exile from their families and Irish society with antiquarian history and links her concerns about gender and heterosexual privilege to questions about the construction of British history and the nation-state.

The ladies lived together in Wales for over forty years. Seward, who met them seventeen years into their residence, writes of their life that the pair "to letter'd ease devote, and Friendship's blest repose."[87] She fondly refers to them as "enchantresses . . . beneath whose plastic wand" the "peculiar graces" of their house and garden "arose."[88] She goes on to describe them as "extraordinary women, who, in the bosom of their deep retirement, are sought by the first characters of the age, both as to rank and talents."[89] Although Seward also employs the word "peculiar" in her account of Plas Newydd, her account of the ladies differs from those published throughout the nineteenth century. An account written by the actor Charles Matthews and published both in John Hicklin's *The Ladies of Llangollen* (1847) and in E. Owens Blackburn's *Illustrious Irishwomen* (1877) offers a sense of the popular perception of the ladies:

> Well, I have seen them, heard them, touched them. The pets, "the ladies," as they are called, dined here yesterday – Lady Eleanor Butler and Miss

Ponsonby, the curiosities of Llangollen mentioned by Miss Seward in her letters, about the year 1760. I mentioned to you in a former letter the effect they produced upon me in public, but never shall I forget the first burst yesterday upon entering the drawing-room, to find the dear antediluvian darlings, attired for dinner in the same manified dress, with the Croix de St. Louis, and other orders, and myriads of large brooches, with stones large enough for snuff-boxes, stuck in their starched neckcloths! I have not room to describe their most fascinating persons. I have an invitation from them, which I much fear I cannot accept. They returned home last night, fourteen miles, after twelve o'clock. They have not slept one night from home for above forty years. I longed to put Lady Eleanor under a bell-glass, and bring her to Highgate for you to look at.[90]

Matthews's account gives a sense of how "out of date" the ladies appeared. Yet Seward's letters, dating from only about fifteen years before Matthews's account, treat the ladies as contemporaries, and she exchanges letters and thoughts with them as equals, while Matthews condescendingly labels them "antediluvian darlings." Although slightly more compassionate, Walter Scott's account of his visit in 1825 resembles Matthews's, "We had read histories and descriptions enough of those romantic spinsters, and were prepared to be well amused; but the reality surpassed all expectation ... Yet it is too bad to laugh at these good old girls; they have long been the guardian angels of the village."[91] Scott continues by linking the ladies to a long-gone revolutionary age: "I was really affected with a melancholy sort of pleasure in contemplating it in the persons of the amiable old ladies who are among the last of its living representatives"; he claims that the ladies have the "air of the world of the 'ancien regime', courteous and entertaining without the slightest affectation."[92] As Scott's and Matthews's letters suggest, the ladies became museum pieces, "curiosities" or "the last ... living representatives" of the previous age. Their retreat became a tourist site, attracting not just Walter Scott, but also Edmund Burke and William Wordsworth. In a letter to Mrs. Parry Price, Seward gives a sense of the ladies' life as curiosities:

> The idea people often express to me of the dull, secluded life the accomplished friends lead is very diverting, since never did people live in such constant society with the great, the learned, and the ingenious. An influx of company so various and incessant obliges them daily to decline appearing to the parties that request permission to see the place ... They thought Sir Watkin Williams Wynne judged wrong in bringing so large a party, 16, to see their place, two days before I arrived. Their appearing to such a number was out of all question.[93]

As Romantic attractions or oddities, the ladies were objects to be placed under a "bell jar" like the antiquarian artifacts that often stood in for lost or waning histories. In her poem, Seward develops connections between the ladies' retreat at Plas Newydd and the stories, objects, and ephemera collected by Thomas Pennant and his antiquarian brethren. Yet instead of treating the ladies with condescension, Seward takes their status as "holdovers" from an earlier age seriously to raise questions about the consequences of the forward march of progress.

Marked by gaps and abrupt turns that invite the reader to determine how the ladies' story complements Welsh and English histories, *Llangollen Vale* articulates an anti-progressive theory of history. Seward begins with what many readers would recognize as history proper, drawing from the English chronicle writers used by Pennant, such as Caxton, Holinshed, and Thomas Rymer. She recounts Owen of Glendower's allegiance to the "hapless" Richard II and "brave Glendour's tears" "embalm[ing]" the Vale's name. Richard II's death leads to the "imperious" Henry's attempt to reduce Cambria to "vassalage" and concludes with the "clashing of arms, and furious shouts of war" that marked Glendower's revolt.[94] Seward draws on the conventions of epic in the opening stanzas. The passage features a singular hero and relates the supernatural circumstances surrounding his birth. Like Pennant, Seward uses Glendower's birth as an opportunity to comment on the national biases built into historical methodologies by contrasting Welsh and English accounts of Glendower's nativity. In a footnote, Seward acknowledges that the Welsh bard Jolo Goch marked the hero's birth with the arrival of a comet; in the English Holinshed's version, the hero's birth coincides with the arrival of a river of blood that filled his father's stables and left "The Steeds paternal, on their cavern'd floor, / Foaming, and horror-struck, 'fret fetlock-deep in gore.'"[95] By mixing bardic histories with English chronicles, Seward points out the limitations of historical methods built around a singular national tradition and emphasizes that progress and development are culturally relative – where the bard finds a harbinger of greatness, the chronicle writer notes a bloody sign of regress. In the poem and in her letters, Seward also reflects Pennant's sense of Glendower as a representative of the Welsh nation. In her letters, she writes that Owen of Glendower "gave" Llangollen Vale "to the Cambrians to boast it as their Welch Thermopylae, by himself and his small army cutting their way through the numerous legion of the English, in a narrow pass at the foot of one of its mountains."[96] She echoes this same sentiment in the poem where she recounts a personified female Cambria watching the "unequal fray" and jumping into battle:

From rock to rock, with loud acclaim, she sprung,
While from her Chief, the routed Legions fled;

Saw Deva roll their slaughter'd heaps among,
The check'd waves eddying round the ghastly dead;
Saw, in that hour, her own Llangollen claim
Thermopylae's bright wreath, and aye-enduring fame.[97]

Here Cambria and "her Chief" Glendower fight side by side in the Welsh Thermopylae. In another displacement of classic ground, which recalls her discussion of the classic ground of Lichfield in her letters, Seward, the "British muse," rewrites Thermopylae and transforms the English into the foreign Persians and the Welsh into the native Spartan heroes, who fight for their nation against great odds.

From the rebellion, she moves into a Romantic mode that Seward associates with Petrarch as well as the bardic poetry made popular by antiquarians like Pennant. The classical analogies from Owen's story are replaced by Romantic comparisons associated with a later period. In the story of Mifanwy Vechan and the poetry of the Bard Hoel, Seward claims that "O! Harp of Cambria, never hast thou known / Notes more mellifluent floating o'er the wires, / Than when thy Bard this brighter Laura sung, / And with his ill-starr'd love Llangollen's echos rung."[98] In her letters, she described the Bard Hoel as "another Petrarch, who sighed and sung of unattainable beauty."[99] Pennant himself uses Tristan as an analogy for Hoel and situates him in the tradition of chivalry and romance.[100] Hoel's "ill starr'd" passion and failure echoes Glendower's failed quest for Welsh independence. Although Seward adapts both the story of Owen of Glendower and Mifanwy Vechan from Thomas Pennant's *A Tour in Wales*, she changes the order of events, positioning the Bard Hoel's failed wooing of Vechan after Glendower's rebellion. Pennant clearly locates Glendower's Rebellion after Hoel's wooing. Not only does Seward mix literary and historical genres, but she also changes chronology and creates a non-linear story for the Vale that privileges modes of telling, contrasts classical and bardic historiography, and offers vastly different, even clashing, perspectives on historical development. A reviewer for the *The Gentleman's Magazine* recognized that the poem experiments with not only history but also poetic genre, claiming that "the poem Llangollen Vale involves in itself the principle of *poetic contrast*."[101]

From the epic and Petrarchan modes, which contain stories of military and sexual defeat, her tone shifts to a gothic and sentimental register. After Hoel's poetry "consecrates" the Vale "to love,"[102] Seward skips several hundred years and moves from thwarted heterosexual desire to the ladies' "vestal lustre" and their "sacred FRIENDSHIP, permanent as pure."[103] The sentimental mode Seward employs in this section of the poem celebrates fellow feeling and sympathy, which are often seen as emotions most successfully cultivated by moderns. Yet Seward's modern feelings exist in a fantastic gothic landscape colored by references to James Thomson's Spenserian *Castle of Indolence*, which she invokes to describe the ladies' renovation of Plas Newydd and its grounds. She recounts Butler and Ponsonby's move to Plas Newydd, which she calls the "fairy palace of the Vale."[104] She relates the improvements the ladies make to the surrounding gardens and praises the gothic library they built. She contrasts the ladies' existence and their gothic "palace" to the imagined repression suffered by the religious community of the Vale's Valle Crucis Abbey, whose denizens "lashed the hours" to "the grim IDOL" of superstition.[105] She wonders if any of the occupants of the Abbey ever felt like the ladies: "Wore one young lip gay Eleanora's smile? / Did Zara's look serene one tedious hour beguile?"[106] Butler and Ponsonby's neogothic retreat recreates in a secular space the same-sex gothic community of the Valle Crucis's nuns. Instead of "lashing" the hours away in superstitious devotions, Butler and Ponsonby allow the refined feelings produced by their same-sex community as well as the arts that arise from such a cultivated emotional state to flourish:

This gentle Pair no glooms of thought infest,
Nor Bigotry, nor Envy's sullen gleam
Shed withering influence on the effort blest,
Which most shou'd win the other's dear esteem,
By added knowledge, by endowment high,
By Charity's warm boon, and Pity's soothing sigh.[107]

Charity, pity, and knowledge, the emotional and intellectual byproducts afforded by modernity and commercial society, are made possible here, paradoxically, by the ladies' status as exiles.

In Seward's letters, the beauty of the Vale comes to seem an extension of the relationship of Butler and Ponsonby. They occupy "a little temple, consecrate to Friendship and the Muses, and adorned by the hands of all the Graces." She finds them "Devoted to each other, their expanded hearts have yet room for other warm attachments."[108] After meeting the ladies, she began corresponding with them both on literary, political, and personal subjects. In a letter to Sarah Ponsonby she writes, "I consider Llangollen Vale as my little Elysium. It is nowhere that my understanding, my taste, and my sentiments luxuriate in such vivid and unalloyed gratification."[109] Seward tried, unsuccessfully, to recreate Llangollen Vale in Lichfield. She had an Eolian harp made, "upon the construction of Miss Ponsonby's."[110] The ladies also sent Seward some of the fruit trees she admired. In return, she sent the ladies a copy of George Romney's picture of *Serena Reading by Candlelight*, which she claims "bears the stamp and image" of Honora.[111] The ladies hung Honora's image in the portrait gallery in their library, leading Seward to exclaim in response to a letter thanking her for the image, "All the obligation of her establishment in the Lyceum of Llangollen Vale is on my side. How could dear Miss Ponsonby speak of it as on yours and her own! I would have given treble the cost of this engraving, for the consciousness that the similitude of the fair idol of my affections is thus enshrined."[112] Honora's portrait joined the ladies' collection of historical and contemporary portraits, which covered the walls of their library. As many critics have noted, by enshrining Honora in Plas Newydd's library Seward may be expressing repressed sexual desire, but she is also creating a new historical record – a queer history that includes female friendship as well as those vanquished by war, unrequited love, and religion. Seward's history celebrates the fine feeling and polish the ladies were famous for generating in their rural retreat, outside modern commercial society. As Mark Salber Philips writes, "Sentimental histories, to put it another way, bring us possible brothers and sisters, not impossible heroes; actuality not exemplarity provides its pedagogical programme."[113] Although the ladies were heroes and comfortably positioned beside figures such as Glendower, they were also Seward's "sisters" who represented an alternative relationship to the world and a "pedagogical programme" that called into question the hierarchically gendered and sexual relationships that structured progressive narratives of the nation-state.

Seward concludes her description of the ladies' Welsh retreat with a critique of history:

> What boasts Tradition, what th' historic Theme,
> Stands it in all their chronicles confest
> Where the soul's glory shines with clearer beam,
> Than in our sea-zon'd Bulwark of the West,
> When, in this Cambrian Valley, Virtue shows
> Where, in her own soft sex, its steadiest lustre glows?[114]

After reading traditional histories and "historic themes" and looking through well-known "chronicles," Seward claims that she finds no better example of virtue than those displayed by the enduring friendship of Butler and Ponsonby. In doing so, she joins the ladies' history to that of the brave Glendower and the devoted Bard Hoel. She also joins sentimental history or a history of feeling to more established historical genres, such as accounts of battle or the bardic poetry that was becoming a feature of antiquarian histories. In her account of Wales, Seward produces an uneven and Ossianic history that collapses temporal and generic barriers, mixing periods as well as conventions from epic, Petrarchan, and sentimental verse. Her epic tale of battle and war from the fifteenth century gives way to a bard's song of love from decades earlier. The ladies' private rebellion, their refusal to marry as their parents demanded, echoes Glendower's refusal to submit to English rule. The Petrarchan poetry Hoel writes to immortalize his undying and unreciprocated passion for Lady Vechan inspires Seward's effort to celebrate the "vestal" harmony of Butler and Ponsonby's friendship. Although Cary's poem on the Vale celebrates Seward as a "British muse," her poem is distinctly local and Welsh. By manipulating generic conventions and temporality, Seward confuses the boundaries between the public and the private, questions linear development, and blurs distinctions between the local and the larger nation-state. Ultimately, *Llangollen Vale* makes British history less English and creates a curious kinship between Celtic rebels, bards, and unconventional women – all those usually beyond the borders of British history.

Although Seward read popular histories from the period includ- ing Robertson and Gibbon, she expressed frustration with historical narratives of great men and imperial conquest that taught through exemplarity. In a letter to her friend Mrs. Monpessan, Seward expresses her distaste for traditional history. Although the text she criticizes, Charlotte Lennox's translation of the *Memoirs of the Maximillan de Bethune, Duke of Sully, Prime Minister to Henry the Great* (1756),[115] is far from traditional, she nevertheless uses it as a platform for a larger discussion of her problems with existing historical methodologies:

> Performing my promise to you, I have attentively read over the first volume of Sully's *Memoirs*. Sometimes it interested me very much; but I waded through a great deal of it fatigued, and without interest. The little pleasure which reading history generally gives me; the slight and fading impression which its events are apt to leave upon my mind, probably results from my total want to taste for splendour, precedence, and power to influence the destiny of others. To me it seems a species of insanity, when a man, whom destiny has made a king, or a minister, sacrifices the lives of his fellow creatures, and produces all the numerous collateral miseries, parental, filial, paternal, and connubial, consequent upon every single deprivation; for what appears to me so little worth the hazard as an extension of empire, and the gewgaws of rank, even up to that troublesome bauble, the imperial scepter.[116]

Seward's *Llangollen Vale* reflects her distaste for "splendour, precedence, and power" as well as the "gewgaws of rank" and "the imperial scepter" that are gained by the "collateral miseries" upon which the "extension of empire" depends. Instead, Seward anticipates in *Llangollen Vale* the queer historiographies of Halberstam, Dinshaw, and Love and what Mark Salber Philips has called "sentimental history." According to Philips, sentimental history privileges emotion and asks readers not to emulate the historical actors they encounter but to feel with them, find affinities, and sympathize with what Seward calls the "collateral miseries" of history. Sentimental history often focuses on the dispossessed, including women and children, and offers "the dignity of narrative as compensation for lifetimes of oppression and exclusion."[117] Like sentimental history, antiquarian history did not focus exclusively on the conquerors but made room for the conquered, whose narratives often read as fragmented and discontinuous instead of as progressive wholes. According to Marilyn Butler, antiquarianism "celebrated oral and popular experience and minority and conquered experience," putting its practitioners and readers "at odds with contemporary Anglican and Tory apologists such as Samuel Johnson, Thomas Warton, and Edmund Burke, who all emphatically linked long tradition and hence cultural legitimacy with the nation-state and its sanctioned cultural expression in Scripture, law, history, and a canon of published great work by known authors."[118] All of the disparate events Seward links through association in the poem – the ladies' exile, the conquest of Wales, the failed romance of the Bard Hoel and Lady Mifanwy Vechan, as well as the lonely and cruel lives she imagines for the nuns of the Abbey of Valle Crucis – turn into "collateral" histories that exist outside of progressive narratives of development, which often depend on the growth of empire and the sexual and economic reproduction upon which a family's legacy depends.

Although modern readers of the poem focus on Seward's celebration of Eleanor Butler and Sarah Ponsonby's relationship, contemporary readers also understood Seward's work as an experiment in historical methodology. Two pieces written on the occasion of the poem's publication understand it as an attempt to reconcile Welsh and British history.[119] A sonnet written by H. F. Cary, one of Seward's closest friends, praises the poem as Seward's noble effort to uncover lost or repressed elements of British history:

> Llangollen's verdant straights, and mountains hoar,
> How shall I dwell enraptur'd on the themes,
> That now th' immortal MUSE of Britain deems
> Worthy her sacred scroll, unmark'd before!

Before these lines, Cary lists the "unmark'd" themes Seward "deems / Worthy her sacred scroll." They include Glendower's "valour," Hoel's "harp," and the "far wanderers from Ieren's coast" and their "shrine" to "friendship's gentle power." In a sonnet published in the May 1796 edition of *The Gentleman's Magazine*,[120] another of Seward's friends, the Reverend W. B. Stevens, frames *Llangollen Vale* as a celebration of Welsh nationalism. Stevens claims that "Tho' Lichfield boast the Mistress of the strain," Seward, despite her English birth, might be seen as the eighteenth-century equivalent of one of the famed Welsh bards. He writes, "Cambria exult! –again a voice divine / Floats on thy hills, as erst entranc'd the ear / Of Freedom, bending from her native shore . . . Rejoice, ye rock-screen'd Vallies! mute no more." Seward's inclusion of Cary's poem as a preface to her 1796 edition of *Llangollen Vale* and her request that Scott include Stevens's poem in the first volume of her *Poetical Works* suggest that she, like Cary and Stevens, also saw this poem as an experiment in historical method as well as a celebration of female friendship.[121] Notably, in Seward's experiment with method the ladies are not responsible for civilizing men or making sure commercial relations progress smoothly. In fact, instead of trying to shape the commercial world, build factories, or encourage industry as do the Bluestocking women of Sarah Scott's *Millennium Hall*, the ladies create a pastoral paradise that exists outside the economic concerns of modern Britain. Seward's poem calls women's role in the civilizing progress into question. Her poem celebrates the ladies' lives in obscurity and their rejection of conventional social and sexual relationships. They create a Plas Newydd, a new home or place, and most significantly a new time.

Madame Genlis's account in her *Souvenirs de Felicie* (1825) of the ladies looking at the ruin of Dinas Bran while reading the Ossian poems aloud suggests that the Ossian poems figured not just in Seward's experiments with history, but also the ladies' own efforts to inscribe themselves into and recreate an alternative history for themselves and their beloved valley.[122] Genlis writes,

> I walked out the whole forenoon with the two friends; nothing can equal the charms of the surrounding scenery and of the prospects which the mountain whose summit they occupy commands; at this elevation they appear the queens of all the beautiful country at their feet. Towards the north they have a view of the village and of a wood; to the south a long river washed the foot of the mountain, and fertilizes meadows of prodigious extent, beyond which is discovered an amphitheatre of hills, covered with intermingled trees and rocks. In the midst of this wild scenery rises a majestic tower, which might be taken for the Pharos of this coast, but is only the ruins of a magnificent castle, once the residence of the prince of the country. This solitary region was doubtless at that time flourishing and populous, now it is abandoned to nature alone; nothing is now to be seen in it but herds of goats, and a few scattered herdsmen sitting upon the rocks and playing upon the Irish harp.

Facing this rustic and melancholy scene the two friends have raised a verdant seat, shaded by two poplars, and thither they told me they often repair in summer to read together the poems of Ossian.[123]

This scene, of the ladies reading Ossian aloud while staring at the ruins of a Welsh prince's castle in a country once populous, records their desire to not just live in the past but also create a new history that "touches" – to borrow from Carolyn Dinshaw – other outsiders like Ossian and privileges affective relationships above "teleological necessity."[124] The Llangollen historiography practiced by Anna Seward, Eleanor Butler, and Sarah Ponsonby makes "backward" feelings and glances not a negative sign of defeat or retreat, but an attempt to structure a new temporality and recover surprising genealogies that include ancestors who exist outside the traditional frameworks of the biological family and the national community.

Notes

1. Anna Seward, *The Poetical Works of Anna Seward*, vol. 1, p. xxvii.
2. Norma Clarke, "Anna Seward," p. 35.
3. Her *Monody on Major Andre* even became a transatlantic literary and political sensation. Although Seward sympathized with the American Revolution, her poem challenged George Washington's treatment of John Andre, who was hung as a spy during the Revolutionary War. He was also an early lover of Seward's companion Honora Sneyd. General Washington found Seward's portrayal of his actions so embarrassing that, after the war, he sent an emissary to Seward with official documents explaining and defending his treatment of Andre. See Margaret Ashmun, *The Singing Swan*, pp. 85–6.
4. In her letters, Seward testifies to the incredible energy required by her readings, even claiming that a reading of *Macbeth* in the 1790s resulted in permanent lung damage.
5. Quoted in Ashmun, *The Singing Swan*, p. 263.
6. Seward, *Poetical Works*, vol. 1, p. xxv.
7. Ibid., p. xxv. In a letter to Joanna Baillie, Scott confesses that he finds most of Seward's verse "absolutely execrable" (Ashmun, *The Singing Swan*, p. 270).
8. Claudia Thomas Kairoff, *Anna Seward and the End of the Eighteenth Century*.
9. In her recent study, Kairoff positions both Johnson and Darwin as Seward's literary fathers and James Boswell as her brother. In adapting these analogies, Kairoff engages with a long tradition of scholarship on Seward that has seen her value largely in terms of the famous men with whom she associated.
10. See Judith Halberstram, *In a Queer Time and Place*, p. 4. Halberstram

argues that "queer time" attempts to think beyond "a middle-class logic of reproductive temporality" that relies on heterosexual marriage, child-bearing, and reproduction. Although Butler – the daughter of a gentleman who, but for an ancestor's transgressions in the rebellion of 1715, might have been the Earl of Ormond – can hardly be described as middle-class, her choice to reject heterosexual marriage and live in Wales with Ponsonby impacted her family financially and disrupted the aristocratic lineages and genealogies upon which the inheritance of money, property, and titles depended.

11. Item 879, Abbotsford Collection. This item contains the unpublished fragments of Seward's juvenile letters that Scott decided to remove from the "Biographical Preface" of her *Poetical Works*. Seward intended these comments on marriage to be published; in the same letter, Seward also writes, "Yet a few more years, O! let me, exempted from the fatigues of domestic economy, read, work, walk, and converse with my Honora!" Scott also excised this comment from the published version. Although Seward's collected letters and poetry were published posthumously by Scott and Archibald Constable, she undertook the bulk of the editing before her death. A copy in Seward's own hand of the table of contents of her *Poetical Works* held in the Abbotsford Collection testifies to this. Both Scott and Constable, in separate prefaces to Seward's poetry and letters, state that they followed Seward's directions as closely as propriety would allow, only excluding letters that might harm or offend those who were still living.

12. See Teresa Barnard, *Anna Seward*. In her valuable biography, Barnard draws on evidence from Seward's unpublished correspondence to challenge Backscheider's and Curran's readings of her poetry, arguing that "it would be wrong to pigeonhole her relationships or her sexuality by twenty-first-century values" (p. 5). As Barnard argues, her attachment to Honora does often seem sororal, and there is evidence of Seward's attachment to men such as Major John Wright in her youth and John Saville later in life. Although she never expressed any clear desire to marry Saville, their relationship was close and passionate, as Barnard has described in her Chapter 3, "'A free Agent': The Powys and Sykes Letters, 1770–1780." Although it seems inaccurate and anachronistic to label Seward a lesbian, as Barnard suggests, her interest in memorializing her attachment to Honora, her admiration for the female community at Llangollen, as well as her refusal of heterosexual marriage does demonstrate her investment in rethinking or queering conventional understandings of the family and romantic attachment.

13. Heather Love, *Feeling Backwards*, p. 8.
14. Anna Seward to Mrs. Powys, 5 February 1802, in Archibald Constable (ed.), *Letters of Anna Seward*, vol. 6, p. 7.
15. Marilyn Butler, "Popular Antiquarianism," p. 35.
16. See Stuart Curran, "Anna Seward and the Dynamic of Female Friendship," and Paula Backscheider, *Eighteenth-Century Women Poets and Their Poetry*, pp. 304–12.
17. Halberstram, *In a Queer Time and Place*, p. 1.
18. Norma Clarke has argued that Seward's letters witness "the profound

cultural shift that took place in the early decades of the nineteenth century in the course of which critical authority became gendered as male" ("Anna Seward: Swan, Duckling or Goose," p. 37).

19. Seward, *Poetical Works*, vol. 1, p. xiii.
20. For useful discussions of literature's contribution to the consolidation of British identity during the eighteenth century, see Robert Crawford, *Devolving English Literature*, and Clifford Siskin, *The Work of Writing*.
21. See John Kerrigan, *Archipelagic English*.
22. Seward to Emma, November 1762, in Seward, *Poetical Works*, vol. I, p. vii.
23. Seward to Walter Scott, 23 September 1806, in Constable, *Letters of Anna Seward*, vol. 6, p. 315.
24. Ibid., p. 315.
25. Seward continually refers to first-generation Bluestockings in her letters, particularly Elizabeth Montagu. She values Montagu as a literary critic and even scolds Boswell for including in his *Journal of a Tour to the Hebrides* (1785) a "passage which records the despot's injustice to Mrs. Montague's ingenious and able Treatise on Shakespeare." See Seward to James Boswell, 26 March 1786, in Constable, *Letters of Anna Seward*, vol. 1, p. 31.
26. Seward to Emma, November 1762, in Seward, *Poetical Works*, vol. 1, p. vi.
27. Ibid., pp. vii–viii.
28. Donna Heiland, "Swan Songs," p. 386.
29. Constable, *Letters of Anna Seward*, vol. 1, p. 7.
30. Ibid., pp. 7 and 8.
31. Seward to Court Dewes, 20 March 1785, in Constable, *Letters of Anna Seward*, vol. 1, p. 54.
32. 7 March 1788, in Constable, *Letters of Anna Seward*, vol. 1, p. 43.
33. For much of the twentieth century, interest in Seward was kept alive by Johnsonians who saw her as the deserving or sympathetic victim of either Johnson's or Boswell's wit. Hesketh Pearson claimed in *Extraordinary People* (London: Harper & Row, 1965) that Boswell "has given the impression, studiously adopted by other Johnsonians, that Anna is not to be trusted. But she is quite as reliable as Boswell sober, and more reliable than Boswell drunk" (p. 106). Yet the intent of Pearson's comment was to deflate Boswell and not elevate Seward. He goes on to argue that Seward is mainly "worth our attention, not as a curiosity of literature but as a good hearted and honest woman who had the pluck to tell Dr Johnson when he was talking twaddle" (p. 95).
34. Samuel Johnson, *Lives of the Most Eminent English Poets*, vol. 2, p. 462.
35. Ibid., p. 462.
36. Seward to Scott, 20 June 1806, in Constable, *Letters of Anna Seward*, vol. 6, p. 277.
37. Seward to Piozzi, 21 December 1789, in Constable, *Letters of Anna Seward*, vol. 2, p. 337.

38. Seward to Scott, 10 July 1802, in Constable, *Letters of Anna Seward*, vol. 6, p. 39.
39. Ibid., p. 39.
40. Seward emerges in her letters as a female variant of Ossian. Her similarity to Ossian authorizes and even authenticates her as a provincial poet. In her critiques of William Wordsworth and Samuel Coleridge, she associates Ossian's powers of perception and poetic vision with her own. In a letter to the Rev. H. F. Cary on Coleridge and Wordsworth, Seward appears astonished by Coleridge's assessment of Wordsworth's poetry as original. She has a particular problem with Coleridge's claim that Wordsworth coined the phrase "green radiance, for the light of the glow-worm" and adds that "Ossian calls the stars green in twenty parts of his poetry, translated and published, before Wordsworth, who is a very young man, was in existence" (Seward to Cary, 4 March 1798, in Constable, *Letters of Anna Seward*, vol. 5, p. 61). Although she denies the possibility that Wordsworth came to his conclusion about the green light of the glow-worm independently, she claims to have come to the same conclusion unaided in her own early youth. According to Seward, before encountering Ossian's poetry, she perceived "the stars and glow-worm as effusing greenish beams." Ossian's publication merely confirms Seward's own native vision: "When Ossian came out, in my early youth, I was charmed to find him confirming, by his epithet of green for the stars, the accuracy of my visual perception" (Ibid., p. 61). Seward and Ossian share an accuracy of perception Wordsworth, post-Ossian, can only imitate. The barriers between Ossian and Seward disappear even further in the letter. In her critique of Coleridge's "Ode on the Departing Year," the two bards' voices meet. She cites two lines from Coleridge's "Ode," "With wild unequal step he pass'd along, / Of pouring on the winds a broken song," and follows her citation by commenting, "The second line is verbatim from Ossian. I believe the inequality of step, as symptomatic of an agonized mind, will not be found in any poet antecedent to my 'Elegy on Cook'" (ibid., p. 57). Coleridge's poem affirms Seward's hypothesis about her proximity and kinship to Ossian and the influence their poetic visions have had on literary history. Ossian's "broken song" and Seward's "inequality of step" from her *Elegy on Cook* become poetic tags and might be read as designations of their own ambivalent and often invisible place in the British literary history Seward attempts to rewrite.
41. Samuel Johnson, *Dictionary of the English Language*.
42. Boswell, *Life of Johnson*, p. 391.
43. In her *Memoirs of the Life of Dr. Darwin* (1804), Seward describes Johnson's attitude toward the Lichfield intelligentsia, which included her father and Erasmus Darwin: "These were men whose intellectual existence passed unnoticed by Dr. Johnson in his depreciating estimate of Lichfield talents. But Johnson liked only worshippers ... [T]hey were not in the herd that 'paged his heels,' but sunk, in servile silence, under the force of his dogmas, when their hearts and their judgments bore contrary testimony" (pp. 75–6). Interestingly, in his preface to Seward's *Poetical Works*, Scott attributes the tension between the Lichfield elite and

Johnson to class-based anxiety rooted in Seward and Darwin's intimate knowledge of Johnson's humble beginnings as the son of a bookseller.

44. Seward to Scott, 29 January 1807, in Constable, *Letters of Anna Seward*, vol. 6, p. 331.

45. Seward's efforts might be likened to the work of the British authors that Howard Weinbrodt examines in *Britannia's Issue*. Like the male authors Weinbrodt studies, Seward creates modern classics that establish a native tradition. Interestingly, instead of explicitly employing analogies to the classical world or rewriting classical scenes, as do the authors in Weinbrodt's study, Seward dispenses with an explicit comparison in her effort to build a separate tradition for the British Isles.

46. David Duff, *Romanticism and the Uses of Genre*, p. 47; Duff's comments on Seward come in the context of a discussion of the Romantic period as a "clash between opposed systems and protocols: between established and emergent codes, generic and anti-generic tendencies" (ibid., p. 46). Seward's collected letters forge an emergent code that resisted both traditional understandings of genre as well as the neoclassical division between the ancients and moderns. Seward's redefinition of a "classic" and a "classic ground" is one instance of the clash or revolution that Duff describes. According to the *OED*, Robert Burns in 1787 was one of the first authors to use "classic ground" as a description of a literary or culture center instead of as a reference to Greece or Rome. Seward's letters provide another early example of this shift.

47. Seward to Scott, 20 June 1806, in Constable, *Letters of Anna Seward*, vol. 6, p. 276.

48. Seward to Mr. Saville, 15 June 1793, in Constable, *Letters of Anna Seward*, vol. 6, p. 265.

49. John Brewer, *Pleasures of the Imagination*, p. 497; see also Harriet Guest's discussion of Seward in her *Small Change*.

50. Susan Manning, *Fragments of Union*, p. 149. See also Penny Fielding's "'Usurpt by Cyclops'" for a related discussion of Seward's treatment of the Severn in her poem "Coalbook Dale." Fielding argues that Seward's poem develops the Romantic concept of the genus loci and that, "unable to reconcile specific places with a wider geography," Seward transforms Coalbrookdale into a discontinuous "felt, singular spot" (p. 154).

51. Manning, *Fragments of Union*, p. 152.

52. Seward, *Poetical Works*, vol. 1, p. 15.

53. Seward to Weston, 23 December 1786, in Constable, *Letters of Anna Seward*, vol. 1, p. 241.

54. Seward, *Poetical Works*, vol. 3, p. 16.

55. Ibid., p. 19.

56. Ibid., p. 21.

57. Ibid., p. 18.

58. Ibid., p. 18.

59. Ibid., p. 15.

60. Quoted in Steve Shankman, "Introduction," *The Iliad of Homer*, trans. Alexander Pope, ed. Steven Shankman (New York: Penguin Classics, 1996), p. 75.

61. See Samuel H. Monk, "Anna Seward and the Romantic Poets," p. 133; for a less biased evaluation of Seward's relation to the Romantics, see David Wheeler's "Placing Anna Seward."

62. Seward to Mrs. Stokes, 25 October 1807, in Constable, *Letters of Anna Seward*, vol. 6, p. 386.

63. Hugh Blair, "Critical Dissertation on Ossian," in Howard Gaskill (ed.), *The Poems of Ossian and Related Works*, p. 382.

64. Seward to Saville, 15 June 1793, in Constable, *Letters of Anna Seward*, vol. 2, p. 260.

65. Ibid, p. 260. Even before Honora married Edgeworth, Seward described her in an Ossianic register and worried that her delicate constitution might end in an early death. In a letter from 1764, she describes the young Honora as "fresh and beautiful as the young day-star, when he bathes his fair beams in the dews of spring" (*Poetical Works*, vol. 1, p. cxviii). Seward, in true Ossianic fashion, seems to have mourned Honora well before her marriage and death.

66. Duff, *Romanticism and the Use of Genre*, p. 149.

67. Sharon Setzer, "'Pond'rous Engines' in 'Outraged Groves,'" p. 78; Donna Coffey, "Protecting the Botanic Garden," p. 155.

68. See Sylvia Bowerbank, *Speaking for Nature*.

69. Curran, "Dynamic of Female Friendship," p. 21.

70. Seward to Butler, 4 June 1798, in Constable, *Letters of Anna Seward*, vol. 4, p. 16.

71. Maureen McLane, *Balladeering, Minstrelsy, and the Making of British Romantic Poetry*, pp. 132–3.

72. Adam Smith, *Theory of Moral Sentiments*, p. 535.

73. Ibid., p. 536.

74. Seward to Count Dewes, 9 March 1788, in Constable, *Letters of Anna Seward*, vol. 2, p. 66.

75. Lord Kames, *Sketches of the History of Man*, vol. 1, p. 122.

76. Ibid., p. 122.

77. Seward to Mrs. Stokes, 31 June 1796, in Constable, *Letters of Anna Seward*, vol. 4, p. 224.

78. Ibid., p. 224.

79. Ibid., p. 224.

80. Seward to Miss Wingfield, 29 October 1796, in Constable, *Letters of Anna Seward*, vol. 4, p. 266.

81. In a note she appends to this letter, Seward claims that Park was previously "unknown" to her. See Anna Seward, Thomas Park to Seward, 9 March 1796, in Constable, *Letters of Anna Seward*, vol. 6, p. 186.

82. Ibid., p. 186.

83. Ibid., p. 186.

84. The nature of the ladies' departure from Ireland became a source of fascination for their contemporaries. In a letter from 1816 to Matthew Weld Hartstonge, Walter Scott writes, "Your account of the ladies of Llangollen reminded me of a sentimental distress which occurred in the course of their first escape (I think they made two) from their friends in the Green Isle. It was told me by a female friend of theirs and I believe it to be strictly true. One of the Ladies I think Miss P. wore man's attire

upon that occasion and acted as escort to the other. That part of her dress which in well regulated families the wife is never suffered to usurp was made of leather. They made part of the way on horseback and encountered a violent rain, before arriving at the inn. The Amazon ignorant of the mode of treating buckskins which had been thoroughly soaked was so imprudent when she laid aside these indispensable articles of clothing as to hang them to dry before a blazing fire. You who are an old yeoman like myself will anticipate the direful consequences. The garments were in the morning perfectly shriveled up and unequal to contain that part of the person which they were designed to receive. How she got out of the scrape whether by adopting the costume of a Scotch highlander or borrowing the breeches of the landlord I must leave to your imagination for the lady who told me the story left it to mine." See *The Letters of Sir Walter Scott 1787–1807*, vol. 4, pp. 224–5.

85. In *An Archive of Feelings*, Ann Cvetkovich argues that the "concept of exile . . . which frequently presumes a place of natural origin and emphasizes the loss of one's nation in the negative sense" can also be a "resource for creating new cultures" (pp. 121–2).
86. Thomas Pennant, *A Tour in Wales*, vol. 1, p. 2.
87. Anna Seward, *Llangollen Vale with Other Poems*, p. 7.
88. Seward to the Rev. Henry White, 7 September 1795, in Constable, *Letters of Anna Seward*, vol. 4, p. 103. Seward appears to have drawn directly from her letters in the composition of *Llangollen Vale*.
89. Ibid., p. 104.
90. Quoted in John Hicklin, *The Ladies of Llangollen*, pp. 12–13.
91. Ibid., p. 13.
92. Ibid., p. 40.
93. Seward to Miss Parry Price, 23 September 1795, in Historical Manuscripts Commission, *Fifteenth Report, Appendix, Part VII, The Manuscripts of the Duke of Somerset, The Marquis of Ailesbury, and The Rev. Sir T. H. G. Puleston, Bart.*, p. 341.
94. Seward, *Llangollen Vale*, pp. 2–3.
95. Ibid., p. 1.
96. Seward to Miss Wingfield, 14 August 1795, in Constable, *Letters of Anna Seward*, vol. 4, p. 92.
97. Seward, *Llangollen Vale*, p. 4.
98. Ibid., p. 5.
99. Seward to Miss Wingfield, 14 August 1795, in Constable, *Letters of Anna Seward*, vol. 4, p. 90.
100. Pennant, *A Tour in Wales*, vol. 1, p. 281.
101. Ibid, p. 413.
102. Seward, *Llangollen Vale*, p. 6.
103. Ibid., p. 6.
104. Ibid., p. 7
105. Ibid., p. 10.
106. Ibid., p. 10.
107. Ibid., p. 11.
108. Seward to Mrs. Mary Powys, 17 November 1795, in Constable, *Letters of Anna Seward*, vol. 4, p. 120.

109. Seward to Miss Ponsonby 30 October 1797, in Constable, *Letters of Anna Seward*, vol. 5, p. 10.
110. Seward to Miss Wingfield, 19 July 1796, in Constable, *Letters of Anna Seward*, vol. 5, p. 230. Despite receiving a drawing of the harp and measurements from Ponsonby, Seward's recreation failed. Unfortunately, the "eastern sash windows" the harp was "made to fit" rarely received a wind "strong enough to wake the sullen slumbers of its many chords."
111. Seward to the Right Hon. Lady Eleanor Butler Lichfield, 4 June 1798, in Constable, *Letters of Anna Seward*, vol. 5, p. 108.
112. Ibid., p. 108.
113. Mark Salber Philips, "On the Advantage and Disadvantage of Sentimental History for Life," p. 55.
114. Seward, *Llangollen Vale*, p. 9.
115. As a memoir, Lennox's history participates in what Mark Salber Philips in *Society and Sentiment* sees as the opening up of historical discourse in the eighteenth century to include the private realm.
116. Seward to Mrs. Monpessan, 5 March 1787, in Constable, *Letters of Anna Seward*, vol. 1, p. 250.
117. Philips, "On the Advantage and Disadvantage of Sentimental History," p. 55.
118. Marilyn Butler, "Popular Antiquarianism," p. 330.
119. Contemporary reviews of the poem also set Ponsonby and Butler's relationship alongside other aspects of the poem. *The European Magazine* 29 (January–June 1796) noted that Llangollen Vale is the spot "where two ladies, the honourable Lady Eleanor Butler and Miss Ponsonby, by not seventeen years residence, have continued the celebrity of this sequestered spot," reminding readers to remember "the view of their cottage" which appeared in the magazine in 1794, while also mentioning Owen of Glendower (p. 260). *The Monthly Review* 20 (May–August 1796) includes the section of the poem on the ladies, but categorizes Seward's work as a historical poem, claiming that it "pursues the history of that delightful retreat, from the time of Glendour, who made it the scene of his enterprising valour, to its present state, dignified and rendered interesting by the residence of an accomplished pair of female friends, Lady Eleanor Butler and Miss Ponsonby; as a tribute or respect to whom, the poem was apparently written" (p. 152). *The Gentleman's Magazine* 79 (January–June 1796) gives each section of the poem equal attention, mentioning "the valour of Owen Glendour, and the poetic love of the Bard Hoel for the lady of the Castle of Dinas Bran." The review concludes by noting that "the vale owes its present éclat to the seventeen years' retirement of two ladies, nobly born and extensively celebrated" (p. 413).
120. *The Gentleman's Magazine* 79 (May–August, 1796), p. 421.
121. Although Scott decided not to include Stevens's poem in his edition of Seward's works, it is listed in the manuscript copy of the table of contents, which Seward prepared for Scott. The manuscript can be found in the Abbotsford Collection, National Library of Scotland.
122. Elizabeth Mavor also paraphrases Genlis's account in *The Ladies of*

Llangollen, and John Brewer mentions Genlis's anecdote in his *Pleasures of the Imagination*.

123. Hicklin, *The Ladies of Llangollen*, p. 22.
124. Carolyn Dinshaw, *Getting Medieval*, p. 2.

Chapter 4

Poetry, Paratext, and History in Radcliffe's Gothic

While the author awaits hypothetical newspaper reviews, literary prizes, and other official recognitions, the epigraph is already, a bit, his consecration. With it, he chooses his peers and thus his place in the pantheon. (Gerard Genette, *Paratexts* 160)

It is tempting to skip or ignore the snippets of poetry Ann Radcliffe used to preface the chapters of her gothic fictions. Although the frequent poetical interludes in Radcliffe's novels take a back seat to most readers' preference for plot, the fragments of poetry dispersed throughout her narratives, when considered together, are more than a distraction. E. J. Clery and Deidre Lynch posit that, once compiled together, her epigraphs compose a canon of vernacular literature.[1] Radcliffe's catalogue includes perennial favorites Shakespeare and Milton, as well as largely forgotten eighteenth-century poets like William Mason and women writers like Charlotte Smith; however, many of the most frequently cited poems recreate elements of Celtic history and culture, such as James Thomson's *The Castle of Indolence* (1748), James Beattie's *The Minstrel* (1777), Thomas Gray's "The Bard" (1757), and James Macpherson's Ossian poems (1760–3). If paratext functions in a novel as what Gerard Genette calls a "boundary," "border," "threshold," or in-between space, the Celtic poems Radcliffe favors negotiate the relationship between, on the one hand, her gothic tales of female imprisonment and terror and, on the other, the political and cultural imbalances created by a predominantly English British state.[2] This chapter argues that Radcliffe's extensive paratextual apparatus in her most famous novel *The Mysteries of Udolpho* (1794) puts her heroine's quest in conversation with the questions of uneven development, imperial expansion, and the contested origins of British character raised by eighteenth-century philosophers and poets.

Genette has suggested that in selecting an epigraph, an author "chooses his peers and his place in the pantheon." Radcliffe's extensive paratextual apparatus positions her not alongside the gothic and female authors with whom she is frequently classed but the poets she most often cites, such as Thomas Gray, William Collins, Macpherson, Beattie, and Thomson – who like Radcliffe found inspiration on the Celtic periphery. A serious consideration of what her biographer Rictor Norton calls the under-examined "'poetic' rather than 'novelistic' features of her oeuvre" challenges the marginal position in which Radcliffe has been placed by studies of the novel.[3] This approach disrupts the position of her gothic fiction in literary history as a "mutation" of realist fiction, often treated in studies of the novel as an afterword or final chapter.[4] Once outside established narratives of the novel, Radcliffe, whom Walter Scott dubs "the first poetess of romantic fiction,"[5] emerges as a descendant of the Ossian craze of the mid-eighteenth century, the Scottish Enlightenment's theories of history that appeared at the same time, and the poetry of the even earlier gothic revival.

The Celtic peripheries or borderlands of *The Mysteries of Udolpho* also suggest that Radcliffe's fiction engages in debates not only about the Revolutionary and Jacobin present of the 1790s to which contemporary critics have devoted so much attention,[6] but also debates over how to interpret Great Britain's past, particularly its variously termed "barbarian," Gothic, or Celtic past. The contested origins of British history become visible in her citations of poetry from the gothic revival and in the discussions of manners and feelings that occur within her narrative, and recall the theories of history and sentiment set forth by the Scottish Enlightenment. Although the gothic revival of the earlier eighteenth century inspired a nostalgia for chivalric feeling and Britain's Gothic past that one finds in Burke's *Reflections on Revolution in France*, it also led writers and readers to think deeply about imperial expansion and British history. The gothic revival has been described by Christine Gerrard as a "strain of literary nationalism" that began with the patriot poetry of the 1730s and writers like Thomson.[7] This early gothic poetry was critical of Robert Walpole's ministry and suspicious of his commitment to economic and imperial expansion. Patriot Whigs, such as Thomson, opposed Walpole and were led by Lord Bolingbroke and later Lord Lyttelton. The patriot Whigs attempted to locate British liberty and civility in a remote gothic past. By creating the native gothic as a historical ideal, they were able to measure the decline of the British state and anticipate a revival of the native customs of Britain, represented by the "Celts, Goths, and Saxons, and their accompanying mythologies," all of which contributed to the creation of the eighteenth-century Gothic movement.[8] Poets often cited by Radcliffe, including Thomson, Gray, Beattie, and Macpherson, have all been characterized as members of the gothic revival and all had ties to the patriot opposition.[9] Born later than Thomson, Macpherson and Beattie were active members of the Scottish Enlightenment, and their poetry also engages with the theories of progress set forth by Scots literati. Notably, the concerns of the gothic revival and the Scottish Enlightenment frequently overlapped; both theorized the influence of Gothic culture on British identity and considered the possibility that imperial expansion, which they understood as analogous to Rome's rise, could lead to a decline of the British state.[10] The poetry within Radcliffe's fiction gestures to this larger discussion of gothic history and historical progress and provides alternative aesthetic and philosophical contexts for her work, contexts that have been occluded by studies that only consider her debt and legacy to other novelists.

This gothic revival and the Scottish Enlightenment raise important questions about established readings of her work. For example, Claudia Johnson has read the *The Mysteries of Udolpho* against Edmund Burke's defense of Marie Antoinette and his attempts to revive a chivalric past populated by feeling men, who would weep over the Revolutionaries' attack on their Queen.[11] Yet these same feeling men, when read alongside Thomson's *Castle of Indolence* or placed in the context of Scottish Enlightenment historiography, appear as overindulgent moderns with dangerously refined emotions. In contrast to the men of feeling discussed by Johnson and others, Radcliffe's heroines, such as *Udolpho*'s Emily St. Aubert, exhibit a Smithean "self-command" or controlled sensibility that transforms them into agents of civilization who, instead of embodying the dangers of modernity, balance the virtues of savage and commercial societies. By tracking her interest in Scottish Enlightenment theories of history and feeling and eighteenth-century Celtic and gothic poetry, it becomes possible to see her as engaging with Enlightenment debates about progress and the role of women in the development of civil society.

The poetical epigraphs within *Udolpho* join Emily's "progress" to eighteenth-century debates about history, the relationship between manners and economic structures, and the place of women in history. As a "password of intellectuality," a means of "integrat[ing] the novel into . . . a cultural tradition,"[12] the epigraphs in *Udolpho* align Radcliffe's fiction with a national literary tradition that dramatizes the damage sustained by Celtic subcultures within Great Britain. This literary tradition betrays a pressing awareness of the pitfalls of British national belonging and the cultural losses and gains produced by imperial expansion. The contested national pasts found within Radcliffe's gothic, like the poetry of the gothic revival and the Ossian craze from which she draws, borrow from post-1688 Whig historiography, which plumbed the ancient history of the British Isles to recover new native models of British character. In doing so, many Whig historiographers reshaped the Celtic past and transformed Gothic and Celtic barbarians into model British citizens. Radcliffe's turn to this brand of Enlightenment historiography allows her to question, as do the first- and second-generation Bluestockings discussed in previous chapters, the imperial basis of British identity and the relationship between women's elevated status in civil society and the commercial gains closely associated with the specters of imperial luxury and decline. Reading the narrative of Emily's journey alongside the epigraphs transforms Radcliffe's novel, and perhaps her gothic aesthetic, into a mode of feminist historiography that provides a framework for questioning and examining the representation of women in historical narrative and their role in civilization's progress.

Radcliffe and Gothic Historiographies

Traditionally, critics read Radcliffe's novels as marking psychological, economic, and political shifts: the creation of the internally riven modern self in Terry Castle's well-known reading and the development of commercial society in E. J. Clery's analysis.[13] These readings seem an inevitable result of the temporal confusion that characterizes Radcliffe's fiction, from the imposition of descriptions of Salvator Rosa and Claude Lorrain's landscapes onto the sixteenth century, to the location of eighteenth-century sentiments and manners in a medieval past. Although Radcliffe's novels undeniably comment on the historical shifts these critics describe, I would like to read Radcliffe's gothic not just as a marker of historical shifts, but as a meta-commentary on the problems involved in producing history, measuring change, and mapping progress. Radcliffe's *Mysteries of Udolpho* participates in the literary and historical shift away from classical gauges of development to a new interest in native and vernacular models. As Suvir Kaul argues, comparisons between the classical ages of Rome and Greece were used not just to inflate British egos and pretensions, but also to warn Britons about the consequences of imperial expansion and the potentially deleterious effects of luxury. The classical model invites analogies to Rome's fall absent from the native gothic, which celebrates the historical and aesthetic achievements of the Saxons and Celts of the British Isles instead of the overreaching citizens of imperial Rome. The paratext of Radcliffe's novels shows her to be working with native and vernacular models of the past and engaging with the historical and aesthetic debates of the mid-eighteenth-century gothic revival in addition to the later philosophical and historical debates of the Scottish Enlightenment. Radcliffe's fiction suggests continuities between these two movements, which are often separated by literary and historical chronologies that separate England from Scotland, the eighteenth century from the Romantic period, poetry from fiction, and fiction from philosophy. Her preference for vernacular poetry and pre-Romantic as opposed to neo-classical poetry echoes the interest of the gothic revival in recovering a native British past and Scottish literati's desire to recover a lost Ossianic world that could rival Ancient Greece and Rome. In fact, the graveyard poets, including Thomson, Gray, and Macpherson, who so influenced Radcliffe's historical method, were also great favorites of Adam Smith, who cited Thomson and Gray in his *Theory of Moral Sentiments* and used Thomson, Gray, and Macpherson as examples in his *Lectures on Rhetoric and Belles Lettres*.[14]

Like Adam Smith, Radcliffe's frequent invocation of these elegiac and backward-looking poets shaped her approach to history and her assessment of the connections between imperial expansion and civilization's progress. In his 1762 *Letters on Chivalry and Romance*, Richard Hurd set forth the aesthetic and historical aims of the gothic revival.[15] In a series of letters modeled on Joseph Addison's *Spectator*, Hurd practices an historically-minded literary criticism, arguing that the characteristics of the gothic that eighteenth-century readers found "unnatural" and irregular were products of a repressed and native gothic past.[16] He defends the gothic and recovers its singular "rules," which he claims were followed by Renaissance poets, particularly Edmund Spenser, whose *Faerie Queene* inspired Thomson's *Castle of Indolence* and James Beattie's *Minstrel*:

> When an architect examines a Gothic structure by Grecian rules, he finds nothing but deformity. But the Gothic architecture has it's [sic] own rules, by which when it comes to be examined, it is seen to have it's [sic] merit, as well as the Grecian. The question is not, which of the two is conducted in the simplest or truest taste; but, whether there be not sense and design in both, when scrutinized by the laws on which each is projected.[17]

In separating the classical principles of literary form from the native and more identifiably British values of the gothic, Hurd makes possible not only competing aesthetic systems but also competing historical ones. According to Hurd, eighteenth-century readers' inability to understand the gothic stems from the historical amnesia that followed the disappearance of the feudal system and the outmoded political structure that accompanied it: "That the Gothic manners of Chivalry, as springing out of the feudal system, were singular, as that system itself: So that, when that political constitution vanished out of Europe, the manners, that belonged to it, were no longer seen or understood."[18] By forging connections between the development of manners, economics, politics, and aesthetics, Hurd's critical approach foreshadows the concerns of the conjectural histories of the Scottish Enlightenment, but without the explicit theorization of the negative as well as positive consequences of commerce on humankind's development. Hurd's efforts to recuperate a gothic aesthetic anticipate Scottish Enlightenment philosophers' treatment of the Ossian poems as a counternarrative to the universal history their stadial theories both trace and critique. Hurd's celebration of the native gothic introduces the possibility that a backward and gothic aesthetic might be an appropriate vehicle for critics of the commercial present and expanding empire of the British nation-state.

Throughout his defense of the gothic, Hurd, like his Scottish Enlightenment contemporaries, "conjectures" about "the rise of chivalry" and its relationship to "feudal government."[19] He suggests that the constant state of war amongst the "feudal chiefs" of the Middle Ages fostered gallantry, chivalry, and an equality between the sexes that included women's participation in war, their ability to inherit property, and the "free commerce of the ladies, in those knots and circles of the great."[20] According to Hurd, the gothic and romance's representation of these characteristics merely "copy from the manners of the times."[21] Even though some readers saw, as Walter Scott suggests, Radcliffe's success as an "evil sign of the times" and a "degradation of public taste,"[22] Radcliffe's gothic, when tied to the earlier gothic revival, can be understood as a critique of the imperial present, an anti-progressive or backward-looking perspective that attempts to create an alternative to a liberal logic that ties commercial and imperial development to the progress of women and the arts. The gothic revival described by Hurd also recuperates an historical model that could be used to suggest that women's progress may be independent of economic development.

Although Hurd and the Scottish thinkers who have been the subject of much of this book came to different conclusions, there are striking similarities between their discussions of gender and progress. Depending on the historical or cultural vantage they selected, Scottish thinkers understood the elevation of women as either cultivating greater humanity and inspiring social progress or creating effeminate men and marking imperial and social decay. As discussed in my second chapter, Lord Kames and John Millar used Ancient Caledonia not only to exert pressure on the stadial schema but also to elevate a native British past above Greek and Roman models in a way that resembles Hurd's treatment of the Middle Ages; however, in Kames's and Millar's work the status of women in Ancient Caledonia resembles that of women in modern commercial cultures. On the other hand, Adam Ferguson, a member of the famous Highland Black Watch Regiment and great admirer of Spartan society, was, of all the Scottish literati, the most hesitant to sanction this gender revolution. He saw the greater equality between the sexes spawned by commercial society as confusing gender roles, and read this confusion as a sign of decay in his *Essay on Civil Society*:

> The increasing regard in which men appear, in the progress of commercial arts, to study their profit, or the delicacy with which they refine on their pleasure, even industry itself, or the habit of application to a tedious employment, in which no honours are won, may, perhaps, be considered as indications of a growing attention to interest, or of effeminacy, contracted in the enjoyment of ease and conveniency.[23]

In Ferguson, the leisure time and busy work created by commercial and imperial expansion mark not just the feminization of society but also a loss of national consciousness, a descent into self-serving pursuits. Ferguson links a revival of national character to the reinstatement of boundaries between the sexes and the imposition of new limits on imperial expansion. Imperial expansion brings with it an "enjoyment of ease and conveniency" that he sees as dangerous because it renders "the individual of less consequence to the public." Radcliffe's first novel, *The Castles of Athlin and Dunbayne* (1789), which was her only novel to be set in Scotland, illustrates the tensions within Scottish thinkers' accounts of gender and progress. The conflict within the novel revolves around two men: Malcolm of Dunbayne, a clan chief who "suffers" his lands to "lie uncultivated" and finds himself "torn by conflicting passions" he cannot control, and the more refined and civilized Earl of Athlin, a peer of Scotland who possesses a heart that "glowed with all the warmth of benevolence."[24] The different manners of Malcolm and the Earl of Athlin exemplify the two poles of the Scottish Enlightenment's stadial theory of history, which posits the existence of four stages of social and economic development. Malcolm personifies the first of four stages in which humans battle the elements and each other for survival and are ruled by "uncultivated" passions. The Earl of Athlin, connected to a larger social and economic network, has time to tame his passions and refine his feelings, qualities that mark the later stages of human development. The hot-blooded warlord, Malcolm, and the cultivated peer, the Earl of Athlin, battle over the Earl's sister Mary, who represents the best of humankind, having a "heart which vibrated in unison with the sweetest feeling of humanity; a mind, quick in perceiving the nicest lines of moral rectitude, and strenuous in endeavouring to act up to its perceptions."[25] Like

Radcliffe's later heroines, Mary finds herself caught between not just men but also rival historical forces, competing temporalities that coexist and offer women alterative futures. *The Castles of Athlin and Dunbayne* suggests that the origins of her gothic fiction are entangled with the questions about gender and progress raised by Scottish stadial history. Radcliffe's first novel not only demonstrates her interest in Scottish historiography, but also provides an additional context for the references to Scottish poetry she makes within *The Mysteries of Udolpho*'s paratext and diegesis.

The oft-commented-on medievalism of her novels clearly, in the spirit of Hurd, attempts to recreate the chivalric and gothic character of an earlier age. Yet Emily St. Aubert's journey to places such as commercial Venice and her immersion in the luxurious trappings of the city also comment on the commercial character of modernity. Instead of clearly mapping a history that either traces the commercial progress of the British Empire or anticipates its decline into luxury and excess, Radcliffe's gothic history critiques teleological development – a position suggested by her famously convoluted and circuitous plots, which borrow heavily from romance, and reinforced in her novel's paratext, which cites poetry, seemingly haphazardly, from numerous periods and sources. Before addressing the curious "progress" Radcliffe traces in the narrative of *The Mysteries of Udolpho*, the next section of this chapter focuses on the progress poetry of James Thomson and James Beattie, two of the poets Radcliffe turns to most often, and suggests that their work provided Radcliffe with a map of civilization's development to set against her own heroine's journey.

Radcliffe and the Scottish Progress Poem

The story of Emily St. Aubert, the heroine of *The Mysteries of Udolpho*, fits uneasily within these debates over the nature of progress, creating an anomalous trajectory for which universal and progressive histories cannot account and suggesting the possibility of another emergent and non-linear feminist history that exists somewhere between the epigraphs and Radcliffe's diegesis. Throughout Radcliffe's novel, excerpts from popular gothic poetry are contrasted with Emily's encounters with unfamiliar sites and environments that represent various states of development. Emily travels from her father's estate, the pastoral La Vallée, to cosmopolitan Venice, and, finally, to the savage environment of Montoni's Udolpho. With the exception of La Vallée, she appears comfortable nowhere. For example, the practiced and polished songs of the

Venetian women Emily encounters are juxtaposed with Emily's taste for "the popular songs of her native province" and the "pathos and simplicity" with which she sings.[26] Likewise, while imprisoned at Udolpho, she is shocked by Montoni's rude and savage treatment of her aunt and his wife, Madame Montoni. Although Emily ultimately marries Valancourt, after his sojourn to the metropolitan Paris they no longer seem to be suitable companions. Emily's inability to acclimate to either the modern metropole or the rude and savage Italian countryside becomes ever clearer when her journey is set against the Scottish progress poems Radcliffe excerpts in the epigraphs of *Udolpho*'s chapters. However obscure or remote, the Scottish borderlands in Radcliffe's novels remain a powerful landscape through which her readers were invited to imagine an alternative to conventional understandings of progress.

Radcliffe's meditation on Emily's vexed relationship to established historical narratives becomes especially conspicuous in her use of two progress poems, Thomson's *The Castle of Indolence* and Beattie's *The Minstrel*. Typically, progress poems involve "an imaginary westward and northward journey of an allegorical entity such as Liberty," and "they trace the birth and historical manifestations of its subject from classical times to the present, conveniently ending in contemporary Britain, the last and therefore best model of civilization and government."[27] In the spirit of the progress poem, both Beattie's and Thomson's verse relates a truncated history of human development, beginning in a rude age located in some Scottish-inspired landscape and continuing to a more complex level of development. Treated ambivalently at best, progress in both poems fails to follow a teleological or linear path. *The Castle of Indolence* moves from an "underdeveloped" landscape with scenes drawn from the Scottish border of Thomson's youth as well as an imaginary Oriental landscape, to an account of the "Knight of Industry" who arrives to civilize this part-Celtic and part-Oriental land accompanied by a bard, a "little Druid Wight / Of withered aspect,"[28] whose "withered" appearance critics agree is a description of Alexander Pope (a curious representation of progress in and of itself). Similarly, in the Preface to *The Minstrel*, Beattie describes the poem as following "the progress of a Poetical Genius, born in a rude age, from the first dawning of fancy and reason, till that period at which he may be supposed capable of appearing in the world as a MINSTREL."[29] Yet the circuitous and gothic byways readers wander through in the Spenserian stanzas of *The Castle of Indolence* and *The Minstrel* contrast starkly with the neat and evenly-paced steps of the neoclassical heroic couplets used, for example, by Pope, "the Druid wight" who Thomson positions as the poet of industry and British moral progress. Beattie recognizes the mixed messages offered by "so difficult a measure," and describes the Spenserian stanzas as admitting "both simplicity and magnificence ... the sententiousness of the couplet, as well as the more complex modulation of blank verse."[30] Both simple and awe-inspiring, a vehicle for basic emotion and complex ideas, the Spenserian stanzas are capable of registering formally the poets' ambivalent perspectives on progress and development. Both poems stage the literary and historical debates surrounding the native gothic's place in British aesthetics and history and explore its role as either a corrective to a corrupt imperial present or a marker of Britons' progress, their acquired distance from gothic barbarity.

Although the protagonists of both poems are male, Harriet Guest and John Barrell have discussed the renewed interest of women writers in James Thomson, particularly Charlotte Smith, Frances Burney, and Mary Hays, arguing that Thomson became for women novelists "a resource and reference point in an increasingly politicized discussion of sentimentality, femininity, and domestic life."[31] For Radcliffe, Thomson's *Castle of Indolence* became a "reference point" for her own interrogation of the relationship between economic and historical progress and the progress of women. "A poet of Empire," Thomson, in his *Liberty* and *Britannia* and his *Castle of Indolence*, explored "historical and geographical explanations for the development and decline of empires, cultures, and civilizations – explanations that provide moral, economic, social, and political lessons for Britain at home and abroad."[32] Suvir Kaul, and to a greater extent Mary Jane Scott, see a Scotsman like Thomson as particularly sensitive to questions of empire and more apt to register and theorize "cultural anxiety" about Britain and its empire than his English counterparts.[33] Thomson's ambivalence about the growth of the British nation-state emerges throughout *The Castle of Indolence*, a two-canto poem that contrasts different perspectives on economic progress. The Knight of the second canto works to eradicate barbarism from his "chosen isle": "The work which long he in his breast had brewed / Now to perform he ardent did devise, / To wit, a barbarous world to civilize."[34] The Knight's bard composes songs on "the speaking strings" of his "British harp" to wake the castle's inhabitants from their indolent and wasted lives.[35] Together the Knight and his bard reveal the territory surrounding the castle to be "a joyless land of bogs."[36] The Knight's industry and the bard's art work to inspire in the citizenry a sense of civic duty. Yet all but one of Radcliffe's epigraphs from *The Castle of Indolence* come from the first canto, which takes a more complicated position on British industry and commerce and fails to reinforce the second canto's clearly articulated trajectory of development, instead expressing a deep and gothic ambivalence. Although we find the familiar warnings about the excesses of the corrupt East, exemplified in Thomson's accusation that the land of indolence delivers "dreams voluptuous, soft, and bland" that originate in an "Arabian heaven,"[37] we also find references to a simpler and native pastoral past, which critics have read as Thomson's description of his boyhood on the Scottish border. In mixing images of an indolent Eastern world and an innocent Scottish past, Thomson explores alternatives to a British modernity that both validate and critique the Knight's work in the second canto.

For example, Radcliffe prefaces the eleventh chapter of *Udolpho*'s third volume with one of Thomson's celebrations of his native Scotland.

> Of innocence, simplicity, and truth,
> To cares estranged, and manhood's thorny ways
> What transport to retrace our boyish plays,
> Our easy bliss, when each thing joy supplied –
> The woods, the mountains, and the warbling maze
> Of the wild brooks![38]

This scrap of poetry is followed by her description in the chapter of the rural retreat of two secondary characters, who have been read as doppelgangers for Emily and her father and function to figure Emily's loss. Like Emily and her father, the Count De Villefort and his daughter find much pleasure in their ancestral domain, which is far from the more sophisticated Paris.[39] Paratextual fragments like this one allow Radcliffe to celebrate retirement and contrast "the simple life" with the complexities of modern life, represented in the novel by Paris and Venice. The Count's celebration of his retirement seems to require his daughter to feel in a similar fashion. When they explore his estate, the "pleasure [that] danced in her eyes" contrasts sharply with the attitude of the Count's wife, whose refined tastes lead her to dislike the estate, which she continually refers to as this "barbarous spot."[40] In this instance, the Count's daughter's gaze sanctions his decision to retreat from the busy world.

If this were the only citation from Thomson's poem, the idea that Radcliffe purposely invoked the underdeveloped Scottish countryside as a reference point or gauge for measuring progress would seem tenuous at best; however, continued references to *The Castle of Indolence* indicate a conscious turn to a larger historical as well as literary framework for her heroine Emily's experiences. Each epigraph and chapter establishes a comparison between two different times and two different places. Excerpts from the first canto of *The Castle of Indolence* set the underdeveloped landscape surrounding Thomson's castle against the Italian countryside outside Udolpho. After Emily's aunt dies, Emily is taken from the castle and placed in a cottage outside its walls for the duration of an attack mounted by Montoni's enemies. Radcliffe begins the chapter on Emily's country sojourn with an epigraph taken from the beginning of the first canto:[41]

> Was nought around but images of rest,
> Sleep-soothing groves, and quiet lawns between,
> And flowery beds that slumberous influence kest,
> From poppies breath'd, and banks of pleasant green,
> Where never yet was creeping creature seen.
> Meantime unnumbered glittering streamlets play'd,
> And hurled every where their water's sheen,
> That as they bicker'd through the sunny glade,
> Though restless still themselves, a lulling murmur made.[42]

Radcliffe equates Emily's country respite from Montoni's tyranny to the peace and unproductive indolence enjoyed by the inhabitants of Thomson's castle. The comparison sets Emily's pastoral idyll outside the walls of Udolpho against the barbarous treatment she receives from Montoni while a prisoner in his Italian castle. Pastoral settings and their ambiguous placement between savagery and modernity offer women in *Udolpho* a respite from the harsh and patriarchal strictures found in rude environments, or the dangerous freedoms created by the economic forces of modernity. The chapter sets Emily's experiences alongside Thomson's conflicted representations of an underdeveloped landscape that borrows Scottish and Eastern elements, mixing images of innocence and nature with poppy-infused dreams that create a dangerous immobility. The epigraph expresses a deep ambivalence about Emily's desire to immerse herself in a pastoral retreat that seems like both a return to a simpler and innocent time, and an escape from the more pressing concerns of the moment.

Other allusions to this first canto and its account of alternatives to the Knight's celebration of progress and industry are more difficult to reconcile with the feelings and experiences of Radcliffe's heroines. Earlier in the novel, in a chapter describing the deferral of Emily and Valancourt's wedding, Radcliffe begins with an epigraph from Thomson's first canto that employs a curious simile, comparing the transformation of the Castle's inhabitants to a Scots shepherd's experience of the second sight. After being ushered into the Castle, the new arrivals are dressed and invited to cease laboring and "do what you will."[43] Soon after, the mass of people that enter magically disappear: "Strait of these endless numbers, swarming round / As thick as idle motes in sunny ray, / Not one eftsoons in view was to be found / But every man strolled off his own glad way."[44] Adding to the disorienting quality of this description, the shift from being among a swarm of people depicted as "idle motes" to isolation, where "Not one eftsoons in view was to be found," is compared to the shepherd's vision:

As when a shepherd of the Hebrid Isles,
Placed far amid the melancholy main,
(Whether it be long fancy him beguiles,
Or that aerial beings sometimes deign
To stand embodied to our sense plain)
Sees on that naked hill, or valley low,
The whilst in ocean Phoebus dips his wain,
A vast assembly moving to and fro;
Then all at once the air dissolves the wondrous show.[45]

According to the author of *A Description of the Western Islands* (1702), Martin Martin, who Mary Jane Scott suggests may have inspired Thomson's description,[46] the second sight allowed Scots to see spectral visions of the future in a material form. Thomson compares the descent of the castle's inhabitants into indolence and luxury, which are associated in the poem with the East, to the vision of a lone Scottish shepherd, who at a distance from his island home and lost on "the melancholy main" sees a vision of a future, depicting "A vast assembly moving to and fro." It is extremely difficult to understand this singular shepherd's vision of a future inhabited by this aimless assembly. Why compare the inhabitants of the castle to the Highland shepherd's vision of a wandering crowd? Could this shepherd's vision of the future hint that progress might result in a backwards descent into luxury and indolence, which appears from the distant perspective of the Hebridean shepherd a "vast assembly," part of a "wondrous show" – phrases that suggest a bustling and increasingly expansive commercial world? Whatever the case, the shepherd occupies a privileged position, able to perceive two realities and perhaps two stages of human development at a single time. Scotland becomes in *The Castle of Indolence* a conduit for the poem's own ambivalence about progress, a place where the past and future coexist and critique the present imperial orientation of the British nation-state. Emily's deferred wedding to Valancourt is likened to this ambiguous vision of the future. Literally "the wondrous show" that was to accompany their nuptials disappears, but the shepherd's vision also serves to remind readers that by not marrying Valancourt, Emily maintains a liminal role, between stages of development, able to see in multiple directions like the Highland shepherd of the epigraph. The paratextual quotations from Thomson's poem suggest that Emily's decided preference for retreat and her inability to assimilate comfortably into a range of environments that she experiences on her journey with Madam

Montoni can be read as part of a larger critique of women's placement in imperial and commercial narratives of British development.

Radcliffe's references to James Beattie's *The Minstrel* raise similar questions about Emily's ability to "progress" or find an orientation on existing historical maps. Maureen McLane in her recent survey of British minstrels examines the relationship between popular eighteenth-century minstrels and developing historical methodologies, arguing that minstrels, somewhere between "prehistoric" bards and "modern" ballad mongers were "liminal" figures who took up the "problematic of periodization."[47] McLane emphasizes the connections between Beattie and the Scottish Enlightenment's conjectural histories. Although best known as a critic of Humean skepticism, Beattie was educated in Aberdeen (like James Macpherson) and later was appointed as a professor of moral philosophy at Marischal College. As McLane argues, the intellectual milieu in which Beattie worked shapes the travels of Edwin, his minstrel. Like many of his Scottish counterparts, Beattie equates the development of the individual from birth to old age with the progress of the nation from "rude" hunting and gathering societies to a later period, in this case the Age of Minstrels – a courtly and, to borrow from Hurd, gothic stopping point preceding the contemporary age of commerce. Adam Ferguson uses a similar analogy in his account of civil society's development: "If, in advanced years, we would form a just notion of our progress from the cradle, we must have recourse to the nursery, and from the example of those who are still in the period of life we mean to describe, take our representation of past manners, that cannot, in any other way, be recalled."[48] By mixing gothic and Scottish Enlightenment tropes in his poem, Beattie interrogates the relationship between individual experience and the larger narrative of the nation. Like Emily, Edwin moves between stages of human development. Yet his trajectory, according to McLane, begins in a feminine and "rude age" in which he is nurtured by an "ancient dame" who uses "riddle's quaint device . . . [to cheer] the shepherds round their social hearth" and extends the masculine "threshold of Enlightenment announced by a severe hermit" who introduces Edwin to the "path of Science."[49] By labeling the early stages of history feminine and the later masculine, McLane deftly identifies one gendered trajectory of progress, but others operate within the poem.[50] Although, as McLane argues, Edwin does progress from his birthplace and the nurturing influence of the village's "beldam" to the "cultivated spot" of the hermit, Beattie dedicates his final revision of the poem in 1784 to his patron, greatest defender, and most critical reader, Elizabeth Montagu. At the end of the first canto, he associates the Bluestocking salonnière Montagu with the best of modernity:

But on this verse if Montague should smile,
New strains ere long shall animate thy frame.
And her applause to me is more than fame;
For still with truth accords her taste refined.
At lucre or renown let others aim,
I only wish to please the gentle mind
Whom Nature's charms inspire, and love of human kind.[51]

Instead of the vulgar trappings of "lucre" and "fame," Beattie aims to reach the "refined" tastes of Montagu, his ideal reader, who possesses the polished and modern manners necessary to appreciate good poetry. Montagu's destabilizing appearance introduces the possibility that the poem also traces a journey to a refined and feminine modernity as well as a passage into a masculine Enlightenment. The competing figures of the hermit, Montagu, and the "ancient dame" remind readers of the multiple eighteenth-century historical models that traced the competing and gendered histories of reason and feeling. Edwin's struggle with these different historical registers gestures toward the difficulty Emily has in projecting herself into any of the competing temporalities she encounters.

Frequently, references to *The Minstrel* and Edwin, who as McLane argues troubles the notion of historical "periodization," complement Emily's own troubled progress through a variety of environments. Beginning several of her chapters with epigraphs from *The Minstrel*, Radcliffe frames Emily's journey from rural France into her Italian prison, Udolpho, with the journey of Edwin to adulthood. The excerpts from *The Minstrel* indicate that Emily moves not just into adulthood but also between stages of development. When Emily's aunt, Madame Cheron, arrives to take Emily from her bucolic home and eventually through the more rugged terrain of Italy, the chapter epigraph taken from *The Minstrel* describes how the poet's perspective shifts once Edwin reaches adulthood. No longer will the poet dwell on the childhood haunts Edwin rambled through in Book I.

I leave that flowery path for aye
Of childhood, where I sported many a day,
Warbling and sauntering carelessly along;
Where every face was innocent and gay,
Each vale romantic, tuneful every tongue,
Sweet, wild, and artless all.[52]

After this stanza, Edwin moves into the more complex and rugged landscape of *The Minstrel*'s Book 2, found beyond a "lonely eminence" where as a young adult Edwin meets the enlightened hermit. Radcliffe selects this stanza to signal the journey into adulthood Emily is about to undertake from the pastoral La Vallée, her father's modest estate, into the refined and modern world of Madame Cheron's Tholouse, the luxurious world of Venice, and finally the savage landscape of Udolpho. In another instance, Radcliffe prefaces a chapter about Emily's journey into the Pyrenees, culminating with the death of her beloved father, with a description of Edwin's perceptions and appreciation of the landscape of his home, the rural "north countrie" or "Scotia":

> In truth he was a strange and wayward wight,
> Fond of each gentle, and each dreadful scene,
> In darkness, and in storm he found delight;
> Nor less than when on ocean-wave serene
> The southern sun diffuse'd his dazzling sheen.
> Even sad vicissitude amus'd his soul;
> And if a sigh would sometimes intervene,
> And down his cheek a tear of pity roll,
> A sigh, a tear, so sweet, he wish'd not to controul.[53]

Moving between historical periods, Emily and Edwin are both "wayward wight[s]," on a historical precipice, unable to find a foothold. Edwin's departure from his native village is, in part, prompted by his distaste for the rude sport and occupations of his companions:

> The exploit of strength, dexterity, or speed,
> To him nor vanity nor joy could bring.
> His heart, from cruel sport estranged, would bleed
> To work the woe of any living thing.
> By trap, or net; by arrow, or by sling;
> These he detested; those he scorn'd to wield:[54]

Edwin finds himself unable to practice the "cruel sport" demanded by the rude age of hunters and shepherds into which he was born. Likewise, Edwin holds himself "remote" from the "rude gambol" of the village dance, enjoying the music from afar.[55] Yet he also finds himself unable to embrace wholly the modern principles described by the hermit. Although he adopts the hermit's philosophical and scientific principles, he cannot abandon the fancy and poetry of his earlier life: "But she, who set on fire his infant heart, / And all his dreams, and all his wanderings shared . . . Still claim the enthusiast's fond and first regard."[56] Edwin's "wayward" qualities make him an unlikely hero for a poem that was supposed to end with his leading his people against an invading army and may, in part, account for its status as an unfinished fragment.[57] The poem's fragmentary status and Edwin's own inability to progress in a legible fashion comment on Emily's own retreat back to La Vallée at the end of the novel. Instead of progress, Radcliffe's gothic historiography appears more interested in restoration, return, and retreat.

Like Edward, Emily shuttles between purportedly simple and more complex stages of human development. She experiences the unevenness of time, beginning in the pastoral French countryside, traveling through excessively polite and cosmopolitan cities in France and Italy, and stopping periodically at the brutal fortress of Udolpho. At the end of the novel, when she inherits the domains of her father, Madame Cheron, and Montoni, she finds herself the legatee of all these stages of development or competing temporalities. Yet, with the exception of her pastoral retreat, she remains comfortable nowhere. Emily belongs to neither a modern feminine world that links luxury, refinement, and commercial expansion to the progress of women, nor a hyper-masculine "savage" world of barely disguised passion and brutal feeling. She insists on enjoying the simple pleasures of rural life at La Vallée, a pastoral space separate from the cosmopolitan centers of commerce and equally distant from the barbarism of Udolpho.

From Paratext to Text: Rereading *The Mysteries of Udolpho*

Radcliffe's citations of Thomson and Beattie's accounts of civilization's progress suggest that her novel and her gothic aesthetic participate in Enlightenment discussions of women, gender, and the mapping of progress. In fact, Emily appears to be caught between warring historical forces, which are embodied by the men and women she encounters throughout the novel. She meets a range of male types: some resemble the militant premodern warriors celebrated by Ferguson, others the chivalrous knights of Hurd's gothic, or the feeling men of Kames and Millar's modern commercial society. She also meets women who possess affected and refined modern manners that repulse her and others who claim savage passions that frighten her. Unlike the men or women she meets, Emily fails to fit into existing schemas of development. Although obviously a civilizing force, she combines modern and refined sentiments with the self-command and stoicism more appropriate to a premodern society.

She does not belong to the savage world of Montoni, the villain of Udolpho. His high passions run without restraint, unregulated by the women surrounding him. He regards women as his inferiors, property to be abandoned in drafty turrets. At one point, he condemns the emerging and modern rule of women, calling his friend and Emily's admirer, Count Morano, "the slave of a petty tyrant" when he pleads for Emily's comfort.[58] Yet, far from epitomizing a modern and feminine civil realm,

Emily remains equally distant from the world of refined feeling embodied by her father St. Aubert and her lover Valancourt, whose emotions lack the measured restraint exhibited by the less demonstrative and more stoic Emily. In the context of Scottish Enlightenment historiography, St. Aubert and Valancourt appear to be effeminate and overindulgent moderns, not – as in Claudia Johnson's reading – throwbacks to Edmund Burke's romantic and chivalric British past. Although St. Aubert educates Emily to suppress her emotions and maintain "fortitude" in the face of disaster, he appears unable to control his own feelings. During Emily's first test, the death of her mother, she "felt the importance of the lessons, which had taught her to restrain her sensibility . . . never had she practised them with a triumph so complete."[59] Emily's victory over grief stands in stark contrast to the reaction of St. Aubert, who frequently has to leave his wife's bedside to "indulge his tears."[60] Emily's restraint and ability to control her emotions also serve to emphasize Valancourt's overindulgence. When Emily tells Valancourt she must leave him for Italy, ending their engagement, he finds himself unable to control his passions. The novel describes him as emotionally imbalanced: "Valancourt, between these emotions of love and pity, lost the power, and almost the wish, of repressing his agitation; and, in the intervals of convulsive sobs, he, at one moment, kissed away her tears, then told her cruelly, that possibly she might never again weep for him."[61] Valancourt's extreme grief culminates in misplaced accusations. Unmoved by Emily's efforts to restrain her grief, he says, "Emily! . . . this, this moment is the bitterest that is yet come to me. You do not – cannot love me! – It would be impossible for you to reason thus coolly, thus deliberately, if you did."[62] Throughout the novel, Valancourt overemotes, and his reactions are without fail disproportionate to the occasion. After being reunited with Emily and hearing about her harrowing imprisonment at the hands of Montoni, Valancourt, "no longer master of his emotions," elevates his period of suffering[63] – the time he spent gambling in Parisian salons – above Emily's ordeal. Instead of greeting Emily with apologies and sympathy, he accuses her of being too frigid: "is it thus you meet him, whom once you meant to honour with your hand – thus you meet him, who has loved you – suffered for you?"[64] Valancourt overvalues his experience in the casinos of Paris and undervalues Emily's time away from him, during which she suffered under the constant threat of rape, the death of her closest living relative, and a near shipwreck. Here, Valancourt's behavior realizes Adam Ferguson's greatest fears: he forgoes the honors he might have won on the battlefield after enlisting in the French army for "tedious employment" and dissipation. Valancourt's decided preference for wandering aimlessly through the scenic Alps or gambling in

Paris, instead of serving Emily or his country, emerges as a symptom of social decay or progress run amuck.

Valancourt's overindulgence contrasts sharply with Montoni's excessive restraint. Montoni's self-discipline at times resembles the stoicism Adam Smith in his *Theory of Moral Sentiments* attributes to and admires in those he designates "savages." In his discussion of custom and fashion, Smith compares the open and transparent emotions of civilized men like Valancourt with those of men who belong to an earlier age. He writes, "The passions of a savage . . . though they never express themselves by any outward emotion, but lie concealed in the breast of the sufferer, are, notwithstanding, all mounted to the highest pitch of fury."[65] Although Montoni is often described as a barely contained volcano, Emily observes and reluctantly admires his talent for disguising his true emotions, beginning with his feigned attraction to her aunt Madam Cheron and extending to his fearless battles to defend Udolpho from neighboring warlords:

> She could scarcely have imagined, that passions so fierce and so various, as those which Montoni exhibited, could have been concentrated in one individual; yet what more surprised her, was that, on great occasions, he could bend these passions, wild as they were, to the cause of interest, and generally could disguise in his countenance their operation in his mind; but she had seen him too often, when he had thought it unnecessary to conceal his nature, to be deceived on such occasions.[66]

Montoni's talent for what Adam Smith praises as "self-command," which enables him to "disguise" his passions, coexists with the "sort of animal ferocity" and determination he exhibits as the captain of the condottieri.[67] As a "stranger to pity and fear," Montoni,[68] unlike Valancourt and St. Aubert, finds no value in the polish, refinement, and humanity that women were believed to introduce into society. As Smith writes in his *Theory of Moral Sentiments*, "the weakness of love, which is so much indulged in ages of humanity and politeness, is regarded among savages as the most unpardonable effeminacy."[69] To Emily, Montoni's "savage" features make him appear like a relic from a previous age. In fact, when exploring the ancient chambers of Udolpho with her maid Annette, Emily comes across a picture of "a soldier on horseback in a field of battle . . . darting his spear upon a man, who lay under the feet of the horse, and who held up one hand in a supplicating attitude."[70] The look of vengeance in the spear-wielding soldier's eye "struck Emily as resembling Montoni."[71] Despite Montoni's barbarism, Emily finds herself admiring him: "Emily felt admiration, but not the admiration that leads to esteem; for it was mixed with a degree of fear she knew not exactly wherefore."[72] Part of Emily's admiration for Montoni stems from their shared stoicism, their ability to exercise self-command and restrain emotion under extreme circumstances.[73] The unnamed "fear" that accompanies her admiration for Montoni may register a suspicion that they are more alike than it at first seems. Montoni himself confirms this suspicion. During a conversation in which he fruitlessly attempts to force Emily to cede her inheritance from her aunt to him, Montoni says, "I am not in the habit of flattering, and you will, therefore, receive, as sincere, the praise I bestow, when I say, that you possess an understanding superior to that of your sex; and that you have none of those contemptible foibles, that frequently mark the female character – such as avarice and the love of power, which latter makes women delight to contradict and to tease, when they cannot conquer."[74] Emily's "superior understanding" allows her to control her passions, and she appears to be without the "avarice" and lust for "power" that marks modern women, who pursue luxury and self-interest.

Despite her uncanny similarities to Montoni, the male character with whom Emily most closely corresponds is the chivalrous Chevalier Du Pont. She meets Du Pont while in prison in Udolpho. Often read as a doppelganger for Valancourt, Du Pont remains by Emily's side and aids in her escape from Udolpho while Valancourt falls prey to the temptations of Paris. Significantly, throughout the novel Du Pont is associated with the music of Ossian, which continually wafts through the text from distant and unnamed sources. Emily recognizes the Chevalier's song not as a portion of Macpherson's Highland epic but her own native music. Emily hears this music after she refuses to sign over her estates to Montoni. While contemplating the various means by which Montoni might choose to punish her, the only comforts she receives are the "notes of distant music" which float into her chamber from a mysterious source:

> In a few moments, their soft melody was accompanied by a voice so full of pathos, that it evidently sang not of imaginary sorrows. Its sweet and peculiar tones she thought she had somewhere heard before; yet, if this was not fancy, it was, at most, a very faint recollection. It stole over her mind, amidst the anguish of her present suffering like a celestial strain, soothing, and reassuring her; – "Pleasant as the gale of spring, that sighs on the hunter's ear, when he awakens from dreams of joy, and has heard the music of the spirits of the hill."[75]

Although Radcliffe identifies these lines in a footnote as a piece of Ossian's most famous epic *Fingal*, Emily renames this song as "one of the popular airs of her native province, to which she had so often listened with delight, when a child, and which she had so often heard her father repeat! To this well-known song, never, till now, heard but in her native country, her heart melted, while the memory of past times returned."[76] In this moment, Emily displaces this Ossianic lament from the Scottish Highlands to medieval Gascony, from a Scottish warrior culture to her father's provincial retreat, his escape from a corrupt and overly refined modern world.

At first, Emily believes Valancourt to be the source of this song. She imagines her beloved Valancourt imprisoned in Montoni's dungeon as a soldier of the French army, instead of (as he is in reality) enjoying a life of dissipation, gambling in Parisian salons and falling under the sway of sophisticated salonnières. Eventually, the source of the music reveals itself as not Valancourt but Du Pont, another young Frenchman who lived near Emily's birthplace, La Vallée, and has long admired her from afar. Although she encountered Du Pont and his mysterious music at La Vallée well before she met Valancourt, she finds herself bound by her promises to Valancourt and unable to accept his attentions. She does agree to escape with Du Pont from Udolpho to France, where she finds shelter with the Count De Villefort and his family. The chivalrous and attentive Du Pont, unlike Valancourt, emerges as a suitable companion for Emily. Instead of lamenting volubly and frequently after Emily rejects him, he enjoys a "deep, but silent melancholy."[77] The Count De Villefort, who becomes Emily's surrogate father, calls Du Pont "a sensible and amiable man."[78] Finally, when Du Pont discovers through a mutual friend that Valancourt's Parisian debauches were not ignominious enough to bar him from accepting Emily's hand, he acts in a disinterested fashion. He tells the Count and Emily of the mistake, restoring his rival's good character and gracefully leaves the novel and Emily without any of Valancourt's hysterics. Readers cannot help but imagine the more peaceful life Emily might have led with the more restrained and like-minded Du Pont, whose sentiments more closely correspond with Emily's own feelings. He remains an Ossianic future-history unfulfilled, a chivalrous knight similar to the ones described by Hurd. Despite his pitch-perfect gothic manners, Du Pont remains curiously out of place. Like the Celtic epigraphs outside the narrative frame, Du Pont points to an alternative narrative or history outside the existing text, which concludes with Emily's marriage to the suspect Valancourt. Du Pont's balanced behavior seems to have no place in the novel's polarizing narrative of civilization, which runs from savage to modern, the masculine Montoni to the much more feminine Valancourt.

Uncomfortable with the luxurious trappings of a feminine and refined modernity, in possession of stoic tendencies yet critical of savage passions, Radcliffe's Emily complicates linear history and the gendered categories imposed on changing human and economic relationships.

Throughout the novel, Emily appears caught between these extremes of human development represented by Montoni and Valancourt – between times, as well as between men. She feels deeply like Valancourt, but exercises a restraint and stoicism associated with Montoni's more "savage" disposition. Despite St. Aubert's own refined sentiments, his education of Emily resembles the Spartan-like training in the suppression of emotion admired by Adam Ferguson, who praises the mothers of the barbarian tribes of Europe who killed their children before being overtaken by the Romans because they "preferred death to captivity."[79] Although the emotional St. Aubert would be incapable of exhibiting a similar sort of self-control, he trains Emily to have the fortitude to withstand adverse circumstances: "He endeavoured, therefore, to strengthen her mind; to enure her to habits of self-command; to teach her to reject the first impulse of her feelings, and to look, with cool examination, upon the disappointments he sometimes threw in her way."[80] With the notable exception of Du Pont, Emily's "self-command" combined with her ability to empathize yet not selfishly over-identify with her fellow humans sets her apart from the other characters in the novel. In opposition to Valancourt, who suffers so demonstrably, "Hers was a silent anguish, weeping, yet enduring; not the wild energy of passion, inflaming imagination, bearing down the barriers of reason and living in a world of its own."[81] Unlike Valancourt and Montoni, Emily also remains mindful of her place in the world and her connection to other people: "The sufferings of others, whoever they might be, called forth her ready compassion, which dissipated at once every obscuring cloud of goodness, that passion or prejudice might have raised in her mind."[82] She troubles the possibility of universal history, a certain map of progress, by belonging to neither commercial society nor the savage world. Like the Celtic bards found on the peripheries of Radcliffe's novel, Emily survives her parents and two infant brothers and becomes an anomaly, the last of her race.

Emily also appears anomalous when compared with many of the other women in the novel, and her interactions with women invite readers to mediate on how women are represented and positioned within narratives of progress. She fails to perform the "excessive refinement" of the Venetian women she encounters.[83] Their "by turns tender, sentimental and gay" manners charm Emily but appear to be more of an artful affectation than a product of genuine feeling.[84] Likewise, the modern and cosmopolitan habits of the Countess De Villefort seem light years away from Emily's simple and native charms. The Countess, instead of playing native songs on a lute or enjoying the simple pleasure of nature like Emily, reads "sentimental novel[s] on some fashionable system of philosophy."[85] The Countess prefers fiction to reality, affecting "an elegant languor, that persuaded her almost to faint, when her favourite reads to her a story of fictitious sorrow; but her countenance suffered no change, when living objects of distress solicited her charity."[86] Although Emily also appreciates literature and writes poetry, her literary pursuits complement and encourage charitable actions. Emily's visits to the poor of her father's home, La Vallée, exhibit an anachronistic sensitivity to actual suffering impossible to duplicate in the modern, contrived, and escapist world of the Countess. Here Emily seems to follow Ferguson's dictates in regards to literature: "the human mind could not suffer more from a contempt of letters, than it does from the false importance which is given to literature, as a business of life, not as a help to our conduct."[87] On the other hand, Emily appears to be equally distant from the too passionate, almost "savage" Laurentini, whose affair a generation earlier with the Marquis De Villefort and role in the poisoning of Emily's aunt the Marquess recall to Emily's maid Annette's mind the "great passions" of the savage Montoni.[88]

References to Celtic histories and literature are also used within the novel's diegesis to reinforce Emily's historically anomalous position and to craft a women's history that challenges the gender binaries used to organize narratives of historical development and the reductive savage and civilized categories in which many of the novel's characters are placed. The novel's diegesis repeatedly puts women's history in dialogue with sympathetic portrayals of the "underdeveloped" Celtic peripheries, which, like the Ossian poems, trouble conventional historical schemas. For example, Radcliffe quotes Celtic-inspired poetry in relation to Madame Montoni's suffering, giving it a national and political, instead of a strictly domestic, import. Upon departing Udolpho for the pastoral cottage in which Montoni intends to shield her from the upcoming battles at the castle, Emily recalls Thomas Gray's poem "The Bard" and uses it as a lens through which to understand the crimes against her, her aunt, and Laurentini that have occurred within the castle. When placed outside the context of Radcliffe's gothic, "The Bard" is unconcerned with the domestic realm and the plight of oppressed wives like Madame Montoni. It celebrates Welsh tradition and examines the purported slaying of the Welsh bards by Edward I as characteristic of England's relationship to its Celtic periphery. Yet Emily quotes from Gray's poem when describing Montoni's crimes against women: "With many a foul, and midnight murder stain'd."[89] In this moment, she associates the Welsh Bard's description of the Tower of London and the many national crimes it has concealed to domestic tyranny and the abandoned turret in which Emily's aunt is imprisoned. In doing so, she likens this tainted

English history to Madame Montoni's imprisonment and the suspicious circumstances surrounding the disappearance of the castle's former owner, Laurentini, whom Emily imagines was also slain by Montoni. The bard's description of the Tower comes within a catalogue of English crimes the Welsh bard relates before he plunges to his death. By suturing Madame Montoni's death to "The Bard," Montoni's domestic tyranny is folded into a long list of English crimes, particularly English violence against the Celtic peripheries. By pairing "The Bard" with the suffering of Madame Montoni, Radcliffe indicates that the darker side of the domestic realm might be likened to the repressed histories of the Celtic peripheries and the underexamined costs of imperial progress.

The epigraph to Chapter 10 of the second volume of *Udolpho*, which details Montoni's imprisonment of his wife, reinforces this alternative reading of Madame Montoni and draws greater attention to Radcliffe's use of "The Bard" within the chapter. The epigraph from Frank Sayers's play *Moina: A Tragedy* makes Madame Montoni into much more than an ill-mannered and self-serving guardian. Significantly, Sayers's play is based on the Ossianic poem "Carthon" and was published in his *Dramatic Sketches of Ancient Northern Mythology* (1790). "Carthon" details the forced marriage of Moina to one of Fingal's ancestors, Clessammor. Soon after marrying Moina, Clessammor is killed by her lover Reuda, and Moina dies not long after in childbirth. Sayers recasts Moina's story as a conflict between the Saxons and the Irish. In his version, Moina is forced to marry Harold, the Saxon conqueror of her Irish people. Her lover, the bard Carril, enters Harold's castle in disguise to save his beloved. Fortuitously for the lovers, Harold dies in battle. But just before Moina and Carril are about to leave for Ireland, the Saxons bury Moina alive with Harold's corpse to satisfy the brutal desires of their gods. Carril arrives too late, only to find Moina dead. Although Madame Montoni's story and Moina's are vastly different, both women are imprisoned by men they hate and made to suffer. Radcliffe quotes the chorus of bards' lament for Moina at the beginning of the chapter: "And shall no lay of death / With pleasing murmur soothe / Her parted soul? / Shall no tear wet her grave?"[90] The chorus of bards within the play fears that Moina, buried in a foreign country, will have no one to mourn over her. Madame Montoni, removed from her native France, imprisoned, and then buried in the lawless Italian countryside, shares a similar fate. Before, Madame Montoni's "coarseness and selfishness" marked her as an unrefined villain. The Ossianic valence ennobles Emily's aunt, who dies in a foreign land to preserve her estates for her niece. Between the epigraph and the narrative proper, another portrait of Madame Montoni emerges – a suggestion that her story might look differently in another historical framework, one which attends more carefully not just to the manners of women, but also to the social and economic forces that keep them on the peripheries of society, as instruments or measures of change instead of historical actors who freely control property and finances. Although Madame Montoni's suffering results from Montoni's savage behavior, the novel's turn to Celtic poetry to explain her difficult circumstances aligns anomalous Celtic histories with Radcliffe's women's history. Radcliffe's novel suggests that women's history like the Celtic histories recreated by Macpherson and Gray complicates the progressive narrative of the British state.

Ultimately, exploring Radcliffe's debt to Celtic literature and Scottish philosophy as well as attending to the overlooked paratextual borders of her novels decenters traditional feminist readings of the female gothic. Beginning with Ellen Moers, feminist critics have productively interpreted Radcliffe's novels as critiques of patriarchy and expressions of women's frustrations with the domestic realm.[91] Attention to Radcliffe's paratext draws attention away from an insular domestic realm and generates new potential questions about the relationship between feminist, Marxist, and postcolonial treatments of history and temporality. Radcliffe critiques the gendered gauges used to manufacture history, and in doing so interrogates the relationship between a society's mode of production and the progress of women. Her fiction refuses universalizing and reductive claims about women's progress and poses an alternative to the rhetoric of imperial expansion, which often characterized the British Empire as not only transforming territories economically but also freeing women from the savage bonds of oppression. Through Emily, Radcliffe fashions a feminist historiography that refuses a universal or linear narrative of progress that relies upon clearly gendered poles of development and denies the dependence of developed sentiments on economic progress. This feminist theory of history found in novels like *The Mysteries of Udolpho* may have influenced the development of the gothic aesthetic, a genre of doppelgangers, split selves, and unexpected repetitions, which mirrors on the individual and psychological level the uneven narrative of history, the refusal of linear and universal maps of human experience, that Radcliffe found in her Celtic sources.

Notes

1. Deidre Lynch, "Gothic Libraries and National Subjects"; E. J. Clery, *Women's Gothic* (Horndon: Northcote House, 2000); see also Janine Barchas, *Graphic Design, Print Culture, and the Eighteenth-Century Novel*

(Cambridge: Cambridge University Press, 2003), which argues that in novels, epigraphs (particularly those in the vernacular) were scarce before Radcliffe's gothic novels.

2. Gerard Genette, *Paratexts*, pp. 1–2.
3. Richard Norton, *The Mistress of Udolpho*, p. 133.
4. William Warner, *Licensing Entertainment*, p. 279.
5. Walter Scott, *Lives of the Novelists*, p. 305.
6. See, for example, Ronald Paulson's classic study, *Representations of Revolution* (New Haven, CT: Yale University Press, 1983).
7. Christine Gerrard, *The Patriot Opposition to Walpole*, p. 105.
8. Ibid., p. 112.
9. Gerrard details Prince Frederick's patronage of James Thomson and the rewards Thomson received for his explicitly "loyal poems," such as *Liberty* and "Ode to His Royal Highness" (p. 63). Beattie's and Macpherson's connections to the Patriot Opposition are less overt; however, as active members of later eighteenth-century Bluestocking salons, they met and were likely influenced by members of the Patriot Opposition, including Elizabeth Montagu's close friends Lord Lyttelton and Lord Bath (William Pulteney). Both Bath and Lyttelton were leaders of the opposition to Robert Walpole, and later in life were regulars at Montagu's Bluestocking salons. They corresponded extensively with Montagu about literature, art, and politics. Notably, both politicians took a particular interest in the Ossian poems.
10. See Samuel Kliger, *Goths in England* (New York: Octagon Books, 1972) for a discussion of the political import of the gothic during the seventeenth and early eighteenth centuries. See also Colin Kidd, *Subverting Scotland's Past* for a discussion of the Ossian poems' contribution to consolidating British national sentiment and the poems' function as a template for native British liberty.
11. Claudia Johnson, *Equivocal Beings*, pp. 95–116.
12. Genette, *Paratexts*, p. 160.
13. Terry Castle, *The Female Thermometer*; E. J. Clery, *The Rise of Supernatural Fiction*.
14. See Adam Smith, *Theory of Moral Sentiments*, for a quotation from *Seasons* ("Winter") and for a quotation from Gray's "Epitaph on Mrs. Clarke," pp. 161 and 165; see also Smith, *Lectures on Rhetoric and Belles Lettres*, pp. 31, 56, and 71, for further quotations from Thomson's poetry, and pp. 127 and 230 for further quotations from Gray.
15. Richard Hurd, *Letters on Chivalry and Romance*; Hurd's treatise closely followed the publication of Ossian and, like the Caledonian poems, has been linked to a renewed interest in the genealogy of British character. See Juliet Shields, *Sentimental Literature and Anglo-Scottish Identity, 1745–1820* for a relevant discussion of the Ossian poems' role in creating "the nation as a sentimental community" (p. 44).
16. Hurd, *Letters*, p. 109.
17. Ibid., p. 61.
18. Ibid., p. 109.
19. Ibid., p. 11.
20. Ibid., p. 17.

21. Ibid., p. 12.
22. Scott, *Lives of the Novelists*, p. 322.
23. Adam Ferguson, *Essay on Civil Society*, pp. 241–2.
24. Ann Radcliffe, *The Castles of Athlin and Dunbayne*, pp. 7, 39, and 4.
25. Ibid., p. 44.
26. Ann Radcliffe, *The Mysteries of Udolpho*, p. 185.
27. William Levine, "Collins, Thomson, and the Whig Progress of Liberty," p. 554.
28. James Thomson, *The Seasons, The Castle of Indolence, and Other Poems*: *Castle of Indolence*, I.xxxiii. All subsequent citations of *The Castle of Indolence* will rely on this edition and cite the canto and stanza numbers.
29. James Beattie, *The Minstrel* (1784), p. xi. Subsequent citations of *The Minstrel* will rely on this edition and cite canto and stanza numbers when referring to the poem.
30. *The Minstrel*, p. xii.
31. John Barrell and Harriet Guest, "Thomson in the 1790s," p. 218.
32. Suvir Kaul, *Poems of Nation, Anthems of Empire*, p. 134.
33. Ibid., p. 2; see also Mary Jane Scott, *James Thomson, Anglo-Scot*.
34. *Castle of Indolence*, II.xiv.
35. Ibid., II.xlvi.
36. Ibid., II.lxxviii.
37. Ibid., I.xlv.
38. Ibid., I.xlviii.
39. Radcliffe, *Udolpho*, p. 475.
40. Ibid., p. 475.
41. Ibid., p. 413.
42. *Castle of Indolence*, I.iii.
43. Ibid., I.xxviii.
44. Ibid., I.xxxix.
45. Ibid., I.xxx.
46. Scott, *James Thomson*, p. 261.
47. Maureen McLane, *Balladeering, Minstrelsy, and the Making of British Romantic Poetry*, p. 434.
48. Ferguson, *Essay on Civil Society*, p. 80.
49. McLane, *Balladeering*, p. 435.
50. See also Maureen McLane, "Dating, Orality, Thinking Balladry." In her essay, McLane reads the "ancient dame" of *The Minstrel*'s Book 1 as a figure for a feminine and oral tradition historicized by antiquarians and ballad collectors. McLane's article argues that the poem stages written history's attempt to relegate a feminine oral culture to a distant past.
51. *The Minstrel*, I.lx.
52. Ibid., II.iii.
53. Ibid., I:xxii.
54. Ibid., I.xviii.
55. Ibid., I.lv.
56. Ibid., II.lviii.
57. See Roger Robinson, "The Origins and Composition of James Beattie's *Minstrel*."
58. Radcliffe, *Udolpho*, p. 200.

59. Ibid., p. 19.
60. Ibid., p. 19.
61. Ibid., p. 154.
62. Ibid., p. 158.
63. Ibid., p. 625.
64. Ibid., p. 625.
65. Smith, *Theory of Moral Sentiments*, p. 302.
66. Radcliffe, *Udolpho*, p. 296.
67. Ibid., p. 358.
68. Ibid., p. 358.
69. Smith, *Theory of Moral Sentiments*, p. 298.
70. Radcliffe, *Udolpho*, p. 232.
71. Ibid., p. 233.
72. Ibid., p. 122.
73. On the relationship between "savage" stoicism and Smith's impartial spectator, see Maureen Harkin, "Adam Smith's Missing History."
74. Radcliffe, *Udolpho*, p. 380.
75. Ibid., p. 386.
76. Ibid., p. 386.
77. Ibid., p. 493.
78. Ibid., p. 565.
79. Ferguson, *Essay on Civil Society*, p. 105.
80. Radcliffe, *Udolpho*, p. 5.
81. Ibid., p. 329.
82. Ibid., p. 279.
83. Ibid., p. 188.
84. Ibid., p. 188.
85. Ibid., p. 476.
86. Ibid., p. 500.
87. Ferguson, *Essay on Civil Society*, p. 34.
88. Radcliffe, *Udolpho*, p. 237.
89. Ibid., p. 407.
90. Ibid., p. 310.
91. Ellen Moers, *Literary Women*, pp. 90–110. Moers's study defined "the female gothic" as a genre that dramatizes women's imprisonment in the domestic realm. Since Moers's study, several critics have developed and enriched her initial claims. See also Kate Ferguson Ellis, *The Contested Castle* and Diane Hoeveler, *Gothic Feminism*.

Chapter 5

Stadial Fiction or the Progress of Taste

Reviewers of Romantic-era novels often cited lack of verisimilitude, particularly in novels written by women, as a major failing. In a review of the Irish novelist Regina Maria Roche's *The Maid of the Hamlet* (1794), a writer for the *British Catalogue* complained that, "The conduct of this Novel is not upon the whole happily managed; the rules of connection and verisimilitude are not sufficiently adhered to: the narrative is too frequently broken, and probability too grossly violated."[1] In addition to "broken" plots that play fast and loose with "the rules of connection," Romantic heroines often possess unimpeachably exquisite tastes and manners; paradoxically, they are reared in rural isolation, far from the bustling modern world in which taste and manners are cultivated. For instance, the heroine of *Maid of the Hamlet*, the beautiful orphan Matilda, although "educated in retirement," was "brought up in elegance," "easily instructed in every accomplishment," and "to these accomplishments [she] united a graceful demeanour and insinuative address."[2] Characters like Matilda act as precursors to more celebrated and familiar Romantic heroines, such as Glorvina from Sydney Owenson's *The Wild Irish Girl* (1806), who possess polished manners and sentiments that appear at odds with the rural landscapes and the ruined or impoverished habitations they occupy. Out of place and often anachronistic, Romantic heroines violate "probability"; although reviewers saw many of these novels and heroines as aesthetically flawed, this chapter argues that these improbable plots and heroines can also be read as figures for the progress of taste, a progress which unfolds as these heroines travel through a variety of social and economic environments.

The central figure of Regina Maria Roche's widely popular *The Children of the Abbey* (1796), Amanda Malvina Fitzalan – whose middle name recalls the most famous female bard of the Ossian poems – typifies the incongruities that mark such heroines. When Lord Mortimer – Amanda Malvina's soon-to-be suitor – discovers her in rural Wales, he is amazed that an inhabitant of one of the rustic "cottage[s]" near his estate could command such refined sensibilities.[3] He sends Howel, the local curate, to explore "the real situation of Amanda,"[4] and her developed tastes instantly enchant the minister:

> The objects about them naturally led to rural subjects, and from them to what might almost be termed a dissertation on poetry... she was a zealous worshipper of the muses, though diffidence made her conceal her invocations to them. She was led to point out the beauties of her favorite authors, and the soft sensibility of her voice raised a kind of tender enthusiasm in Howel's soul; he gazed and listened, as if his eye could never be satisfied with seeing, or his ear with hearing. At his particular request, Amanda recited the pathetic description of the curate and his lovely daughter from the "Deserted Village" – a tear stole down her cheek as she proceeded. Howel softly laid his hand on hers, and exclaimed, "Good heavens, what an angel!"[5]

Their conversation, which becomes a "dissertation on poetry," reveals Amanda to be familiar with a full range of British authors, and she proves herself capable not only of apprehending but also profess-ing divine beauty in her critical commentary and brief recitation of Goldsmith. Lord Mortimer's description of Amanda a few pages later transforms her from an ideal percipient of taste and beauty to an ideal object of aesthetic appreciation:

> Lord Mortimer regarded her with a degree of tender admiration; an admira-tion heightened by the contrast he drew in his mind between her and the gen-erality of fashionable women he had seen, whom he often secretly censured for sacrificing too largely at the shrine of art and fashion. The pale and varied blush which mantled the cheek of Amanda at once announced itself to be an involuntary suffusion; and her dress was only remarkable for its simplicity; she wore a plain robe of dimity, and an abbey cap of thin muslin, that shaded, without concealing, her face, and gave to it the soft expression of a Madonna; her beautiful hair fell in long ringlets down her back, and curled upon her forehead.[6]

Admittedly, Amanda's "tender" poetry recitations and natural "Madonna-like" beauty can wear thin on readers who are looking for a rounder character. A reviewer for the *British Catalogue* cited Amanda's "too romantic" character as the only flaw in a novel other-wise "very entertaining and well-written."[7] Amanda's status as both an ideal observer and object of aesthetic appreciation cannot help but make her seem out of place in the world she inhabits. Typically, critics read Romantic-era heroines such as Amanda Malvina as a byway in the novel's development, a gothic throwback to the romances of earlier periods or a less fully realized version of the domestic heroines featured in Mary Poovey's and Nancy Armstrong's classic studies.[8] Instead of seeing these fictions as failures or footnotes within larger narratives of the novel's development, this chapter looks at these fictions in the context of Romantic aesthetics, particularly as efforts to imagine what Scottish aesthetic theorists called a "progress of the arts." In this context, the Romantic-era heroines of Roche and her contemporaries appear as aesthetic ideals or, to borrow from Hume, "standard[s] of taste," which are developed and tested in these fictions through the encounters of heroines such as Amanda Malvina with the "particular manners and opinions" of representative cultures and stages of development.[9]

Like much Romantic-era fiction, as Fiona Price has argued, Roche's work fits uneasily into conventional discussions of Romantic aesthetics,[10] which usually revolve around Immanuel Kant, Edmund Burke, and the canonical poetry of the period. When placed in the context of Scottish aesthetic theory, the typical Romantic-era heroine reads as figuring standards of beauty, delicacy, and manners. These standards emerged through comparing aesthetic preferences and practices from a number of economic and social environments and extracting from these comparisons general principles. Roche's potential contribution to the aesthetic theory of the period gains additional credence when her work is set against another Irish contemporary, Maria Edgeworth. Although Caroline Percy, the English heroine in Edgeworth's *Patronage* (1814), appears superficially to have little in common with Amanda Malvina, both heroines embody an aesthetic ideal of unattainable and improbable perfection that has troubled readers. Rosamond, Caroline's sister, acknowledges Caroline's irksome perfections when she compares her sibling to the average heroine: "you shall not be my heroine; you are too well proportioned for a heroine – in mind, I mean: a heroine may – must have a finely proportioned person, but never a well-proportioned mind. All her virtues must be larger than life; all her passions those of a tragedy queen."[11] Rosamond's comments participate in a meta-commentary on the contemporary novel and point to Caroline's failures as a fictional character. Significantly, Caroline's perfect physical and mental "proportions" resemble the body and mind of Amanda Malvina. Both Caroline and Amanda Malvina (who, although a master of her perfectly tuned sentiments, is never a fashionable "tragedy queen") possess simple tastes and work to restrain their passions. Their "finely proportioned" exteriors mimic the regular "proportions" of their intellects. Despite the unfitness of Caroline's temper for the role of heroine and Amanda Malvina's refusals to respond as passionately as the improbable circumstances that surround her seem to dictate, Edgeworth and Roche use their finely tuned sensibilities to measure various regional and national sensibilities against the universal standard of perfection these heroines embody.

Roche's and Edgeworth's novels invite readers to question the particular aesthetic sensibilities associated with the various economic and social environments contained within the British archipelago and sometimes – as in the case of Edgeworth's West Indian-themed *Belinda* – the larger British Empire. Amanda Malvina travels throughout the British Isles, from the pastoral landscape of rural Wales to London's Portman Square. Although *Patronage*'s Caroline Percy remains in England, she assesses the merits of a variety of suitors, who embody English, French, and continental tastes. In Edgeworth's *The Absentee*, Grace Nugent moves between London and the Irish periphery assessing everything from décor and sociability to economic practices. The plots of these novels use national and regional comparisons to measure historical and social development. This comparative approach, as we have seen, grew out of Scottish stadial history and was developed in the history, poetry, and philosophy of the Scottish Enlightenment; this comparative method also informed aesthetic theories from the same period, including David Hume's "Of the Standard of Taste" (1757), Hugh Blair's *Lectures on Rhetoric and Belles Lettres* (1783), Lord Kames's *Elements of Criticism* (1762), and Dugald Stewart's *Philosophical Essays* (1810). Blair, for example, in his *Lectures*, finds that the "internal sense of beauty, which is natural to men" becomes most apparent when developed economic and social conditions allow these sensibilities to flourish.[12] He writes,

> When we refer to the concurring sentiments of men as the ultimate test of what is to be accounted beautiful in the arts, this is to be always understood of men placed in such situations as are favourable to the proper exertions of Taste. Everyone must perceive, that among rude and uncivilized nations, and during the ages of ignorance and darkness, any loose notions that are entertained concerning such subjects carry no authority. In those states of society, Taste has no materials on which to operate. It is either totally suppressed, or appears in its lowest and most imperfect form. We refer to the sentiments of mankind in polished and flourishing nations; when arts are cultivated and manners refined: when works of genius are subjected to free discussion, and Taste is improved by Science and Philosophy.[13]

Like the contemporary treatises on the history of manners discussed in previous chapters, by John Millar, Adam Ferguson, Lord Kames, and Adam Smith, these Scottish aesthetic theories traced the progress of taste from "rude and uncivilized nations" to "polished and flourishing" commercial cultures; however, instead of focusing on identifying major historical shifts, these works theorize the impact historical and economic development had on the progress of art and the development of taste. This chapter reads these aesthetic treatises alongside the work of Roche and Edgeworth to develop a theory of "stadial fiction," a generic tag that emphasizes the engagement of women writers with measuring aesthetic progress in their fictions through a comparative methodology that examines aesthetic shifts as indicators of economic and social development.

Stadial fiction also reflects on the various labels that have been used to describe the Romantic-era novel's engagement with historical discourse. These generic categories include the gothic novel, the gothic romance, the historical novel, the national as well as fashionable tale, and the novel of manners. An era of experiment in the novel's development, the Romantic period witnessed a proliferation of styles, which resist stable generic tags. Gary Kelly, Marshall Brown, and David Duff have characterized the Romantic novel as revising existing poetic, philosophical, and historical traditions.[14] Kelly argues that "sharp generic distinctions were not part of Romantic literary culture; on the contrary, breaking the bounds of form was a recurrent rhetorical gesture."[15] More recently, David Duff argues that a "new perception of time" and an increasing awareness of the "historical relativism of cultural forms" in the Romantic era encouraged authors to deploy genre self-consciously as a means of reflecting on historical and aesthetic shifts.[16] Radcliffe's adaptation of progress poetry in her gothic fiction, and Edgeworth's and Roche's investment in contrasting Celtic, cosmopolitan, and regional aesthetics extend Duff's comments on Romanticism as an era of generic interaction, "a dialectic of innovation and archaism."[17] At the risk of further complicating an already complex terrain, I would like to reframe the debate over genre and the Romantic-era novel by uncovering Roche and Edgeworth's engagement with Scottish theories of historiography and aesthetics. Despite the different approaches developed in these novels, they all engage with contemporary aesthetic debates about the value of "rude" and "refined" art. In fact, the narrative tension within these novels often builds on conflict created by a clash of indelicate or overly polished and artificial tastes with delicate or natural sentiment. This chapter begins by setting forth a fuller definition of stadial fiction and concludes by illustrating how this more capacious category helps us to understand the contributions of Edgeworth and Roche to Romantic aesthetics as well as Enlightenment historiography.

Defining Stadial Fiction

The framework of stadial fiction reaches beyond what Anne H. Stevens has called the extant "limiting categories" used to classify late eighteenth- and early nineteenth-century fiction and puts novels in conversation that have been separated by hard-to-shake generic tags.[18] Accounts of Romantic-era fiction by women have been shaped retrospectively by Walter Scott's discussion of the genres of gothic and historical fiction in the introduction and postscript of his 1814 *Waverley*. Scott famously chose for *Waverley* the subtitle "'Tis Sixty Years Since" in order to set himself apart from Ann Radcliffe and her school. He writes:

> Had I, for example, announced in my frontispiece, "Waverley, a Tale of other Days," must not every novel reader have anticipated a castle scarce less than that of Udolpho, of which the eastern wing had long been uninhabited, and the keys either lost, or consigned to the care of some aged butler or house-keeper, whose trembling steps, about the middle of the second volume, were doomed to guide the hero, or heroine, to the ruinous precincts?[19]

Although Scott expressed admiration for Radcliffe's "style" of genius in his *Lives of the Novelists*, his comic depiction of *The Mysteries of Udolpho* in *Waverley* linked the gothic to romantic melodrama, pre-dictable plots, and flat characters. This is not to say that Scott wholly dismissed late eighteenth-century women's fiction. Although he defines himself against Radcliffe and the gothic romances her fiction repre-sented, including the works of Roche, he describes his brand of histori-cal fiction as indebted to – or even derived from – Maria Edgeworth's Irish novels. In *Waverley*'s postscript, he announces that he attempted "to emulate the admirable Irish portraits drawn by Miss Edgeworth."[20] In the preface to his collected works, which appeared in 1829, Scott writes, "I felt that something might be attempted for my own country, of the same kind with that which Miss Edgeworth so fortunately achieved for Ireland –something which might introduce her natives to those of the sister kingdom, in a more favourable light than they had been placed hitherto, and tend to procure sympathy for their virtues, and indulgence for their foibles."[21] Despite the attention drawn by recent studies to the influence of women writers from Charlotte Lennox to Sophia Lee on the development of historical fiction,[22] the origin story of the historical novel frequently begins with Scott's *Waverley* and the distinctions he draws between gothic and historical fiction.

Critics such as Ina Ferris, Katie Trumpener, and Juliet Shields have complicated Scott's definition of the historical novel and women's con-tribution to the genre by emphasizing the differences between Scott's historical fiction and the national tale. They see the national tale as a genre primarily shaped by women writers with more subversive politi-cal agendas than the more conservative politics associated with Scott. In this formulation, the national tales of Maria Edgeworth and Sydney Owenson disrupt the progressive temporality of the British nation and voice the "grievances" of an Irish nation within Great Britain while either holding out the promise of "transcultural union" or voicing a separatist politics.[23] On the other hand, the historical novels of Scott work to forge a singular British nation that locates disputes between England and the Celtic periphery safely in an antiquarian or romantic past.[24] Despite the different political and cultural investments of the historical novel and the national tale, these works stand for historical rigor and particularity in addition to a direct engagement with politics and economics absent from gothic novels, which create a more fantastic past without the scholarly footnotes and editorial apparatuses that often accompany the fiction of Owenson, Edgeworth, and Scott. While engaging with the questions about gender and genre raised by Trumpener and Ferris, this chapter shifts the discussion away from generic hierarchies that associate Edgeworth with either the more intellectual historical novel or the overtly political national tale. As Claire Connolly argues in her study of Irish fiction, attention to the overtly political national tale has made it difficult to account for many of Edgeworth's novels, including *Patronage*, and the generic constraints of the national tale have obscured the range of genres that Irish authors used to process political and cultural issues;[25] the more inclusive category of stadial fiction puts Edgeworth's and Roche's work in dialogue with writers both inside and outside of Ireland who were interested in tracing a cross-cultural and transnational development of manners and sentiment. The social, or the "mores and manners, the special province of women," which Shields argues made it possible for women writers of the national tale to intervene in debates over political and cultural identity, were also central to the fashionable tales and gothic novels of the same period.[26] The social, cultural, and aesthetic debates that infuse the more fantastic and feminine worlds of the gothic and Romantic traditions also belong in this larger conversation, which has been dominated by the historical novel and later the national tale, about the novel's participation in the mapping of social progress throughout the British Empire.

The category of stadial fiction reconciles these overlapping genres, which share troubling similarities and tend to collapse into one another as they do in Edgeworth's *Castle Rackrent* (1800), which has been classified as a gothic novel, a historical novel, and a national tale. Instead, this group of disparate novels belongs to one genre, stadial fiction.[27] The umbrella of stadial fiction foregrounds these novelists' concern with examining the influence of the four-stage theory of history, which has been described in the first chapter of this book, on aesthetic categories. It also creates new intersections between novels that have been difficult to think about together because of narrow generic types, such as Roche's gothic romance *The Children of the Abbey*, national tales such as her

The Contrast and Edgeworth's *Absentee*, and novels of manners such as Edgeworth's *Patronage* and *Belinda*. This group of novels, which, like stadial history, contrast the aesthetic sensibilities of different nations and ages, shifted discussions of historical development from men to manners and taste.

In tracing the journeys of their heroines through a variety of social environments and historical stages, these novels illustrate the difficulties in identifying a cross-cultural aesthetic standard and confront a number of obstacles to mapping a progress of taste that recall eighteenth- and early nineteenth-century Scottish treatises on aesthetics. Philosophers influenced by Adam Smith's *Lectures on Rhetoric and Belles Lettres* and David Hume's essay "On the Standard of Taste" (1757) also addressed the relationship between aesthetic and cultural development. Although Hume, Smith, and the Scottish philosophers who followed them offered slightly different perspectives on the origins and progress of taste, each theory related moral development to the refinement of taste in some fashion. For example, Hume's much-discussed "standard of taste" associates the sentiment of approbation essential to aesthetic evaluation with belief in a moral standard: "And where a man is confident of the rectitude of that moral standard, by which he judges, he is justly jealous of it, and will not pervert the sentiments of his heart for a moment, in complaisance of any writer whatsoever."[28] He also argues that modern sentiments and tastes are more likely to be refined, delicate, and just: "The want of humanity and of decency, so conspicuous in the characters drawn by several of the ancient poets, even sometimes by HOMER and the GREEK tragedians, diminishes considerably the merit of their noble performances, and gives modern authors an advantage over them."[29] Hume insists that cross-cultural and historical comparisons are requisite to developing a delicacy of taste, which he defines as "the source of all the finest and more innocent enjoyments, of which human nature is susceptible."[30] He argues that, "Wherever you can ascertain a delicacy of taste, it is sure to meet with approbation; and the best way of ascertaining it is to appeal to those models and principles, which have been established by the uniform consent of experience of nations and ages."[31] The Scottish philosophers of taste who followed Hume and women novelists of the Romantic era shared his interest in "ascertaining a delicacy of taste" and the feeling of approbation it produced by traversing in their philosophy and fiction the "experience of nations and ages."

After the publication of Hume's influential essay, Hugh Blair, Lord Kames, and Dugald Stewart wrote more extensive treatises on aesthetics, many of which became popular textbooks in British and American universities. Hugh Blair's *Lectures on Rhetoric and Belles Lettres* and

Lord Kames's *Elements of Criticism* went through several editions throughout the eighteenth and nineteenth centuries.[32] Dugald Stewart's *Philosophical Essays* (1810), which included an extensive discussion of taste, beauty, and the sublime, was also widely read. Although emotion and sensibility, which are often used interchangeably in these treatises, require intellect and reason to develop appropriately, all of these accounts privilege the perceiver's capacity to feel as the prime guarantor of good taste. Blair provides a typical account of emotion's preeminence in Scottish aesthetics. He argues that reason merely assists emotion in forming aesthetic judgments: "sensibility to beauty" is the primary requirement for the apprehension of good taste, but "reason . . . assists taste in many of its operations, and serves to enlarge its power."[33] He concludes that "Delicacy leans more to feeling; Correctness to reason and judgment."[34] Women also read Blair's treatise and the work of his fellow literati; the engagement of the Bluestockings, particularly in the salons of Elizabeth Montagu, with Blair and Kames has been recounted in Chapter 2. In the following generation of Scottish literati, Dugald Stewart, as Pam Perkins has recently established, had a network of female correspondents and readers, including Elizabeth Hamilton and Maria Edgeworth,[35] who cited Stewart extensively in her *Letters to Literary Ladies* (1795). Blair, Kames, and Stewart all argued that there was a comparative or relative component to socially and culturally specific definitions of taste and beauty and clearly borrowed, as did Hume, from the comparative method developed in Scottish historiography.

Despite their acknowledgement that a universal standard of taste might be found through their comparative methodologies, the discussions of aesthetics found in these treatises stress the culturally and nationally relative values of beauty and delicacy as well as the influence economic development has on the refinement of natural taste. Despite his defense of ancient Caledonian society in his "Dissertation on the Poems of Ossian," Blair argues in his *Lectures* that the proper balance between feeling or reason can be found primarily in developed societies:

> One may have strong sensibility, and yet be deficient in delicate Taste. He may be deeply impressed by such beauties as he perceives, but he perceives only what is in some degree coarse, which is bold and palpable; while chaster and simpler ornaments escape his notice. In this state Taste generally exists among rude and unrefined nations. But a person of delicate Taste both feels strongly, and feels accurately.[36]

Blair's discussion of the relative nature of taste concludes with a rhetorical question meant to make the trajectory of taste's refinement or development concrete: "For is there any one who will maintain that the Taste of a Hottentot or a Laplander is as delicate and as correct as that of a Longinus or an Addison? Or, that he can be charged with no defect or incapacity who thinks a common news-writer as excellent an Historian as Tacitus?"[37] Interestingly, Blair's scale of development in this concrete example does not follow a clear spatial or temporal trajectory and reveals the unevenness of the progress of taste that he means to describe. While Tacitus, Longinus, and Addison are read as examples of developed taste, Hottentots and Laplanders as well as the "common news-writers" of eighteenth-century Britain possess underdeveloped sensibilities. Blair registers here a suspicion of modernity, placing the modern Addison in an ancient and classical age and displacing rude or common London news-writers to distant and savage equatorial and far northern climes. In doing so, he troubles the equation of developed tastes with modern commerce and its instruments such as print culture, which can inspire an advance, as in the case of Addison, or a devolution, as in the case of an average Grub Street hack. Similarly suspicious of modernity, Lord Kames writes: "A gradual progress from simplicity to complex forms and profuse ornaments, seems to be the fate of all the fine arts: in that progress these arts resemble behavior, which, from original candour and simplicity, has degenerated into artificial refinements."[38] Yet, like Blair, he generally favors modernity and views delicate and correct taste to be an offshoot of a developed society: "men, originally savage and brutal, acquire not rationality nor delicacy of taste till they be long disciplined in society."[39] His praise for modernity is qualified by his concern, perhaps most fully articulated by Adam Ferguson in his unequivocal critique of modernity *Essay on Civil Society*, that developed societies will descend into voluptuousness and opulence; Kames warns that "the delicacy of taste above described ... must be improved by education, reflection, and experience: it must be preserved in vigour by living regularly, by using the goods of fortune with moderation, and by following the dictates of improved nature, which give welcome to every rational pleasure without indulging in excess."[40] Like the novels of Roche and Edgeworth, which measure the aesthetic standard embodied in their heroines against a number of environments and social settings, these treatises on taste struggle to chart a clear aesthetic progress. More variable and relative than universal, the progress of taste in these treatises remains difficult to define yet a key measure of development.

Following Blair and Kames, Dugald Stewart, a contemporary of Roche and Edgeworth, agreed that a delicate sensibility is the chief requirement for good taste, arguing that "where there is no sensibility, there can be no taste."[41] Like Blair and Kames, he also suggests that sensibility must be balanced with education and refinement: "Taste does not consist in sensibility alone . . . it is susceptible of improvement from culture, in a higher degree perhaps than any other power of the mind."[42] Although Stewart encourages the development of refined and delicate tastes, he too believes that danger accompanies taste's progress: "in a mind where delicacy of sensibility is extreme, the acquisition of correct taste is, in ordinary cases, next to impossible."[43] He builds his theory of aesthetic progress by using the development of an individual's taste from childhood to adulthood as an analogy for the aesthetic progress of nations: "From the admiration of colours, the eye gradually advances to that of forms; beginning first with such as are most obviously regular. Hence the pleasure which children, almost without exception, express, when they see gardens laid out after the Dutch manner; and hence the justness of the epithet childish, or puerile, which is commonly employed to characterize this species of taste; – one of the earliest stages of its progress both in individuals and in nations."[44] Although the Dutch with their highly developed commercial system certainly do not qualify as a "savage" nation, the artificial boundaries and distinct colors and shapes found in their gardens exemplify the "unnatural" and degenerative tastes created by an overly refined commercial culture. He also finds ostentatious displays of dress and furniture to be infantile: "in articles of dress or of furniture, a passion for gaudy decoration is justly regarded as the symptom of a taste for the Beautiful, which is destined never to pass the first stage of infancy."[45] Although there is far from universal agreement on a standard of taste, these Scottish thinkers shared a common belief that social and economic development can cultivate taste and, paradoxically, a suspicion that progress might be circular and that developed tastes merely recall the savage appetites of distant ages and places.

To solve this dilemma, Scottish philosophers, like the heroines in Romantic-era novels, worked to separate false and indelicate feeling from the genuine sentiments they aped. Blair argues that taste is required to distinguish "between affected and natural ornament."[46] All of these accounts also associate "correct taste" as well as "natural taste" with beauty; however, natural beauty becomes very difficult to separate from artifice. The difficulty these philosophers have in distinguishing beauty from its uncanny and artificial other resembles the efforts of Roche and Edgeworth to establish a standard and distinguish their heroines from their less worthy foils and doppelgangers. Often the identification of true beauty depends on a difficult-to-define feeling. According to Blair, material beauty and the sympathetic feelings that create society can be recognized by a shared sensation. He claims that "the social virtues . . . of a softer and general kind," such "as compassion, mildness, friendship and generosity . . . excite in the beholder a sensation of pleasure, so much akin to that produced by Beautiful external objects, that, though of a more exalted nature, it may with propriety be classed under the same head."[47] Kames attempts to define beauty by theorizing two different classes: relative and intrinsic beauty. He associates relative beauty with utility, whereas intrinsic beauty "is discovered in a single object viewed apart without relation to any other;"[48] however, he claims that a "delightful object" appears when "these two beauties collide."[49] Intrinsic beauty and relative beauty share the principles of "regularity, uniformity, proportion, order, and simplicity."[50] Regularity, simplicity, and usefulness are qualities that also define Romantic heroines like Caroline Percy and Amanda Malvina, who, although beautiful in isolation, shine when set against their peers. Stewart builds on Kames's sense of relative beauty and finds that understanding beauty requires comprehending the "perception of relations" or beauty's relationship to external things as well as ideas:

> Place beauty in the perception of relations, and you will have the history of its progress from the infancy of the world to the present hour. On the other hand, choose for the distinguishing characteristic of the beautiful in general, any other quality you can possibly imagine, and you will immediately find your notion limited in its application of the mode of thinking prevalent in particular countries, or at particular periods of time.[51]

By placing their ideally beautiful heroines against a variety of social and cultural environments, Roche and Edgeworth invite the "perception of relations" described by Stewart and help trace the history of beauty's progress theorized in Kames's *Elements of Criticism*.

Although beauty in these treatises is often aligned with feminine categories such as delicacy, these philosophers do not explicitly assign beauty to a particular sex, in contrast to Burke. Notably, Stewart spends much of his time critiquing Burke's approach as too partial because he concentrated "(unconsciously perhaps) on female beauty as his standard."[52] The aesthetic philosophers of the Scottish Enlightenment adapted a more gender-neutral approach, yet their cross-cultural studies of beauty resemble the journeys of the heroines in Roche and Edgeworth's novels, just as the plots of their novels develop the comparative approach of the Scottish Enlightenment. The delicate and refined heroines who star in these novels negotiate a variety of environments, from rural Ireland and Wales to fashionable London, and either benefit from or become victims of the lasting effects of regular or irregular educations. While navigating these very different cultural and social terrains, these heroines often exhibit a delicacy of taste and beauty that emerges through the process of cultural and historical comparison. Although Scott's novels have typically been read as marking the end of the Scottish Enlightenment, the productions of his female contemporaries and predecessors, including Edgeworth and Radcliffe, to whom he gestures in the preface of *Waverley*, engage with the same questions of historical method, temporality, and social progress as Scott and the Scottish writers and philosophers who came before him. The novels of his female contemporaries focus on measuring the social value of typically feminine categories like beauty, elegance, and refinement in relation to developing social, commercial, and imperial structures. Like Scott's hero Edward Waverley, whose refined manners and overly developed literary sensibilities seem out of place in the Highlands of Scotland as well as the commercial world of London, the heroines of Romantic-era fiction struggle to reconcile their refined tastes and sensibilities with the different social and economic climates that they encounter. In these novels, taste gauges the differences between the four nations that coexisted within the British Isles as well as the continent and beyond. Ultimately, the heroine who can transcend these different sensibilities suggests the possibility of a standard of taste that might find a unity among these different communities.

Maria Edgeworth and the Cultivation of Taste

Edgeworth's debt to Scottish philosophy and aesthetic theory appears throughout her work. Adam Smith's *Wealth of Nations* has been acknowledged by several critics, including Marilyn Butler and Fraser Easton,[53] as an influence on her Irish novels. Smith's theory of political economy, his account of Scotland's efforts to modernize, and his critiques of absenteeism were read by Maria and her father Richard Lovell Edgeworth as applicable to the Irish case. Traces of her interest in the Scottish Enlightenment can be found in her fiction and prose. In a chapter of *Belinda* entitled "Rights of Woman," Harriet Freke finds Belinda reading Smith's *Theory of Moral Sentiments* as well as Dr. John Moore's *Travels*, which contrasted the manners of different European nations and cultures. In this example, the Scottish Enlightenment not only acts as an alternative to Freke's parody of Wollstonecraft's radical egalitarianism, but also highlights women's role in cultivating manners and refining the emotions necessary to make commerce humane and to keep civilization civilized – a responsibility the masculine Freke abdicates throughout the novel.[54] The subtitle of Edgeworth's *Castle Rackrent* (1800), "a tale of other times," originated with the Ossian poems, as Stevens has also argued, and links the novel to the Ossian poems' important intervention in debates over the progress of civiliza-tion.[55] In this regard, *Castle Rackrent* builds on Macpherson's and the Scottish Enlightenment's effort to incorporate Celtic history and manners into readers' contemporary understanding of the evolution of British identity.[56] Edgeworth also emphasized women's role in the civilizing process in her *Letters for Literary Ladies*, which includes a reference to Stewart's "observation" that learned men might benefit from marriages to "literary ladies." In the same work, she also cites Stewart's *Elements of the Philosophy of the Human Mind* (1792), arguing that women are better able to cultivate their understandings because they are not distracted by the business concerns that Stewart argues narrow a writer's understanding.[57] She also gestures toward Scottish historiography in developing her own theory of women's role in cultivating civil society, and the Scottish comparative method shapes her belief that negative attitudes toward educated women will one day disappear. She writes, "it seems probable that the faults usually ascribed to learned ladies, like those peculiar to learned men, may have arisen in a great measure from circumstances which the progress of civilization in society has much altered."[58] Employing the comparative method of Scottish historiography, she compares contemporary descriptions of "learned ladies" as "peculiarities" to the descriptions of the learned men of the distant past as magicians or a "class of necromancers."[59] She claims that the "progress of civilization in society" will act as a correc-tive and "alter" contemporary representations of educated women as it transformed medieval understandings of educated men.

Within this context, it becomes possible to read Edgeworth's novels, particularly *Ennui*, *The Absentee*, and *Patronage*, as not just national tales or novels of manners but aesthetic treatises or stadial fictions that compare the sensibilities and tastes of a variety of men and women from different national and colonial spaces. *The Absentee* and *Ennui*, which are usually categorized as national tales and belong to Edgeworth's *Tales of Fashionable Life*, detail the deleterious effects on absentee landlords of leaving Ireland for the fashionable life of London; usually considered separately, *Patronage* leaves Irish concerns behind and engages with the class politics of English society. Significantly, although it was not completed on time, *Patronage* was also originally intended to be part of *Tales of Fashionable Life*.[60] All of the novels share a concern with the relationship of sensibility and taste to economic and historical structures. *The Absentee* and *Patronage* share a particular concern with women's contribution to the civilizing process, and Fiona Price has argued that Edgeworth's *Tales of Fashionable Life* present "a complex view of the relationship between taste and nation."[61] Although the luxurious indulgences and dissipated tastes of the Earl of Glenthorn, the main character of *Ennui*, also demonstrate Edgeworth's engagement with taste and its relationship to the economic and political character of Ireland, Glenthorn does not possess the self-command of either Grace Nugent or Caroline Percy, the delicate and admired heroines of *The Absentee* and *Patronage*. The delicacy of taste possessed by both Grace and Caroline elevates them above the other characters in the novels and allows them to compare national tastes and developmental differences in a way that resembles the ideal observer described by Hume and his contemporaries. Unlike the Earl of Glenthorn, they both embody an aesthetic standard and act as arbiters of good taste.

With her aptly chosen name, Grace Nugent in *The Absentee* functions to correct the Clonbrony family's aesthetic excesses, and by correcting their tastes she simultaneously helps restore their economic independence. Long absent from their Irish estate, the family is forced to return to Ireland after Lady Clonbrony falls victim to fashion. In London, Lady Clonbrony wastes the family's fortune on luxurious excesses to impress her English friends. Early on in the novel she hosts a gala featuring a Turkish tent, Alhambra tapestries, and a Chinese pagoda. The patchwork of Eastern references built into her décor illustrates her fall into excess and echoes conjectural history's persistent alignment of the East with overindulgence and sensuousness without a moral purpose.[62] When the English Mrs. Dareville seeks to insult Lady Clonbrony's décor, she focuses her attention on the useful objects: "And how good of you, my dear lady Clonbrony, in defiance of bulls and blunders, to allow us a comfortable English fireplace and plenty of Newcastle coal in China! – And white marble – no! white velvet hearthrug painted with beautiful flowers – O! the delicate, the *useful* thing!"[63] Mrs. Dareville mocks the Irish Lady Clonbrony's haphazard mixture of fashionable chinoiserie with traditional English décor; yet the childish and dissipated Lady Clonbrony finds herself most "vexed by the emphasis on the word useful."[64] Lady Clonbrony understands fashionable taste as the ability to replicate luxurious Eastern and English interiors in, as she says, a "correct, and appropriate, and quite picturesque" fashion.[65] Unfortunately, her superficial understanding of good taste fails to connect taste to a utilitarian or moral purpose, and her efforts to create a tasteful interior fail miserably. By merely imitating current fashion, Lady Clonbrony's house, like her dress, appears "excessively fashionable in each of its parts," yet "altogether, so extraordinarily unbecoming, as to be fit for a print-shop."[66]

When the London decorator Mr. Soho presents his ridiculous plan for the gala, Grace Nugent attempts to correct him with "propriety and delicacy."[67] Instead of directly insulting Mr. Soho's dubious tastes, she uses her "superior intelligence" to make him "magnify the ridicule" within his plan until even Lady Clonbrony refuses to adopt some of the more outrageous suggestions made by the decorator. Grace is not only delicate, but also "pleasing and graceful," and "the good sense, the taste, she showed ... prevented Lady Clonbrony from doing any thing preposterously absurd, or exorbitantly extravagant."[68] Grace combines her delicacy of taste with a preference for simplicity and Irish life that the fashionable absentee Lady Clonbrony despises. When Lady Clonbrony accuses her of being a "partisan of Ireland," Grace defends her nation, saying "Ireland had been a friend to me: that I found Irish friends, when I had no other; an Irish home, when I had no other."[69] When the Clonbronys' son, Lord Colambre, travels to Ireland to inspect his father's estate, he finds the Irish temperament to be almost as charming as Grace: "The hospitality of which the father boasted, the son found in all its warmth, but meliorated and refined; less convivial, more social ... Lord Colambre found a spirit of improvement, a desire for knowledge, and a taste for science and literature."[70] Lord Colambre becomes almost as enamored with Ireland as he is of his cousin Grace, whose abilities to gauge the differences between London society and Irish life become a testament to her own delicacy of taste. *The Absentee* offers the simplicity and superiority of Grace and Ireland as anecdotes to the dissipated life led by the Clonbronys in fashionable London;[71] Grace acts as an aesthetic ideal mediating between nations and aesthetic sensibilities.

Patronage also contrasts national aesthetics and links taste to propriety and moral development. At the same time that the novel critiques the outmoded economics of patronage through its account of the success of the Percys' self-sufficient sons, it mobilizes Caroline Percy as a standard against which to contrast the different values and sensibilities of different classes and nations. Through this comparative methodology, the novel recommends not just the mobility of the modern commercial world inhabited by the Percy brothers, but also a modern sensibility or taste that complements this changing world. Caroline, who embodies all the tenets of good taste, becomes a vector for these cultural and social comparisons. The many suitors she rejects throughout the novel and her female rivals, who always fall short, become part of the novel's comparative methodology. As the standard of taste within the novel, Caroline Percy joins a beautiful exterior with delicate manners: "She was beautiful, and of an uncommon style of beauty. Ingenuous, unaffected, and with all the simplicity of youth, there was a certain dignity and graceful self-possession in her manner, which gave the idea of a superior character."[72] Caroline also possesses cultivated sensibilities instilled in her by her parents. When her brother Godfrey claims that "sensibility is the foundation of every thing that is most amiable and charming, of every grace, of every virtue in woman,"[73] his father agrees but qualifies his son's observation, adding that the virtuousness of sensibility "depends upon how it is governed, whether sensibility be a curse or a blessing to its possessor, and to society."[74] Like Grace Nugent, Caroline's self-command sets her apart from other women.

Illustrated through her interactions with a number of rival beauties and suitors, Caroline's superior feelings and behavior attempt to mark the difficult-to-identify boundary between universal beauty and taste, and the fleeting and relative effects of artifice and fashion. When confronted with Caroline's "delicate charm,"[75] the fashionable Lady Angelica attempts to show that "whatever might be her abilities, her knowledge, or her charms, these must all submit to a superior power – the power of fashion."[76] Lady Angelica uses art to draw attention back to herself, but her "fashionable *technical* tattle" of marriages and divorce amongst the ton fails to embarrass or distract Caroline, who uses her "strange power of abstraction" to distance herself from Lady Angelica.[77] Caroline's superior beauty and taste even attract Lady Angelica's fashionable suitor Sir James Harcourt. Despite his efforts, Caroline immediately sees through "the full fire of his flattery" and his "assumed appearance."[78] Similarly, she also proves herself to be superior to her fashionable relatives the Miss Falconers, drawing the attention of the beautiful and celebrated Georgiana Falconer's suitors. Yet she finds neither of the Clay brothers, whose attention the Falconers cultivate, suitable. The French Clay affects French sensibilities and is described as an "imitation of those who were ridiculous, detested, or unknown, in good society at Paris; and whom the nation would utterly disclaim as representative of their morals or manners."[79] Likewise, his brother the English Clay embodies the worse stereotypes of English society. Alfred Percy describes the English Clay as "a cold, reserved, proud, dull looking man . . . All that belongs to Mr. Clay, of Clay-Hall, is the best of it's kind, or, at least, *had from the best hand in England*. Everything about him is English; but I don't know whether this arises from love of his country, or contempt of his brother."[80] Ultimately, Caroline rejects the divisive battle of national tastes parodied by the Clay brothers and falls in love with the cosmopolitan Count Altenberg, who, although German, has an English mother and hopes to find a wife in England: "In England, where education, institutions, opinion, manners, the habit of society, and of domestic life, happily combine to give the just proportion of all that is attractive, useful, ornamental, and amiable to the female character."[81] He believes English women possess ideal sensibilities, even citing Elizabeth Montagu's *Essay on Shakespeare* as evidence of English women's perfect taste and ability to mediate between national sensibilities: "Even Voltaire had some tinge of national prejudice, as well as other men. It was reserved for women, to set us in this instance, as in many others, an example at once of superior candour, and superior talent."[82] The count describes Caroline as combining the aesthetic sensibilities of a number of nations:

> the noble simplicity of character that was once the charm of Swisserland, joined the polish, the elegance, that was once the pride of France; a woman possessing an enlarged, cultivated, embellished understanding, capable of comprehending all his views as a politician, and a statesman; yet without the slightest wish for power, or any desire to interfere in public business, or political intrigue . . . It was reserved for Count Altenberg, to meet in England with a woman of sensibility, exquisite, generous as any German romance could conceive, yet without exaggeration in expression, or extravagance in conduct, repressed, regulated, treasured for the happiness of him who could merit such a heart.[83]

Despite never having left England, Caroline personifies the best of a host of nations, a cosmopolitan mixture or a universal standard against which other women are judged and often found lacking. In Count Altenberg, Caroline discovers someone whose self-command and refined sensibilities match her own. Despite his strong feelings for Caroline, his "dignity, tenderness, and passion" are tempered by his "too delicate [and] too well-bred" sensibilities.[84]

Through Caroline, Edgeworth presents a treatise on aesthetics that draws from sources like Montagu's *Essay* and is clearly influenced by Scottish discussions of aesthetics that employed a stadial methodology. Caroline acts to resolve the aesthetic dilemma discussed by Scottish theorists of taste and described in Edgeworth's novel by her brother Alfred Percy's mentor, the Chief Justice, who notably tests Alfred's power of judgment and fitness for the law in an extended discussion about theater and taste. The Chief Justice argues that "we do not always know what we mean by art, and what by nature; that the ideas are so mixed in civilized society, and the words so inaccurately used, both in common conversation, and in the writing of philosophers, that no metaphysical prism can separate, or reduce to their primary meaning."[85] Although readers never learn the details of this important conversation, the novel notes that the judge next "touched upon the distinction between art and artifice" and that the "conversation branched out into remarks on grace and affectation, and thence to the different theories of beauty, and taste, with all which he played with a master's hand."[86] Although the Chief Justice reinforces the link between cultivated tastes and a healthy society, the novel refuses to allow him center stage and merely alludes to abstract elements of his conversation. Rather, Edgeworth's philosophical meditation on taste is performed through the actions of Caroline, who attempts to transcend national biases and acts as a "metaphysical prism," parsing the differences between natural and artificial beauty as well as natural and fashionable taste. The novel even includes a citation from Hume's "Of the Delicacy of Taste and Passion" when describing the origins of Caroline's sensibilities and her mentor Mrs. Hungerford:

> An elegant and just distinction has been made by a philosophical writer between *delicacy of passion and delicacy of taste*. One leading to that ill governed sensibility which transports the soul to ecstacy, or reduces it to despair, on every adverse or prosperous change of fortune; the other enlarging our sphere of happiness, by directing and increasing our sensibility to objects of which we may command the enjoyment, instead of wasting it upon those over which we have no control. Mrs. Hungerford was a striking example of the advantage of cultivating *delicacy of taste*.[87]

Through Caroline Percy, Edgeworth not only theorizes, as did Hume and his Scottish contemporaries, the balance a delicacy of taste requires between command and feeling, but also illustrates how such command might be exerted in society and the particular responsibility delicate and feeling women have for controlling their passions and cultivating the tastes of those who surround them. By illustrating the principles of correct, delicate, and natural taste through the actions of fictional characters like Caroline, who read more like philosophical abstractions or ideals than real people or round characters, Edgeworth's stadial fictions create a philosophical terrain upon which readers might trace a progress of taste.

Regina Maria Roche and Stadial Aesthetics

Although Edgeworth and Roche remain at a significant distance from each other in early nineteenth-century and contemporary critical discourse, putting these two authors in conversation with each other makes it possible to rethink the conventional categories used to discuss Romantic-era fiction. Despite Roche and Edgeworth's shared engagement with theorizing the progress of taste, Edgeworth enjoyed serious critical attention during her lifetime and still does today. In part, this is due to literary history's tendency to read Edgeworth as exceptional and Roche as representative. Edgeworth herself initiated this narrative by distancing herself from her contemporaries and insisting that she wrote not novels but tales, which attempted something more philosophical and pedagogical. Her work drew praise from Walter Scott and Jeremy Bentham,[88] who also positioned her as an exception, and lengthy reviews of her fictions appeared in British periodicals such as *The Edinburgh Review*, *The Monthly Catalogue* and *The Critical Review*. Edgeworth remains an important presence in contemporary critical discussions of Romanticism. Marilyn Butler has done much to recover the details of her life and make her fiction central to understanding the Romantic period. Katie Trumpener and Ina Ferris have positioned her as one of the progenitors of the national tale. Despite the work of Miranda Burgess, who has pointed out that Roche also employed the subtitle "tale" and has read her *Children of the Abbey* as "heralding techniques" that would later mark Edgeworth's and Owenson's national tales,[89] Roche is still read primarily in the context of the sensational novels of her publisher William Lane's Minerva Press, and little time has been devoted to Roche's fiction and its relationships to genres other than the gothic; yet, like Edgeworth, she wrote stadial fictions, which were indebted to the poetry of the Scottish Enlightenment and the Scottish comparative mode of historiography.

One of the most popular and widely read novelists of the late eighteenth and early nineteenth century, Roche was dismissed by critics in the Romantic era and figures, if at all, as a footnote or marginal presence in literary criticism. Her links to the Minerva Press, and Isabella Thorpe's inclusion of Roche's *Clermont* (1798) in the list of "horrid" novels she provides Catherine Morland in Jane Austen's *Northanger Abbey*, have made it difficult to develop other contexts for her fiction. Admittedly, the unlikely coincidences and saccharine romances that mark her fiction can be tiresome, yet much is lost by examining her work solely within the context of the Minerva Press.[90] Like Edgeworth, Roche intervened in period debates about the relationship between aesthetic development and economic progress. For instance, Amanda Malvina in *The Children of the Abbey* moves between agricultural communities in Wales and commercial London, commenting on the different modes of sociability and taste prevalent in each place. Similarly, one of Roche's later national tales, *The Contrast* (1828), compares social and economic development in England, Ireland, and Wales. *The Contrast*, although not as well-known as *The Children of the Abbey*, perhaps because it was published after the heyday of the Minerva Press, provides important biographical information about Roche that connects the themes and settings of her earlier gothic fiction to her later regional fiction, such as *The Munster Cottage Boy* (1820), and makes a case for her investment in the comparative historical methodology developed in Scottish philosophy and the Romantic-era novel.

Written in an effort to recover Roche and her husband's fortunes after they lost her paternal estate in Ireland, *The Contrast* includes extensive discussions of absenteeism, incumbrances, and the loss of its heroine Helena's fortune through the influence of corrupt agents. Published by subscription, the novel was supported by William Wordsworth, Robert Southey, and L. E. L. (Letitia Elizabeth Landon). Through the 1820s and early 1830s, Roche continually appealed for financial support to the recently established Royal Literary Fund.[91] In a lengthy letter to the committee, Roche details her experience as an absentee landowner in Ireland and proves her familiarity with the economic particularities of Irish absenteeism. Roche's complex explanations of rents, interest, and incumbrances initially seem at a distance from the world of her popular novels, such as *Clermont* and *The Children of the Abbey*, which are often understood to eschew reality and historical particularity, using "ruins, abbeys, or castles . . . only to rouse sentimental broodings in the characters."[92] Roche's biography, like Edgeworth's well-documented life, connects the gothic ruins in her fiction to not just the emotional states of her characters but also Irish history and economics. Instead of reading her work as a pale imitation of her contemporaries Edgeworth, Sydney Owenson, and Walter Scott, as Natalie Schroeder has suggested, Roche's fiction can be read as a part of the larger field of stadial fiction in which writers like Edgeworth worked, an attempt to engage with important unresolved questions about the nature of progress and its relationship to imperial and economic development.[93] In this regard, although her heroines, whose delicate constitutions are often nurtured in rude circumstances, might strain credulity – as Macpherson's Ossian did in the eighteenth century – they also gesture toward a desire to separate manners and aesthetic progress from a progressive teleology that sees economic development as the motor of civil society and women's progress.

The letters from Roche to the Royal Literary Fund reveal that after declaring bankruptcy in 1802, her husband was forced to begin the process of selling Roche's "patrimony," which was in King's County, Ireland and left to her by her father, Captain Blundell Dalton. Roche describes being tricked by a lawyer, John Buswell, who later became a MP for Ireland:

> Through means of this description Mr. Buswell acquired a knowledge of our affairs, and in particular of the estate which had dissolved to me. This estate consisted of an undivided moiety of certain lands in the King's County Ireland, on which existed heavy incumbrances, which however having been greatly exaggerated, and the profit rent being represented as not more than a few pounds annually, Mr. Buswell managed to become the purchaser of Mr.

Roche's life interest in the property from his assignees for the small sum of fifty pounds.

Before entering further into the subject I beg to observe that the patrimony alluded to consisted of an undivided moiety of the Estate of Monastereris in the King's County Ireland. The other moiety being possessed by a different branch of the family. The talent and ingenuity of Mr. Buswell enabled him so speciously to represent to the commissioners and assignees of my husband that the incumbrances before mentioned affected only that moiety of the estate that belonged to me, and consequently the interest annually due thereon was stated to be so great as to reduce the clear rent after meeting the above claims to the trifling sum of eight pounds six and three pence. Now I trust the fallacy of this statement will appear evident in the sequel of my narrative. In 1804, my property had so much increased in value as to induce Mr. Buswell to make offers for the purchase of my reversionary interest in the estate after the decease of my husband. Our necessities at this period were so great, and the professions of friendship on the part of Mr. Buswell so encouraging as to induce a compliance with his proposals, and the more so seeing he possessed a claim on Mr. Roche for professional services which he professed to have settled. Under these circumstances I was obliged to part with my property to avoid a greater evil, and to accept of two hundred pounds for that property which will presently be shewn to yield upwards of that sum annually clear of all demands.

Mr. Buswell after thus purchasing my husband's life interest for 50 pounds, and my own for 200 pounds, continued to enjoy the fruits of his bargain till 1812 by which time his annual profit from my estate had, by his own confession so largely increased.[94]

Roche experienced first-hand the financial difficulties represented in Edgeworth's fiction as well as in her own: the deleterious effects of incumbrances, subleases, extensive litigation, deceptive agents, absenteeism, and corrupt politicians. She admits in her novel *The Contrast* that her fiction had become a way of alleviating her financial difficulties, her only means of support, assuring those "who may be strangers to her history" that "at no period of her life did she take up the pen under difficulties and afflictions so overwhelming, and must therefore trust to their generous candour to overlook or excuse the defects they may meet with in her Work now submitted to them."[95] As an Irish landholder living much of her life in England, her personal experience with the economic and social unevenness of the British archipelago suggests that the emotional states, delicate sensibilities, and range of tastes described in her novels should be seen as part of contemporary debates over the relationship between aesthetics and the economics of progress.

Although written well before Roche's bankruptcy, *The Children of the Abbey* illustrates her enduring interest in the economic and aesthetic differences between the four nations of the British Isles. The novel follows the movements of its heroine Amanda Malvina between

Devonshire, the North of Wales, Scotland, Ireland, and even the fashionable Portland Square in London, noting the manners and the modes of production and consumption practiced in each place. Amanda Malvina is known for her "refined and cultivated tastes,"[96] which appear to be a product of her Ossianic sensibilities. References to the Ossian poems, as in Radcliffe's *Mysteries of Udolpho*, denote the developed tastes of Amanda Malvina and her immediate family, who are cultured yet untainted by the overly refined tastes and emotions found in Southern England. For example, the heroine's brother is named Oscar Fitzalan, after Ossian's son. A blind harper even wanders through the novel, singing Ossianic verse. When the heroine describes her first encounter with the harper, she sees him through an Ossianic frame: "The venerable appearance of the musician, the simple melody of his harp, recalled to Amanda's recollection the *tales of other times*, in which she had so often delighted: it sent her soul back to the ages of old, to the days of other years, when bards rehearsed the exploits of heroes, and sung the praises of the dead."[97] This encounter with the harper is followed by a long quotation of Ossianic verse. References to Ossian proliferate, and readers soon discover that the heroine's deceased mother was named Malvina.[98] In the Highland poems, Malvina tragically survives her betrothed, Ossian's son Oscar, and keeps Ossian company in the waning days of his life. Although she dies before Ossian, she resembles him in that she exists both as an actor in the events Ossian recalls and in the nostalgic time after the disappearance of their race, when he relates the history of his people. In *The Children of the Abbey*, the heroine's father and her mother meet in Scotland, where her father is "quartered [with his regiment] in a remote part of that kingdom."[99] When Fitzalan first encounters Malvina, she is singing a "Scotch air" and "she looked like one of the beautiful forms which Ossian so often describes: her white dress fluttered in the wind, and her dark hair hung disheveled around her."[100] The heroine Amanda Malvina absorbs her mother's name and her taste for Scottish verse. Like the Malvina of the Ossian poems, Amanda Malvina of *The Children of the Abbey* also acts as a mediator, traveling "between times," and repeatedly crosses the borders separating the regions and nations of the British Isles.

From Scotland, Amanda Malvina travels to North Wales, where she immerses herself in the pastoral simplicity of her nurse's family, the Edwins, a name which is meant to remind readers of the title character in James Beattie's popular *The Minstrel*. When she moves with her father to Ireland, she notes the underdeveloped condition of the Irish and, like Adam Smith and later Edgeworth, critiques absenteeism:

the wretchedness so often conspicuous among many of the lower rank, fill her not only with compassion, but surprise, as she had imagined that liberty and a fruitful soil were generally attended with comfort and prosperity. Her father, to whom she communicated this idea, informed her that the indigence of the peasants proceeded in a great degree from the emigration of their landlords.[101]

Here Roche, an Irish author like Edgeworth, reveals an investment in political economy and uneven development that foreshadows Edgeworth's Irish novels. Once in London, Amanda also exhibits an awareness of the dangers of commercial and social refinement. The daughter of the absentee landlord, Lady Euphrasia, who spends most of the year at her fashionable Portman Square residence, appears at a ball "scarcely able to support her delicate frame . . . her languishing eyes [are] half closed."[102] When noticed by admirers, she appears "like a proud sultana in the midst of her slaves,"[103] recalling the decadent aristocratic women whom Mary Wollstonecraft in *A Vindication of the Rights of Woman* associates with the East. Roche's heroine emerges as an antidote to Lady Euphrasia and the decay spawned by highly developed societies and economies that remove landholders from their tenants and land, and lead them away from the origins of their capital to fashionable commercial centers such as London. Unlike Lady Euphrasia, Amanda's simple adornments and manners create a favorable "contrast" in the hero's mind between her and "the generality of fashionable women he had seen, whom he often secretly censured for sacrificing too largely at the shrine of art and fashion."[104] Like the heroines and heroes of Ossianic verse and later Edgeworth's Caroline Percy, Amanda cultivates her passions and tastes without becoming a victim to the excesses of advanced commercial culture. She models the aesthetic ideal theorized in the treatises of Blair, Kames, and later Stewart.

The title of *The Contrast* makes explicit the comparative mode in which Roche works and reminds readers of both Edgeworth's *Patronage*, which contrasts the Percys and the Falconers,[105] and the Scottish historical method. Not only does the novel compare Sicily, rural Ireland, London, and Wales, but it also contrasts the tastes and sensibilities of its two heroines: Adelaide, who was educated by her suffering mother in Wales, and Helena, who was reared by her fashionable grandmother in London. In the course of the novel, both heroines marry Irish landowners, but the overly refined tastes of Helena lead to her demise, while the cultivated sensibilities and self-command of Adelaide result in a happy marriage.

Helena is the daughter of Sir Maurice Rossglen, who married her mother, an English heiress, to save his heavily entailed estate in Ireland.

Despite the mercenary motives behind their marriage, the two enjoy a happy yet brief union that ends with the birth of Helena and the death of her mother. Rossglen allows Helena's grandmother to raise her among London's fashionable set, including the Bridgemores, who act as Helena's guardians and financial agents after her grandmother's death. Before dying himself, Rossglen brings Helena back to Ireland, where she meets his new wife and daughters as well as his wife's son from her first marriage, Sigismund Mountflorence, whose paternal estate is about to be lost due to long-standing incumbrances. Rossglen hopes Helena and Mountflorence will marry, enabling Mountflorence to use Helena's fortune to save his estate. Oddly, what prevents Helena and Mountflorence from enjoying their lives together is not the complex circumstances surrounding Mountflorence's patrimony, but Helena's own inability to demonstrate delicacy and command over her sensibilities and passions. Although "all those fugitive graces that belong to sensibility were hers," the poor fashionable education provided by her grandmother in London gave her "an innate consciousness of superiority," which prevents her from seeing the good in her stepmother and sisters until she has offended them almost beyond repair. Rossglen's wife sees Helena's inability to communicate as more a "fault of education than of nature,"[106] and Helena feels her own insufficiencies when she compares herself to her father's other daughters: "while in all the light and elegant accomplishments of the day, she had no cause to fear competition, she was by no means as well read in various parts of history and science as her sisters, educated as they were, under the immediate eye of a watchful and accomplished mother."[107]

Despite her growing appreciation of her father's family, Helena returns to London after his death and, through the evil machinations of the Bridgemores, comes to believe herself slighted by her Irish family. She immerses herself in London fashion, but is transformed by the sensibilities and newfound tastes Ireland awakened in her: "a thousand times gladly would she have exchanged, if in her power, these brilliant scenes, where she shone so preeminent, for those romantic ones in which she had been first awakened to a knowledge of her own perceptions, and taught to value them as they ought to be."[108] When she tries to exercise her newfound feelings in London, one of her close companions remarks that "sentiment is not quite so much the fashion, my love, as it was, so we'll dispense with the quotation you were giving."[109] Her pride and the Bridgemores' duplicitousness lead her to cut off communication with her Irish family, only to discover that Mr. Bridgemore, acting as her agent, has lost or stolen the better part of her enormous fortune. In shame, she leaves London for a rented estate in Wales, where she enters a gothic nightmare. Her rented house, a partial ruin itself, is mysteriously broken into by her former suitor Sir Osbert, who tricks her into marriage. Osbert has become a typical gothic villain, and Helena soon learns that he is not just a corrupt aristocrat but also a murderer living in exile. Soon after their marriage, she escapes Sir Osbert and comes to believe him lost at sea. Eventually, Mountflorence finds Helena in Wales and they marry. Yet her experiences in fashionable London and gothic Wales have changed her: "her looks continued so delicate that Mountflorence could not help contemplating her as a drooping flower."[110] At first, Helena appears to recover, but while she is living with Mountflorence in Ireland, Sir Osbert unexpectedly appears. His appearance makes Helena into a bigamist, and she dies bemoaning her own inability to control her feelings: "why endued with feelings to render this circumstance such a source of suffering?"[111] She concludes that she has always been too sensitive to thrive in the fashionable world of London and too sophisticated to respond as she would have wished to her Irish family. Helena's death appears to be a direct result of her own inability to integrate her sensibilities into her environment. The various genres she travels through, from the gothic novel she inhabits in Wales to the novel of manners she experiences in London, act to theorize the complex relationship of nation, taste, and economic development. Instead of achieving a universal or cosmopolitan standard as did Edgeworth's Caroline Percy, Helena finds herself a victim of her education and faulty sensibility.

The circumstances surrounding her foil (and sometimes doppelganger) Adelaide's birth and upbringing are as complex as Helena's. Like Helena, she is motherless, a victim of the evil Sir Osbert, and exiled for a period in Wales. Her future husband, Horatio De Montville, first discovers her in a ruined gothic castle in Sicily. After De Montville travels to Ireland to meet the wife his uncle has chosen for him, he begins to see Adelaide again under a number of mysterious circumstances. De Montville soon discovers that Adelaide is in fact his uncle's long-lost daughter as well as his intended bride. Although Adelaide wants to marry, she stalls the ceremony until she can clear her reputation, which had been damaged by her selfless desire to shield her friend Sophia Courtney from the social stigma of her illicit connection with Sir Osbert. The naïve Sophia consents to a clandestine marriage with Sir Osbert, but after Sir Osbert reveals that the marriage ceremony was a farce, Sophia realizes that her reputation has been lost and becomes ill. In an effort to recover Sophia's fame, Adelaide arranges for a secret meeting with Sir Osbert in an attempt to persuade him to marry her friend. Instead of listening to her plea, Sir Osbert attempts to abduct Adelaide, who quickly escapes, but appearances lead the public to believe that she had consented to an elopement. To protect the reputation of her friend and her friend's family, Adelaide remains silent and refuses to defend herself, despite the trial this experience is for her "sensitive and delicate mind."[112] Angry at Adelaide's refusal to marry, her father Lord Le Poer banishes her to Wales, where she escapes marriage to a Welshman named Madoc, who is discovered to be a fortune hunter and a bigamist. Adelaide runs from Wales to London, arriving "more dead than alive."[113] Ultimately, her father discovers both that her guardian in Wales was in league with Madoc and that Adelaide's failure to follow his commands to marry De Montville was not due to obstinacy, but her extreme delicacy. He immediately repents and forgives his daughter. After discovering this secret, her father feels his own baseness: "I now begin to comprehend all ... and this generous, though certainly romantic, creature – romantic, in risking her own happiness for that other, I flung from my cold bosom, as unworthy of being taken to it!"[114] She marries De Montville and they enjoy a happiness that was impossible for the more fashionable and corrupted Helena. Unlike Helena, Adelaide learns in Wales "how to command her feelings, that being one of the earliest lessons taught her by her suffering mother."[115] Where Helena succumbs to marriage with Sir Osbert out of desperation and loneliness, and soon after marries Mountflorence without revealing her previous marriage to Sir Osbert, Adelaide refuses to "dissemble."[116] Unlike Helena, Adelaide resists the fashionable world and possesses a stoic self-command that allows her to suffer the suspicions of her family and the public and resist succumbing to the wishes of her father and De Montville until her reputation has been vindicated. Interestingly, she remains unmarked by any particular nation and transcends the Italian, Irish, Welsh, and English environments she occupies, embodying a universal or even cosmopolitan balance that Helena failed to achieve.

By contrasting the different sensibilities of these two heroines, their educations, and the different environments they travel through, Roche's novel theorizes the difficulties entailed in measuring aesthetic progress in a way that resembles Edgeworth's fiction and the aesthetic treatises of Blair, Kames, and Stewart. Like her contemporaries, Roche believes that the appropriate and most productive use of feeling comes from one's ability to command the passions and demonstrate a delicacy of taste that can sustain itself despite national and historical differences. Although Edgeworth's more reserved heroines Caroline Percy and Grace Nugent at times read like a critique of Roche's Amanda Malvina or Adelaide, they all share a delicacy of taste that has been perfected by their experience of different environments. Like the aesthetic treatises of the Scottish Enlightenment, Edgeworth's and Roche's stadial fictions should be read as complex meditations on the relationship between nature and artifice, aesthetics and education, as well as the historical and economic progress of taste. These Romantic-era heroines, often dismissed as irksome in their perfections, might be better read as embodiments of a philosophical ideal, standards of taste, than simply as flat characters. Their notable lack of complexity enables them to trace the progress of taste and beauty through a host of socially and economically variable environments.

By the beginning of the nineteenth century the female warriors of the Ossian poems, who were addressed in the first chapter of this study, have morphed into the heroines of Romantic-era fiction – characters like *The Absentee*'s Grace Nugent and *The Children of the Abbey*'s Amanda Malvina. The historical and aesthetic dilemmas dramatized in the Ossian poems, the salons of first- and second-generation Bluestockings, and the philosophy of the Scottish Enlightenment strangely reemerge in the fiction of Radcliffe, Roche, and Edgeworth. Although initially the female bards and warriors, who possess refined sensibilities, yet are not afraid to wield a bow, seem categorically different from their novelistic doubles, the self-command that enabled Ossianic women to revenge their lovers' deaths instead of dissolving into tears resembles the self-command that prevents *The Patronage*'s Caroline Percy from falling prey to the Clays or *The Contrast*'s Adelaide from giving in to Sir Osbert's, and later her father's, demands. Surprisingly, this genealogy, which connects the Ossian poems and the Scottish Enlightenment to the poetry of the Bluestockings and the novels of Radcliffe, Edgeworth, and Roche, allows us to read these heroines' self-command not only as looking forwards to the Victorian angel in the house, but also backwards. They echo the struggle of female warriors and bards to resist emerging narratives of civilization, and the desire of the Ladies of Llangollen to retreat from society in the queer utopia of their beloved Welsh valley. The masculine self-command Smith assigned to a rude age survives in these Romantic-era heroines' resistance to the fashionable world of London and a civilizing process that too easily aligns commercial development with the elevation of the feminine and the refinement of sensibility.

Notes

1. Review of *The Maid of the Hamlet* in *British Critic* (June 1794), p. 695.
2. Regina Maria Roche, *The Maid of the Hamlet*, p. 5.
3. Regina Maria Roche, *The Children of the Abbey*, p. 48.

4. Ibid., p. 48.
5. Ibid., p. 49.
6. Ibid., p. 53.
7. Review of *The Children of the Abbey* in *British Catalogue* (January 1798), p. 77.
8. Nancy Armstrong, *Desire and Domestic Fiction*; Mary Poovey, *Uneven Developments*.
9. David Hume, *Essays Moral, Political, and Literary*, p. 243.
10. Fiona Price in *Women Writers and the Aesthetics of Romanticism* argues that "[during] this period, disputes over taste frequently took place in marginalized forms themselves," including "the Gothic, the sentimental novel, the romance, and the tale" (p. 2). Price suggests that these novels were responsible for democratizing taste and integrating taste into the quotidian and domestic environments often discussed in these novels.
11. Maria Edgeworth, *Patronage*, vol. 6, p. 71.
12. Hugh Blair, *Lectures on Rhetoric and Belles Lettres*, p. 17.
13. Ibid., p. 18.
14. Marshall Brown, "Poetry and the Novel"; Gary Kelly, *English Fiction of the Romantic Period, 1789–1830*.
15. Kelly, *English Fiction of the Romantic Period*, p. 42.
16. David Duff, *Romanticism and the Uses of Genre*, p. 121.
17. Ibid., p. 20.
18. Anne H. Stevens, *British Historical Fiction before Scott*, p. 7.
19. Walter Scott, *Waverley*, p. 33.
20. Ibid., p. 493.
21. Ibid., p. 493.
22. See Ruth Mack's *Literary Historicity* for a discussion of the development of the historical novel in the eighteenth century. Mack argues that a shift in emphasis from exemplary history to social histories led to a reevaluation of the relationship between history and experience. She finds this shift in historical method discussed in the eighteenth-century novel and history "proper." Her discussion of Charlotte Lennox's *The Female Quixote* and its engagement with history as a relative and non-linear discourse provides a relevant context for my discussion of women writers' contribution to the development of historical fiction.
23. In *Bardic Nationalism*, Katie Trumpener outlines the differences between the national tale and the historical novel: "The national tale before *Waverley* presents national character as a synecdoche of an unchanging cultural space: here nationalism is a self-evident legacy, the result of unbroken continuity and a populist community that unites aristocracy and folk. The historical novel draws heavily on this vision of national continuity, but it posits the moment of nationalism as a further stage of historical development: only through the forcible, often violent, entry into history does the feudal folk community become a nation, and only through dislocation and collective suffering is a new national identity forged" (p. 142). Ina Ferris in *The Romatic National Tale and the Question of Ireland* presents a complementary definition: "the national tale is not simply a fiction that takes national matters of manners for its subject . . . but a fiction that

locates itself in a contentious zone of discourse in order to articulate the grievances of a small people" (p. 50).

24. In *Scott's Shadow*, Ian Duncan makes a similar claim, arguing that "authentic cultural identities" reemerge in Scott's fiction as "aesthetic effects" (p. 98).

25. Claire Connolly, *A Cultural History of the Irish Novel, 1790–1829*, p. 4.

26. Juliet Shields, *Sentimental Literature and Anglo-Scottish Identity, 1745–1820*, p. 136.

27. Ian Duncan's discussion of the early nineteenth-century novelist John Galt in *Scott's Shadow* provides an additional context for the fictions of Edgeworth and Roche. As Duncan argues, Galt develops in his fiction the category of "theoretical history" (p. 216). Indebted to the Scottish Enlightenment, Galt's "theoretical histories" use "reason, experience, and common sense" to impress morals upon readers (p. 16). Galt's project might be compared to Edgeworth's desire to use the principles of the Scottish Enlightenment to reform the romantic proclivities of her female contemporaries and transform the novel into a pedagogical instrument.

28. Hume, "Of the Standard of Taste," in *Essays Moral, Political, and Literary*, p. 247.

29. Ibid., p. 246.

30. Ibid., p. 236.

31. Ibid., p. 237.

32. In *Enlightenment and the Book*, Richard Sher writes, "Lord Kames's *Elements of Criticism* . . . went to a tenth British edition in 1824 and an eleventh in 1839 (in addition to a large number of nineteenth-century editions in America)" (p. 91). See also Robert Crawford (ed.), *The Scottish Invention of English Literature*.

33. Blair, *Lectures on Rhetoric and Belles Lettres*, p. 11.

34. Ibid., p. 14.

35. See Pam Perkins, *Women Writers and the Edinburgh Enlightenment*, pp. 104–6, for a discussion of Elizabeth Hamilton's engagement with Dugald Stewart's philosophy. See Marilyn Butler, *Maria Edgeworth* for a discussion of the influence of Stewart as well as the Scottish Enlightenment on Edgeworth's writing.

36. Blair, *Lectures on Rhetoric and Belles Lettres*, p. 14.

37. Ibid., p. 15.

38. Lord Kames, *Elements of Criticism*, vol. 1, p. 147.

39. Ibid., vol. 2, p. 725.

40. Ibid., vol. 2, p. 727.

41. Dugald Stewart, "On Taste," in *The Collected Works of Dugald Stewart*, vol. v, p. 366.

42. Ibid., p. 340.

43. Ibid., p. 366.

44. Dugald Stewart, "On the Beautiful," in *The Collected Works of Dugald Stewart*, vol. v, p. 205.

45. Ibid., p. 256.

46. Blair, *Lectures on Rhetoric and Belles Lettres*, p. 7.

47. Ibid., p. 48.

48. Kames, *Elements of Criticism*, vol. 1, p. 143.
49. Ibid., p. 143.
50. Ibid., p. 144.
51. Ibid., p. 192.
52. Ibid., p. 221.
53. Butler, *Maria Edgeworth*, p. 76; Fraser Easton, "Cosmopolitical Economy."
54. In Maria Edgeworth's *Belinda*, Harriet Freke, perhaps the most indelicate of all the women in Edgeworth's fiction, ridicules Belinda's reading: "'What have you here?' continued Mrs. Freke, who did not choose to attend to this question, exclaiming as she reviewed each of the books on the table in their turns, in the summary of language of presumptuous ignorance. 'Smith's *Theory of Moral Sentiments*—Milk and water! Moore's *Travels*—Hasty pudding! *La Bruyere*—Nettle porridge! This is what you were at when I came in, was it not?' said she, taking up a book in which she saw Belinda's mark, '*Essay on the Inconsistency of Human Wishes*. Poor thing! Who bored you with this task?'" (pp. 227–8).
55. The phrase "tale of other times" appears in "The War of Caros," a poem that describes Ossian's son Oscar's attempt to untangle the legacy and history of his forefathers. Sophia Lee's *The Recess* (1783), an important early historical novel, also uses this Ossianic phrase as its subtitle, suggesting additional continuities between the Ossianic poetry and the gothic and historical novel.
56. Richard Lovell Edgeworth's second wife and Anna Seward's beloved companion Honora Sneyd Edgeworth loved Ossianic verse. Edgeworth's lifelong devotion to Honora (despite her early death and his remarriage) suggests that the poems were probably quite popular in the Edgeworth household.
57. See Maria Edgeworth, *Letters for Literary Ladies*, p. 26.
58. Ibid., p. 18.
59. Ibid., p. 18.
60. In the introduction to the Pickering & Chatto edition of *Patronage*, vol. 6, Butler explains that, "At the end of 1811 RLE called a halt, on the ground that *Patronage* was far too long to fit into the series. He suggested Maria should make a second Irish tale to match *Ennui* in the first, by merging the play called *The Absentee* (which has a lord from England traveling incognito in Ireland) with the Irish émigré family in *Patronage* (who were originally patients of Dr Erasmus Percy in London)" (p. x).
61. Price in *Women Writers and the Aesthetics of Romanticism* argues that Edgeworth's *Tales of Fashionable Life* "present a complex view of the relationship between taste and nation," and views the "cross-class sympathy" inspired in novels like *Ennui* and *The Absentee* as reflective of English, particularly fashionable London's, interference with the relationship between landlord and tenant that structured traditional Irish life (p. 153).
62. Price argues that Edgeworth's "work has a utilitarian drive that is difficult to equate with the influential Kantian position on taste" (p. 115). Although Scottish thinkers such as Adam Smith refused to align taste and utility and separated the useful from the moral and correct, other Scottish

thinkers, particularly those of the common sense school, saw utility as a just product of good taste.

63. Maria Edgeworth, *The Absentee*, vol. 5.
64. Ibid., p. 31.
65. Ibid., p. 32.
66. Ibid., p. 32.
67. Ibid., p. 15.
68. Ibid., p. 15.
69. Ibid., p. 59.
70. Ibid., pp. 65–6.
71. In *The Cultural History of the Irish Novel*, Claire Connolly reads Lady Clonbrony's focus on things, furniture, and objects in a slightly different fashion. In a larger argument about the "frangibil[ity]" of not only the Irish Union but also Romantic-era Irish fiction (p. 45), she draws attention to Lady Clonbrony's refusal to return to Ireland unless the family replaces the house's outdated damask chairs, which have become stained and worn in the family's absence. Grace agrees to replace the ruined upholstery and ultimately the chairs themselves, which are burned. Connolly reads this as a sign of waste and excess that exceeds and troubles the restoration and renewal that the family's return and Grace's marriage are supposed to represent (pp. 25–6).
72. *Patronage*, vol. 1, p. 13.
73. Ibid., p. 49.
74. Ibid., p. 49.
75. Ibid., p. 151.
76. Ibid., p. 154.
77. Ibid., p. 154.
78. Ibid., p. 161.
79. *Patronage*, vol. 2, p. 39.
80. *Patronage*, vol. 1, p. 252.
81. *Patronage*, vol. 2, p. 52.
82. Ibid., p. 44.
83. Ibid., p. 52.
84. Ibid., p. 190.
85. *Patronage*, vol. 1, p. 224.
86. Ibid., p. 224.
87. *Patronage*, vol. 2, p. 102.
88. In the introduction to the Pickering & Chatto edition of *Patronage*, vol. 1, Butler notes that Bentham praised *Patronage* in Leigh Hunt's *Examiner* (p. xxiii).
89. Miranda Burgess, "The National Tale and Allied Genres," p. 41; in her essay, Burgess argues that the designator "tale" was also a "marker of what are now called Gothic novels," and her discussion of Roche's influence on Edgeworth and Owenson does much to enrich our understanding of the national tale's complex evolution.
90. Deborah McLeod's unpublished Ph.D. thesis *The Minerva Press* argues that the Minerva Press itself has been unfairly characterized as just a gothic press: "The Minerva Press produced many works other than novels and many types of novels other than gothic and sentimental romances" (p. 13).

91. See Jennie Batchelor, *Women's Work*, pp. 143–84. Batchelor convincingly argues that the establishment of the Royal Literary Fund did much to construct "gendered divisions between, for example, the genius and the hack, the useful and the ornamental, the professional and the popular and the mind and the body" that "degraded" and devalued women's contributions to the literary marketplace (pp. 148–9). In this sense, Roche's association with the Literary Fund, like her association with the Minerva Press, worked to devalue her contributions to literary history.

92. Devendra P. Varma, "Introduction," p. ix.

93. Natalie Schroeder expresses doubts about Roche's investment in Ireland in "Regina Maria Roche and the Early Nineteenth-Century Irish Novel": "Mrs. Roche's Irish interests are very hard to define consistently ... Ultimately, Mrs. Roche's regional novels leave us with more questions than answers. Were the seemingly serious feelings that are expressed in *The Traditions of the Castle* simply make-believe passions, like the thunderstorms in Gothic fiction, turned on for effect? Were these opinions espoused only for the occasion of a new book, or were they something that Mrs. Roche, as a native Irish woman of some national standing, really believed? How deeply was Mrs. Roche really concerned with the Irish problem? Until we know more about Regina Maria Roche's life and background, the answers to these questions will remain a minor mystery" (p. 130).

94. Letters to the Royal Literary Fund, Loan MS 96, Case 590, British Library.

95. Regina Maria Roche, *The Contrast*, vol. 1, p. xv.

96. Roche, *The Children of the Abbey*, p. 58.

97. Ibid., p. 8.

98. In linking her heroine to Malvina, Roche follows a number of other late eighteenth and early nineteenth-century plays, songs, and novels that adopt Malvina as a central character. The early nineteenth-century transnational Malvina industry included, for example, Sophie Cottin's four-volume novel *Malvina* (1802), which was translated from the French.

99. Roche, *The Children of the Abbey*, p. 11.

100. Ibid., p. 16.

101. Ibid., p. 171.

102. Ibid., p. 184.

103. Ibid., p. 184.

104. Ibid., p. 53.

105. The title also recalls Edgeworth's short story "The Contrast," which was published in her *Popular Tales* (1804) and, as Marilyn Butler argues, served as the inspiration for *Patronage*. See Marilyn Butler, "Introductory Note," *Patronage*, p. ix.

106. *The Contrast*, vol. 1, p. 22.

107. Ibid., p. 119.

108. *The Contrast*, vol. 2, p. 165.

109. Ibid., p. 155.

110. *The Contrast*, vol. 3, p. 213.

111. Ibid., p. 255.

112. *The Contrast*, vol. 2, p. 269.
113. Ibid., p. 239.
114. Ibid., p. 268.
115. Ibid., p. 57.
116. Ibid., p. 69.

Epilogue: Women Writers in the Age of Ossian

This book has explored alternatives to antagonistic narratives of women writers and Enlightenment thought. Women did not, for the most part, write philosophical treatises or political pamphlets, but their literary endeavors made charting historical and social progress during the Enlightenment a cross-cultural and comparative exercise. Their work also popularized Enlightenment historiography in novels, poetry collections, and even in the periodical press. A timeline published in December of 1773 by *The Lady's Magazine*, perhaps the most popular and longest-running women's periodical in the English-speaking world,[1] testifies to women's widespread engagement with shaping historical accounts of progress. In "A Chronological Account of the most remarkable Discoveries in the Arts and Sciences," Sophia Amelia, a pseudonymous contributor, makes a claim for women as particularly positioned to develop a global history of the arts. She describes her history as

> a chronological series of events, which very few of the gentlemen know any thing of, and if in boarding-schools my own sex would amuse themselves with the following table by questions and answers I am confident they would puzzle one half of the curates, and six-eighths of the rectors and vicars in the kingdom.[2]

Beginning in 1900 BCE with Abraham, "in whose time sculpture was supposed to be invented," and ending in 1763 CE, the timeline concludes with "Harrison, an Englishman, [who] constructed an instrument to find out the longitude,"[3] making it possible to apprehend the world as a uniform space. Significantly, Sophia Amelia's account of humankind's progress breaks national boundaries and ranges widely across temporal and geographic divides. As well as including aesthetic and moral milestones, such as "700 [BCE] Archilochus, inventor of iambic verse ... 500 [BCE] Confucius, the Chinese moralist ... 1025 [CE] Gui d' Arezzo, invented musical notes,"[4] Sophia Amelia mentions Hippocrates, John

Harvey, and Isaac Newton. A recent invention of Joseph Priestley, the timeline attempted to represent universal history.[5] Sophia Amelia's basic chronology aspires to universality and also reminds readers of the social histories of the Scottish Enlightenment, which blended commercial advances with artistic and moral developments, such as 527 BCE, when "the first silkworm eggs were brought to Europe," and 1702 BCE, which marks "the invention of Dresden china."[6] Interestingly, the only artist from the British Isles Sophia Amelia mentions within her history is the Ossian poet. He figures prominently as the lone entry listed in the first 500 years of the Common Era:

> After Christ
> 250 Ossian, the British poet.
> 527 The first silkworm eggs were brought to Europe.
> 757 The first [pipe] organs were sent from Constantinople to France.
> 1025 Gui d'Arezzo, invented musical notes.
> 1110 Invention of chess.
> 1200 Poetry flourished in Germany.

Sophia Amelia's selection of Ossian rather than Shakespeare, the more contemporary Samuel Richardson, or even one of the women writers who were frequently profiled in the pages of *The Lady's Magazine*, such as Lady Mary Wortley Montagu or Elizabeth Carter, reinforces many of the themes of this book. Ossian connected women to Enlightenment historiography and its practice. His poetry provided women writers— from the well-known and canonical to the pseudonymous—with an opportunity to think about the feminine refinement of the arts and to situate this progress in a cross-cultural and even global context. Sophie Amelia's curious timeline, which combines gender and aesthetics with a transnational approach to understanding the nature of progress, reflects the interests and concerns of the feminine Enlightenment this book attempts to chart. It suggests that women writers from this period might be more productively situated in an Age of Ossian, which extends from the middle of the eighteenth to well into the nineteenth century, bridging the gap between the eighteenth century and the Romantic periods. This Ossianic framework also provides a starting point for thinking about the impact of Anglophone and global approaches to literature on feminist literary historiography.

Although not nearly as temporally or geographically wide-ranging as the territory covered by Sophia Amelia, my study also makes a case for Ossian's significance. The Ossian poems were an important pivot between women writers and Scottish Enlightenment philosophers. Ossian connects women writers to a host of conversations: the role of emotion and gender in historical narrative, the nature of British versus English history, and the debates surrounding the development of universal and global historiographies. Ossian's incredible popularity outside Scotland has been recounted by Howard Gaskill, Dafydd Moore, and, most recently, James Mulholland, who sees Ossianic poetry as key to mapping a global aesthetics of poetic voice.[7] Ossian's popularity also makes possible a new history of women's writing, one that looks far beyond the British domestic sphere. The Bluestockings' adoption of Malvina as a model for their own philosophical and literary pursuits, Seward's Ossianic "songs of grief," and Edgeworth's "tales of other times" evidence women writers' attempts to wrestle with the questions the poems posed about imperial development, progress, and women's role in mapping civilization. Women writers' affinity for Ossianic poetry creates an interesting history itself that crosses national and temporal boundaries and connects discontinuous places and times, such as Ossian's ancient Caledonia, the Ladies of Llangollen's Welsh ruins, and Ann Radcliffe's gothic France and Italy. Following this Ossianic bent in women's writing invites reading across genres, cultures, and nations in a way that resembles the methods of Scottish historiographers, who also drew on Ossian in creating their comparative histories. Ultimately, this study does not suggest a universal women's history or a singular trajectory of progress, but it does gesture toward the value of reading in a non-linear and comparative fashion within women's literary history. Far from being future-oriented or teleologically driven, many women writers looked backwards, imitating ancient fragments in order to create new histories or challenge old ones. The recovery or recreation of outmoded poetic forms also shaped new prose genres, and fragments and relics of supposedly long-gone cultures inspired a reconsideration of women's status and treatment in a modern era.

Women writers' engagement with Ossian and Enlightenment historiography inevitably raises questions about feminist literary historiography, which has recently been wrestling with methodological questions and attempting both to develop aesthetic criteria for women's literature and to think beyond the problematic association of women writers with the domestic novel. In recent and important studies, Betty Schellenberg, Paula Backscheider, and Susan Staves have troubled, in different ways, the investment of feminist critics in domestic fiction. In her study of women writers and British print culture, Schellenberg expresses "dissatisfaction with the standard frameworks used" in discussing the achievements of mid-eighteenth-century women novelists, who, she finds, are too persistently associated with domesticity and the constraints of the separate sphere hypothesis.[8] Schellenberg's careful examination of women writers' contributions to the print marketplace in a range of genres has troubled simplistic elisions of women writers with the heroines of their domestic fictions. Echoing Schellenberg's concerns, Backscheider has argued for the importance of eighteenth-century women's poetry, and Staves has drawn attention to drama, letters, and the translations of influential women like Elizabeth Carter. Women writers' engagement with Ossianic poetry provides another alternative mode for thinking about women's literary history; by rewriting and revising Ossian's poetry in verse and novels and adapting Scottish modes of historiography to literature, women writers shaped the social and literary structures that informed the larger British Empire. The historical and geographical comparisons this mode of thought invited were pervasive: even when writing novels, women writers' concerns with love, desire, and marriage were often structured by comparisons to women throughout history and around the world.

The Age of Ossian also provides new metaphors for women's literary history that trouble women writers' relationship to the familial and domestic. Staves, in thoughtful readings of Samuel Johnson and Charlotte Lennox as well as Sarah and Henry Fielding, suggests mid-century women writers "won acceptance by playing the roles of daughters, sisters, or wives to literary men."[9] Anna Seward and Elizabeth Montagu, who are perhaps most famous for refusing to position themselves as the sisters or daughters of Samuel Johnson, explicitly aligned themselves with the Ossianic bard – the last of his race – and, in doing so, stepped outside the heterosexual and English family, choosing cross-cultural, transnational, and queer affinities. This counternarrative of women writers in the Age of Johnson, or what this study would call an Age of Ossian, resonates with Paula Backscheider's work on friendship poetry, which she sees as providing "an alternate discourse within the genre of poetry and within the larger culture";[10] and certainly the poetry produced by Anna Seward and her Bluestocking predecessors might be effectively categorized as friendship poetry that rethinks issues of progress, inheritance, production and reproduction in ways that challenge both the patriarchal family and the insular national one.

Discussions of aesthetics and women's writing might also be complicated in productive ways by an Ossianic frame that interrogates the feminine progress of the arts and its complex and contradictory relationship to commercial and imperial development. Feminist literary historiographers worry that a preoccupation with projects of recovery has led to a lack of attention to aesthetic merit. In their different ways, Backscheider, Staves, and Schellenberg agree that women's literary history should be subject to aesthetic criteria, suggesting that social and biographical frameworks have overshadowed literary merit. Staves argues that "not all writing by women is the proper object of literary study";[11] Backscheider sorts her chapters by "poetic kinds" instead of individual writers in order to discern who is "worthy of remembrance";[12] in a related vein, Schellenberg examines eighteenth-century reviews in order to identify transhistorical "aesthetic value[s]" that might be used to frame women's writing.[13] My own interest in troubling the divisions between masculine philosophical treatises and feminine novels and poems prevents me from making such hard and fast generic distinctions or adducing literary value in the way some of these critics might want; yet tracing women writers' interest in Ossian reveals their awareness of the political and social stakes of aesthetic practice and judgment. Women writers' discussions and adaptations of Ossian betray their awareness that aesthetic practice and aesthetic merit are culturally specific and often function as a gauge of development. Ossian provides a new window for thinking about a range of issues related to women and aesthetics, from women writers' deployment of refined and rude poetic forms to the popularity of impossibly accomplished and delicate heroines in gothic fiction. In other words, women writers' self-awareness of the cultural significance of their own aesthetic practices, and the ways their literary works might be used to measure not only their individual artistic value but also the progress of their culture or nation, connect their work to philosophical debates over the nature of aesthetic value and complicate judgments of literary merit that rely on universal gauges. If rendering aesthetic value is not universal but culturally and nationally specific, how do we understand an oft-dismissed poem like Anna Seward's "Rich Auld Willie," which she contributed to Walter Scott's *Minstrelsy of the Scottish Border*, or even one of the many oriental tales that appeared in *The Lady's Magazine* and were written by anonymous and pseudonymous women writers like Sophia Amelia?

Ossianic thinking encouraged women writers to imagine in transnational and cross-cultural directions, habits of mind that resemble the comparative logic that structured Scottish Enlightenment historiography. For Scots such as Macpherson and Blair, Ossian may have provided both a Scottish cultural heritage and a way for Scots to integrate themselves into a larger British identity. For women writers, Ossian functioned very differently. The women writers of this study embraced Ossian's inauthenticity and hybridity and used him to craft associations that unsettled standard national, political, and familial frameworks. By adapting Ossian as an origin, women writers were paradoxically able to deny the importance of origins. To begin with Ossian is to begin both in the lost recesses of the ancient British Isles, and with a fiction. Tracing a women's literary history from Ossian can be both maddening and joyful. Ossian invites an ironic critique of the process of making history, a historiography that highlights gaps, blind spots, and the fragility of origins.

Notes

1. For a recent discussion of *The Lady's Magazine*, see Jenny Batchelor, "'Connections, which are of service . . . in a more advanced age.'"
2. Sophia Amelia, "A Chronological Account of the most remarkable Discoveries in the Arts and Sciences," p. 639.
3. Ibid., pp. 639–41.
4. Ibid., pp. 639–41.
5. See Daniel Rosenberg, "Joseph Priestley and the Graphic Invention of Modern Time."
6. Sophia Amelia, "A Chronological Account," p. 639.
7. See James Mulholland's *Sounding Imperial*, particularly Chapter 3, "Scotland and the Invention of Voice."
8. Betty Schellenberg, *The Professionalization of Women Writers in Eighteenth-Century Britain*, pp. 7–8.
9. Susan Staves, *A Literary History of Women's Writing in Britain, 1660–1789*, p. 230.
10. Paula Backscheider, *Eighteenth-Century Women Poets and their Poetry*, p. 194.
11. Staves, *A Literary History*, p. 5.
12. Backscheider, *Eighteenth-Century Women Poets*, p. xxvi.
13. Schellenberg, *The Professionalization of Women Writers*, p. 120.

Bibliography

Primary Sources

Manuscripts
The Abbotsford Collection, National Library of Scotland.
The Abercairny Collection, National Records of Scotland.
The Montagu Collection, Huntington Library.
Letters to the Royal Literary Fund, Loan MS 96, Case 590, British Library.

Print
Alexander, William, *The History of Women* (Edinburgh, [1779] 1783).
Beattie, James, *The Minstrel* (London, [1771–4] 1784).
Blair, Hugh, *Lectures on Rhetoric and Belles Lettres*, ed. Linda Ferreria and
    Michael Halloran (Carbondale: Southern Illinois Press, [1783] 2005).
Boswell, James, *The Journal of a Tour to the Hebrides*, ed. Peter Levi (New
    York: Penguin, [1786] 1984).
Boswell, James, *Life of Johnson*, ed. R. W. Chapman and J. D. Fleeman
    (Oxford: Oxford University Press, [1791] 1998).
Carter, Elizabeth, and Catherine Talbot, *Letters between Elizabeth Carter and
    Catherine Talbot, from the Year 1741–1770*, ed. Rev. Montagu Pennington,
    2 vols (London: 1808).
Edgeworth, Maria, *Letters for Literary Ladies* (London: Everyman, [1795]
    1993).
Edgeworth, Maria, *Belinda* (New York: Oxford University Press, [1801] 2008).
Edgeworth, Maria, *The Absentee*, in *The Works of Maria Edgeworth*, vol. 5
    (London: Pickering & Chatto, [1812] 1999).
Edgeworth, Maria, *Patronage*, in *The Works of Maria Edgeworth*, vols 6–7
    (London: Pickering & Chatto, [1812] 1999).
Ferguson, Adam, *Essay on Civil Society*, ed. Fania Oz-Salzberger (Cambridge:
    Cambridge University Press, [1767] 1995).
Hicklin, John, *The Ladies of Llangollen* (Chester, 1847).
Historic Manuscripts Commission, *Fifteenth Report, Appendix, Part VII, The
    Manuscripts of the Duke of Somerset, The Marquis of Ailesbury, and The
    Rev. Sir T. H. G. Puleston, Bart.* (London, 1898).
Home, Henry [Lord Kames], *Sketches of the History of Man* (Edinburgh, 1774).
Home, Henry [Lord Kames], *Elements of Criticism* (Indianapolis: Liberty Fund,
    [1785] 2005).

Hume, David, *Essays Moral, Political, and Literary* (Indianapolis: Liberty Fund, [1777] 1985).

Hurd, Richard, *Letters on Chivalry and Romance* (London, 1762).

Johnson, Samuel, *Dictionary of the English Language*, 2 vols (London, 1756).

Johnson, Samuel, *A Journey to the Western Islands of Scotland*, ed. Peter Levi (New York: Penguin, [1775] 1984).

Johnson, Samuel, *Lives of the Most Eminent English Poets* (Oxford: Oxford University Press, [1781] 1959).

Macpherson, James (trans.), *Fingal, an ancient epic poem, in six books: together with several other poems, composed by Ossian the son of Fingal* (London: T. Becket and P. A. De Hondt, 1762).

Millar, John, *Origin of the Distinction of Ranks* (Edinburgh, [1771] 1783).

Montagu, Elizabeth, *An Essay on the Writing and Genius of Shakespear* (London, [1769] 1785).

Pennant, Thomas, *A Tour in Wales*, vol. 1 (London, 1778).

Radcliffe, Ann, *The Castles of Athlin and Dunbayne* (New York: Oxford University Press, [1789] 1995).

Radcliffe, Ann, *The Mysteries of Udolpho* (New York: Oxford University Press, [1794] 1998).

Roche, Maria Regina, *The Children of the Abbey* (Philadelphia, [1796] 1870).

Roche, Maria Regina, *The Maid of the Hamlet* (London, 1800).

Roche, Maria Regina, *The Contrast* (London, 1828).

Scott, Walter, *Lives of the Novelists* (London: Oxford University Press, [1821–4] 1906).

Scott, Walter, *The Letters of Walter Scott, 1787–1807*, ed. H. J. C. Grierson (London: Constable & Co. Ltd, 1932).

Seward, Anna, *Llangollen Vale with Other Poems* (London, 1796).

Seward, Anna, *Memoirs of the Life of Dr. Darwin* (London, 1804).

Seward, Anna, *The Poetical Works of Anna Seward*, 3 vols, ed. Walter Scott (Edinburgh, 1809).

Seward, Anna, *Letters of Anna Seward: Written Between the Years 1784 and 1807*, 6 vols, ed. Archibald Constable (Edinburgh, 1811).

Smith, Adam, *The Wealth of Nations* (New York: Prometheus Books, [1776] 1991).

Smith, Adam, *Theory of Moral Sentiments*, ed. Ryan Hanley (New York: Penguin, [1790] 2009).

Smith, Adam, *Lectures on Jurisprudence*, ed. R. L. Meek, D. D. Raphael and P. G. Stein (Oxford: Oxford University Press, 1978).

Smith, Adam, *Lectures on Rhetoric and Belles Lettres*, ed. J. C. Bryce (New York: Cambridge University Press, 1983).

Sophia Amelia, "A Chronological Account of the most remarkable Discoveries in the Arts and Sciences," *The Lady's Magazine* (Dec 1773), pp. 639–41.

Stewart, Dugald, *The Collected Works of Dugald Stewart, vol. v: Philosophical Essays* (Edinburgh, 1855).

Talbot, Catherine, *Reflections of the Seven Days of the Week* (London, 1770).

Thomson, James, *The Seasons, The Castle of Indolence, and Other Poems*, ed. James Sambrook (Oxford: Clarendon Press, 1986).

Wollstonecraft, Mary, *A Vindication of the Rights of Woman*, ed. Deidre Shauna Lynch (New York: W. W. Norton & Co., [1792] 2009).

Secondary Sources

Ahmed, Sara, *The Cultural Politics of Emotion* (Edinburgh: Edinburgh University Press, 2004).

Appiah, Kwame Anthony, *Cosmopolitanism: Ethics in a World of Strangers* (New York: W. W. Norton & Co., 2006).

Arendt, Hannah, *On the Human Condition* (Chicago: University of Chicago Press, 1958).

Armstrong, Nancy, *Desire and Domestic Fiction: A Political History of the Novel* (New York: Oxford University Press, 1990).

Ashmun, Margaret, *The Singing Swan* (New York: Greenwood Press, [1931] 1968).

Backscheider, Paula, *Eighteenth-Century Women Poets and Their Poetry: Inventing Agency, Inventing Genre* (Baltimore: Johns Hopkins University Press, 2005).

Barchus, Janine, *Graphic Design, Print Culture, and the Eighteenth-Century Novel* (Cambridge: Cambridge University Press, 2003).

Barnard, Teresa, *Anna Seward: A Constructed Life* (Aldershot: Ashgate, 2009).

Barrell, John, and Harriet Guest, "Thomson in the 1790s," in Richard Terry (ed.), *James Thomson: Essays for the Tercentary* (Liverpool: Liverpool University Press, 2000), pp. 217–46.

Batchelor, Jennie, *Women's Work: Labour, Gender, Authorship, 1750–1830* (New York: Manchester University Press, 2010).

Batchelor, Jennie, "'Connections, which are of service . . . in a more advanced age': *The Lady's Magazine*, Community, and Women's Literary History," *Tulsa Studies in Women's Literature* 30:2 (2011), pp. 245–67.

Baucom, Ian, *Specters of the Atlantic: Finance Capital, Slavery, and the Philosophy of History* (Durham, NC: Duke University Press, 2005).

Benjamin, Walter, *Illuminations*, trans. Harry Zohn (New York: Schocken Books, 1969).

Bowerbank, Sylvia, *Speaking for Nature: Women and Ecologies of Early Modern England* (Baltimore: Johns Hopkins University Press, 2004).

Bowers, Toni, *Force or Fraud: British Seduction Stories and the Problem of Resistance, 1660–1760* (New York: Oxford University Press, 2011).

Brewer, John, *Pleasures of the Imagination: English Culture in the Eighteenth Century* (Chicago: University of Chicago Press, 2000).

Brown, Laura, *Ends of Empire: Women and Ideology in Early Eighteenth-Century English Literature* (Ithaca, NY: Cornell University Press, 1993).

Brown, Marshall, "Poetry and the novel," in Richard Maxwell and Katie Trumpener (eds), *The Cambridge Companion to Fiction in the Romantic Period* (Cambridge: Cambridge University Press, 2008), pp. 107–28.

Burgess, Miranda, "The National Tale and Allied Genres," in John Wilson Forster (ed.), *The Cambridge Companion to the Irish Novel* (Cambridge: Cambridge University Press, 2007), pp. 39–59.

Butler, Marilyn, *Maria Edgeworth: A Literary Biography* (Oxford: Oxford University Press, 1990).

Butler, Marilyn, "Popular Antiquarianism," in Iain McCalam (ed.), *The Oxford Companion to the Romantic Age: British Culture, 1776–1832* (New York: Oxford University Press, 1999), pp. 328–37.

Carey, Daniel, and Lynn Festa (eds), *The Postcolonial Enlightenment:*

Eighteenth-Century Colonialism and Postcolonial Theory (New York: Oxford University Press, 2009).

Castle, Terry, *The Female Thermometer* (New York: Oxford University Press, 1995).

Chandler, James, *England in 1819: The Politics of Literary Culture and the Case of Romantic Historicism* (Chicago: University of Chicago Press, 1999).

Clarke, Norma, "Anna Seward: Swan, Duckling, or Goose," in Jennie Batchelor and Cora Kaplan (eds), *British Women's Writing in the Eighteenth Century: Authorship, Politics and History* (New York: Palgrave Macmillan, 2005), pp. 34–47.

Clery, E. J., *The Rise of Supernatural Fiction* (Cambridge: Cambridge University Press, 1999).

Clery, E. J., *The Feminization Debate in Eighteenth-Century England: Literature, Commerce and Luxury* (New York: Palgrave, 2004).

Climenson, Emily (ed.), *The Queen of the Bluestockings, Her Correspondence from 1720–1761*, vols 1 and 2 (London: John Murray, 1906).

Coffey, Diane, "Protecting the Botanic Garden: Seward, Darwin, and Coalbrookdale," *Women's Studies* 31 (2002), pp. 141–64.

Connolly, Claire, *A Cultural History of this Irish Novel, 1790–1829* (Cambridge: Cambridge University Press, 2012).

Crawford, Robert, *Devolving English Literature* (New York: Oxford University Press, 1992).

Crawford, Robert (ed.), *The Scottish Invention of English Literature* (New York: Cambridge University Press, 1998).

Curley, Thomas M., *Samuel Johnson, the Ossian Fraud, and the Celtic Revival in Great Britain and Ireland* (Cambridge: Cambridge University Press, 2009).

Curran, Stuart, "Anna Seward and the Dynamic of Female Friendship," in Lilla Mana Crisafulli and Cecilia Pietropoli (eds), *Romantic Women Poets: Genre and Gender* (Amsterdam: Rodopi, 2007), pp. 11–21.

Cvetkovich, Ann, *An Archive of Feelings: Trauma, Sexuality, and Lesbian Public Cultures* (Durham, NC: Duke University Press, 2003).

DeLucia, JoEllen, "A Delicate Debate: Mary Wollstonecraft, the Bluestockings, and the Progress of Women," in Enit Steiner (ed.), *Called to Civil Existence: Mary Wollstonecraft's A Vindication of the Rights of Woman* (Amsterdam: Rodopi, 2014), pp. 113–30.

Dinshaw, Carolyn, *Getting Medieval: Sexualities and Communities, Pre- and Postmodern* (Durham, NC: Duke University Press, 1999).

Duff, David, *Romanticism and the Uses of Genre* (New York: Oxford University Press, 2009).

Duncan, Ian, "Primitive Interventions: Rob Roy, Nation, and World System," *Eighteenth-Century Fiction* 15:1 (2002), pp. 81–102.

Duncan, Ian, *Scott's Shadow: The Novel in Romantic Edinburgh* (Princeton: Princeton University Press, 2007).

Easton, Fraser, "Cosmopolitical Economy: Exchangeable Value and National Development in Adam Smith and Maria Edgeworth," *Studies in Romanticism* 42:1 (2003), pp. 99–125.

Eger, Elizabeth, "Luxury, Industry and Charity: Bluestocking Culture Displayed," in Maxine Berg and Elizabeth Eger (eds), *Luxury in the Eighteenth Century* (New York: Palgrave, 2003), pp. 190–204.

Eger, Elizabeth, *Bluestockings: Women of Reason from Enlightenment to Romanticism* (Basingstoke: Palgrave, 2010).

Elias, Norbert, *The Civilizing Process*, trans. Edmund Jephcott, ed. Eric Dunning, Johan Goudsblom and Stephen Mennell (Malden, MA: Blackwell Publishing, [1978] 2000).

Ellis, Kate Ferguson, *The Contested Castle: Gothic Novels and the Subversion of Domestic Ideology* (Chicago: University of Illinois Press, 1989).

Ferris, Ina, *The Romantic National Tale and the Question of Ireland* (New York: Cambridge University Press, 2009).

Fielding, Penny, *Scotland and the Fictions of Geography* (Cambridge: Cambridge University Press, 2008).

Fielding, Penny, "'Usurpt by Cyclops': Rivers, Industry, and Environment in Eighteenth-Century Poetry," in Evan Gottlieb and Juliet Shields (eds), *Representing Place in British Literature and Culture, 1660–1830* (Aldershot: Ashgate, 2013), pp. 155–72.

Gaskill, Howard (ed.), *The Poems of Ossian and Related Works* (Edinburgh: Edinburgh University Press, 1996).

Gaskill, Howard (ed.), *The Reception of Ossian in Europe* (New York: Continuum, 2004).

Genette, Gerard, *Paratexts: Thresholds of Interpretation*, trans. Jane E. Lewin (Cambridge: Cambridge University Press, 1997).

Gerrard, Christine, *The Patriot Opposition to Walpole* (Oxford: Clarendon Press, 1994).

Gibbon, Luke, "The Sympathetic Bond: Ossian, Celticism, and Colonialism," in Terrence Brown (ed.), *Celticism* (Amsterdam: Rodopi, 1996), pp. 274–91.

Glover, Katharine, *Elite Women and Polite Society in Eighteenth-Century Scotland* (Woodbridge: Boydell Press, 2011).

Greiner, Rae, "Sympathy Time: Adam Smith, George Eliot, and the Realist Novel," *Narrative* 17:3 (2009), pp. 291–311.

Griffin, Robert J., *Wordsworth's Pope: A Study in Literary Historiography* (Cambridge: Cambridge University Press, 1995).

Guest, Harriet, *Small Change: Women, Learning, and Patriotism, 1750–1810* (Chicago: University of Chicago Press, 2000).

Halberstram, Judith, *In a Queer Time and Place: Transgender Bodies, Subcultural Lives* (New York: New York University Press, 2005).

Harkin, Maureen, "Smith's Theory of Moral Sentiments: Sympathy, Women, and Emulation," *Studies in Eighteenth-Century Culture* 24 (1995), pp. 173–90.

Harkin, Maureen, "Adam Smith's Missing History: Primitives, Progress, and the Problems of Genre," *ELH* 72:2 (2005), pp. 429–51.

Heiland, Donna, "Swan Songs: the Correspondence of Anna Seward and James Boswell," *Modern Philology* 90 (1992–3), pp. 381–91.

Hoeveler, Diane, *Gothic Feminism: The Professionalization of Gender from Charlotte Smith to the Brontës* (University Park: Pennsylvania State University Press, 1998).

Hunt, Lynn, *Inventing Human Rights* (New York: W. W. Norton & Co., 2007).

Johnson, Claudia, *Equivocal Beings: Politics, Gender, and Sentimentality in the 1790s* (Chicago: University of Chicago Press, 1995).

Kairoff, Claudia Thomas, *Anna Seward and the End of the Eighteenth Century* (Baltimore: Johns Hopkins University Press, 2012).

Kaul, Suvir, *Poems of Nation, Anthems of Empire* (Charlottesville: University of Virginia Press, 2000).

Kelly, Gary, *English Fiction of the Romantic Period, 1789–1830* (New York: Longman, 1989).

Kelly, Gary, *Revolutionary Feminism: The Mind and Career of Mary Wollstonecraft* (New York: Palgrave, 1995).

Kelly, Gary, "Bluestocking Feminism," in Elizabeth Eger, Charlotte Grant, Clíona Ó Gallchoir, and Penny Warburton (eds), *Women, Writing, and the Public Sphere* (Cambridge: Cambridge University Press, 2001), pp. 163–80.

Kelly, Gary, Elizabeth Eger, Judith Hawley, Jennifer Kelly and Rhoda Zuk (eds), *Bluestocking Feminism: Writings of the Bluestocking Circle, 1738–90*, vols 1–6 (London: Pickering & Chatto, 1999).

Kerrigan, John, *Archipelagic English: Literature, History, and Politics, 1603–1707* (New York: Oxford University Press, 2008).

Kidd, Colin, *Subverting Scotland's Past: Scottish Whig Historians and the Creation of an Anglo-British Identity, 1689–1830* (New York: Cambridge University Press, 1993).

Levine, William, "Collins, Thomson, and the Whig Progress of Liberty," *Studies in English Literature* 34 (1994), pp. 553–77.

Looser, Devoney, *British Women Writers and the Writing of History* (Baltimore: Johns Hopkins University Press, 2000).

Love, Heather, *Feeling Backwards: Loss and the Politics of Queer History* (Cambridge, MA: Harvard University Press, 2007).

Lynch, Deidre, "Gothic Libraries and National Subjects," *Studies in Romanticism* 40.1 (2001), pp. 29–48.

Lynch, Deidre, "Bluestockings," *The Oxford Encyclopedia of British Literature*, vol. 1, ed. David Scott Kastan (New York: Oxford University Press, 2006).

Mack, Ruth, *Literary Historicity: Literature and Historical Experience in Eighteenth-Century Britain* (Stanford: Stanford University Press, 2009).

Manning, Susan, *Fragments of Union: Making Connections in Scottish and American Writing* (New York: Palgrave Macmillan, 2002).

Major, Emma, *Madam Britannia: Women, Church, and Nation, 1712–1812* (New York: Oxford University Press, 2012).

Marshall, David, *The Figure of Theater: Shaftesbury, Defoe, Adam Smith, and George Eliot* (New York: Columbia University Press, 1986).

Mavor, Elizabeth, *The Ladies of Llangollen: A Study in Romantic Friendship* (London: Michael Joseph, 1971).

McLane, Maureen, "Dating, Orality, Thinking Balladry: of Milkmaids and Minstrels in 1771," *The Eighteenth Century: Theory and Interpretation* 47 (2006), pp. 131–49.

McLane, Maureen, *Balladeering, Minstrelsy, and the Making of British Romantic Poetry* (New York: Cambridge University Press, 2008).

McLeod, Deborah, *The Minerva Press*, unpublished Ph.D. thesis (University of Alberta, 1997).

Meek, Ronald, *Social Science and the Ignoble Savage* (Cambridge: Cambridge University Press, 1976).

Moers, Ellen, *Literary Women* (Garden City, NY: Doubleday & Company, Inc., 1976).

Monk, Samuel H., "Anna Seward and the Romantic Poets: A Study in Taste," in Leslie Griggs (ed.), *Wordsworth and Coleridge: Studies in Honor of George McLean Harper* (Princeton: Princeton University Press, 1939).

Moore, Dafydd, "Heroic Incoherence in James Macpherson's The Poems of Ossian," *Eighteenth-Century Studies*, 34.1 (2000), pp. 43–59.

Moore, Dafydd, *Enlightenment and Romance in James Macpherson's The*

Poems of Ossian: Myth, Genre and Cultural Change (Burlington, VT: Ashgate, 2003).

Moore, Dafydd (ed.), *Ossian and Ossianisms*, 4 vols (London: Routledge, 2004).

Moran, Mary Catherine, "The Commerce of the Sexes," in Frank Trentmann (ed.), *Paradoxes of Civil Society* (New York: Berghahn Books, 2000), pp. 61–84.

Mulholland, James, *Sounding Imperial: Poetic Voice and the Politics of Empire, 1730–1820* (Baltimore: Johns Hopkins University Press, 2013).

Muthu, Sankar, *Enlightenment against Empire* (Princeton: Princeton University Press, 2003).

Myers, Sylvia Harcstack, *The Bluestocking Circle: Women, Friendship, and the Life of the Mind in Eighteenth-Century England* (Oxford: Clarendon Press, 1990).

Norton, Richard, *The Mistress of Udolpho* (New York: Leicester University Press, 1999).

O'Brien, Karen, *Women and Enlightenment in Eighteenth-Century Britain* (New York: Cambridge University Press, 2009).

Perkins, Pam, *Women Writers and the Edinburgh Enlightenment* (Amsterdam: Rodopi, 2010).

Philips, Mark Salber, *Society and Sentiment: Genres of Historical Writing in Britain, 1740–1820* (Princeton: Princeton University Press, 2000).

Philips, Mark Salber, "On the Advantage and Disadvantage of Sentimental History for Life," *History Workshop Journal* 65 (2008), pp. 49–64.

Pocock, J. G. A., *Virtue, Commerce, and History* (Cambridge: Cambridge University Press, 1985).

Pocock, J. G. A., *Barbarism and Religion: The Enlightenments of Edward Gibbon, 1737–1764*, vol. 1 (Cambridge: Cambridge University Press, 1999).

Pocock, J. G. A., *Barbarism and Religion: Narratives of Civil Government*, vol. 2 (Cambridge: Cambridge University Press, 2001).

Pohl, Nicole, and Betty Schellenberg (eds), *Reconsidering the Bluestockings* (San Marino: Huntington Library, 2003).

Poovey, Mary, *Uneven Developments: The Ideological Work of Gender in Mid-Victorian England* (Chicago: University of Chicago Press, 1988).

Potkay, Adam, "Virtue and Manners in Macpherson's Poems of Ossian," *PMLA* 107.1 (1992), pp. 120–30.

Potkay, Adam, *The Fate of Eloquence in the Age of Hume* (Ithaca, NY: Cornell University Press, 1994).

Price, Fiona, *Women Writers and the Aesthetics of Romanticism* (Aldershot: Ashgate, 2009).

Reddy, William, *The Navigation of Feeling: A Framework for the History of Emotions* (New York: Cambridge University Press, 2001).

Rendall, Jane, "Virtue and Commerce: Women and the Making of Adam Smith's Political Economy," in Ellen Kennedy and Susan Mendus (eds), *Women in Western Political Philosophy* (Brighton: Wheatsheaf Press, 1987), pp. 44–77.

Rendall, Jane, "Tacitus Engendered: 'Gothic Feminism' and British Histories, *c.*1750–1800," in Geoffrey Cubitt (ed.), *Imagining Nations* (New York: Manchester University Press, 1998), pp. 57–74.

Rendall, Jane, "Clio, Mars and Minerva: The Scottish Enlightenment and the Writing of Women's History," in T. M. Devine and J. R. Young (eds),

Eighteenth Century Scotland: New Perspectives (East Linton: Tuckwell Press, 1999), pp. 134–51.

Rizzo, Betty, *Companions without Vows* (Athens, GA: University of Georgia Press, 1994).

Robinson, Roger, "The Origins and Composition of James Beattie's *Minstrel*," *Romanticism* 4:2 (1998), pp. 224–40.

Rosenberg, Daniel, "Joseph Priestley and the Graphic Invention of Modern Time," *Studies in Eighteenth-Century Culture* 36 (2007), pp. 55–103.

Rothschild, Emma, *Economic Sentiments: Adam Smith, Condorcet, and the Enlightenment* (Cambridge, MA: Harvard University Press, 2001).

Rothschild, Emma, *The Inner Life of Empire* (Princeton: Princeton University Press, 2011).

Ryan, Dermot, "'The Beauty of That Arrangement': Adam Smith Imagines Empire," *Studies in Romanticism* 48:1 (2009), pp. 101–19.

Schellenberg, Betty, *The Professionalization of Women Writers in Eighteenth-Century Britain* (New York: Cambridge University Press, 2006).

Schroeder, Natalie, "Regina Maria Roche and the Early Nineteenth-Century Irish Novel," *Eire-Ireland* 19:2 (1984), pp. 116–30.

Scott, Mary Jane, *James Thomson, Anglo-Scot* (Athens, GA: University of Georgia Press, 1988).

Sebastiani, Silvia, "Race, Women, and Progress in the Late Scottish Enlightenment," in Barbara Taylor and Sarah Knott (eds), *Women, Gender and Enlightenment* (New York: Palgrave Macmillan, 2007), pp. 75–96.

Sebastiani, Silvia, *The Scottish Enlightenment: Race, Gender, and the Limits of Progress*, trans. Jeremy Carden (New York: Palgrave, 2013).

Sen, Amartya, *The Idea of Justice* (Cambridge, MA: Harvard University Press, 2009).

Setzer, Sharon, "'Pond'rous Engines' in 'Outraged Groves': The Environmental Argument of Anna Seward's 'Colebrook Dale,'" *European Romantic Review* 18:1 (2007), pp. 69–82.

Sher, Richard, *Church and University in the Scottish Enlightenment: The Moderate Literati of Edinburgh* (Princeton: Princeton University Press, 1985).

Sher, Richard, *Enlightenment and the Book* (Chicago: University of Chicago Press, 2010).

Shields, Juliet, *Sentimental Literature and Anglo-Scottish Identity, 1745–1820* (New York: Cambridge University Press, 2010).

Siskin, Clifford, *The Work of Writing: Literature and Social Change in Britain, 1700–1830* (Baltimore: Johns Hopkins University Press, 1998).

Sorensen, Janet, *The Grammar of Empire in Eighteenth-Century British Writing* (New York: Cambridge University Press, 2000).

Stafford, Fiona, *The Sublime Savage: A Study of James Macpherson and the Poems of Ossian* (Edinburgh: Edinburgh University Press, 1988).

Stafford, Fiona, *The Last of the Race: the Growth of a Myth from Milton to Darwin* (New York: Oxford University Press, 1994).

Staves, Susan, *A Literary History of Women's Writing in Britain, 1660–1789* (Cambridge: Cambridge University Press, 2006).

Stevens, Anne H., "'Tales of other times': A Survey of British Historical Fiction, 1770–1812," *Cardiff Corvey*, December 2001, http://www.cardiff.ac.uk/encap/journals/corvey/articles/cc07_n03.html (last accessed 29 June 2014).

Stevens, Anne H., *British Historical Fiction Before Scott* (New York: Palgrave Macmillan, 2010).

Taylor, Barbara, *Mary Wollstonecraft and the Feminist Imagination* (New York: Cambridge, 2003).

Temple, Kathryn, *Scandal Nation: Law and Authorship in Britain, 1750–1832* (Ithaca, NY: Cornell University Press, 2002).

Thomson, Derick S., *The Gaelic Sources of Macpherson's Ossian* (Edinburgh: Oliver & Boyd, 1952).

Trumpener, Katie, *Bardic Nationalism: The Romantic Novel and the British Empire* (Princeton: Princeton University Press, 1997).

Varma, Devendra P., "Introduction" to Regina Maria Roche's *Clermont* in *The Northanger Set of Jane Austen Horrid Novels* (London: Folio Press, 1968).

Warner, William, *Licensing Entertainment: The Elevation of Novel Reading in Eighteenth-Century Britain*, 1684–1750 (Berkeley: University of California Press, 1998).

Weinbrodt, Howard, *Britannia's Issue: The Rise of Literature from Dryden to Ossian* (New York: Cambridge University Press, 2007).

Whitcomb, Helen Randall, *The Critical Theory of Lord Kames* (Northampton, MA: Departments of Modern English of Smith College, 1944).

Wheeler, David, "Placing Anna Seward: The 'Genius of Place', Coalbrookdale, and 'Colebrook Dale,'" *New Perspectives of the Eighteenth Century* 5:1 (2008), pp. 30–40.

Index